The Virtuous Vice
Globalization

Edited by
Siamack Shojai
and
Robert Christopherson

PRAEGER

Westport, Connecticut
London

Library of Congress Cataloging-in-Publication Data

The virtuous vice : globalization / edited by Siamack Shojai and Robert
   Christopherson.
       p. cm.
   Includes bibliographical references and index.
   ISBN 0-275-96810-3 (alk. paper)
      1. International economic relations.   2. Globalization—Economic aspects.
   3. Globalization—Social aspects.   4. Globalization—Political aspects.
   5. Globalization—Environmental aspects.   I. Title: Globalization.   II. Shojai,
   Siamack.   III. Christopherson, Robert W.
   HF1359.V57   2004
   303.48'2—dc21   2003053620

British Library Cataloguing in Publication Data is available.

Library of Congress Catalog Card Number: 2003053620
ISBN: 0-275-96810-3

First published in 2004

Praeger Publishers, 88 Post Road West, Westport, CT 06881
An imprint of Greenwood Publishing Group, Inc.
www.praeger.com

Printed in the United States of America

The paper used in this book complies with the
Permanent Paper Standard issued by the National
Information Standards Organization (Z39.48-1984).

10   9   8   7   6   5   4   3   2   1

For Roya and Lori

Contents

Preface

The topic of globalization has become the major theme of many academic disciplines and a source of ongoing research and inquiry by many in academia and industry. Unfortunately, there seems to be some confusion and misconception in the current debate surrounding globalization. Many still do not differentiate between internationalization and globalization of the economy. The multifaceted nature of issues of globalization adds to the complexity and fragmentation of the debate. There is also a general tendency among economists to study globalization in a purely economic context and only consider other aspects of the process in a peripheral mode. This book, arranged in two parts, provides a mix of major aspects of the debate in a multidisciplinary approach. Part I deals with the meaning and the roots of globalization. It provides a discussion of different definitions and processes of globalization, as well as the global economic impact of intensification of international trade and investment.

Political, social, and cultural ramifications of globalization business and the economy are discussed in Part II. The ever-changing nature of nation-states and the erosion of national sovereignty of governments are fully discussed in this part. In addition, globalization issues related to labor, the environment, education, and women are raised and presented in a forward-looking fashion, which would open the debate beyond the immediate concerns of policymakers and analysts in the field. The role of nongovernmental organizations and international institutions, as well as international organizations, in coping with the fallout of globalization is also addressed in this part. This volume can be used as a reference book for many courses in the areas of international business, international economics, international finance, and the global economic and business environment. It provides an intellectually stimulating picture of many relevant issues in this area for further study, analysis, and research by those in academia and the interested practitioners in the field. We believe the subject of the volume is of compelling interest to the professional and academic community.

A book of this nature can be put together only with collaboration of experts in many diverse areas of liberal arts and business studies. We are grateful to our colleagues from many prestigious colleges and universities for participating in this project. Parts of this volume were presented at the 2001 meeting of the Eastern Economic Association in New York City. Special thanks are due to Professors Behzad Yagmaian and Kudret Topyan for participating in the session as discussants and to Professor Dominick Salvatore for chairing the session. Also, we are indebted to those colleagues who read the chapters and provided editorial assistance. Praeger Publishers deserves to be mentioned for its professional and dedicated service in bringing this volume to your library. We would like to thank Beverly Cross and Connie Nephew from the School of Business and Economics at Plattsburgh State University of New York for providing dedicated and caring secretarial support for this project. The seeds of this project were culminated during a semester when Siamack Shojai was on a sabbatical leave at Manhattan College. Dean James Suarez and Manhattan College deserve his sincere appreciation for this opportunity. We are solely responsible for any shortcomings of the book.

Siamack Shojai
Robert Christopherson

Part I

The Meaning and Economic Consequences of Globalization

1 Introduction: The Meaning of Globalization and Internationalization

Siamack Shojai and Robert Christopherson

Former President Ronald Reagan once asked Mikhail Gorbachev to tear down the Berlin Wall. The wall came down in 1989, Gorbachev and his glasnost were overthrown, and, finally, the Soviet Union was dismantled. The demise of the Soviet Communist system encouraged former President George Bush to declare the triumph of liberal democracy and a new beginning for mankind under the banner of "New World Order." Also, it did not take Francis Fukuyama long to publish his now often-cited and well-read book titled *The End of History and the Last Man*, in 1992. Fukuyama announced the triumph of capitalism over Soviet Communism as the last station in Karl Marx's dialectic vision of humans' destiny. The class struggle and its entire antagonistic material dialectics were gone and the world was faced with the challenge of how to cleanse the remaining pockets of communist resistance to the New World Order. However, with dialectical economic class conflicts over, George Huntington, in his summer 1993 article in *Foreign Affairs*, opened our eyes to the idea of "clash of civilizations." The cultural and religious contests between fundamentalists and moderates and between Muslims, Jews, Christians, and Confucians would bring the world to the brink of new and unknown conflicts and disasters—perhaps a preview to the events of September 11, 2001. Huntington's tale of clash of civilizations does not present a vision of the world system beyond a metaphysical view; however, he provides some general policy implications to guide Western policymakers.

Then came the buzzword *globalization*. In all walks of life and every corner of the world, politicians, businessmen, college professors, policymakers, ayatollahs, and students all became numbed by the globaphilia. Many have used globalization and internationalization interchangeably with little regard for a nuance understanding of the two processes. James Rosenau (1997, 360) observes that globalization has become the latest buzzword to which observers resort when things seem different and seemingly unaccounted for. Former prime minister of the Netherlands, Ruud F. M. Lubbers, in his popular course on trends in economics and social globalization offered at Harvard University, cites the work of Jan Aart Scholte (1997) and presents some of the noted definitions of globalization by renowned authors and scholars. Accordingly,

- Globalization refers to all those processes by which the peoples of the world are incorporated into a single society, global society. (Albrow, 1990)
- Globalization can . . . be defined as the intensification of worldwide social relations which link distant localities in such a way that local happenings are shaped by events occuring many miles away and vice versa. (Giddens, 1990)
- The characteristics of the globalization trend include the internationalizing of production, the new international division of labor, new migratory movements from South to North, the new competitive environment that generates these processes, and the internationalizing of the state . . . making states into agencies of the globalizing world. (Cox, 1994)
- The world is becoming a global shopping mall in which ideas and products are available everywhere at the same time. (Kanter, 1995)
- Globalization is what we in the Third World have for several centuries called colonization. (Khor, 1995)
- Globalization entails an accelerating rate and/or higher level of economic interaction between people of different countries, leading to a qualitative shift between nation-states and national economies. (Baker, Epstein, and Pollin, 1998)

The first four quotes seem to refer to globalization as a process, which shrinks the distance among states and results in a global village. The path to the global village is carved by an intensification of international trade and social relations. But the internationalization of production, division of labor, and migratory movements have all been with us for decades if not for centuries (Zevin, 1992; Sachs and Warner, 1995; Rodrick, 1998). If the promised global village ever materializes, what are its characteristics and what would be the state of the New World system? Martin Khor's reference (1995) to the colonial era proclaims that globalization has been with us for decades and it is a world system in which one power conquers another, takes over the territory, dictates the rules of commerce, and eliminates all form of governance by the indigenous people except governance at a municipal level. To Dean Baker, Jerry Epstein, and Bob Pollin (1998) the acceleration of economic interaction among nations or an intensive internationalization of the economy (internationalization) leads to a qualitative shift in the relationship between nation-states and national economies (globalization). Paul Hirst and Grahame Thompson (1999) clearly warn us about the dangers of not distinguishing between trends toward a more intensive internationalization and strong versions of globalization thesis—particularly, when the two become confused and are used interchangeably to describe both globalization and internationalization in the vast literature on this topic. To them the strong version of globalization thesis requires a new view of the international economy.

In some circles a more integrated and open international economy became synopses with globalization of the economy. To others, a mere intensification of international economic ties or the lack thereof has been the main focus of debates on globalization of the economy. Since the principal parties to these transactions and economic activities are national economies, we refer to this as a phenomenon of growing interconnection among national economies—a greater intensification of international economy and not necessarily a globalization of the economy.

Massive capital flows during the post–World War II era, particularly capital flows during the post–Cold War era, have been the focus of many debates on globalization. However, in a post–Bretton Woods era of floating exchange rates, higher levels of capital flows and currency trading reflect the changed nature and structure of the international monetary system as opposed to a substantial qualitative evolution in a borderless global capital market. Hirth and Thompson (1999) present a model of international economy, where principal parties and actors are national economies with a greater interconnection through intensification of trade and investments. In this model of international economy, trade leads to national specialization and division of labor internationally; however, centrality of investments overshadows trade among nations. This is supported by the fact that in 1995 the annual volume of foreign exchange trading was fifty times that of world exports, and daily currency trading has surpassed $1.5 trillion in the global marketplace. In a world system of international trade and investments, the strategic nature of nations' independence is preserved and international events may penetrate or permeate the national economy mainly indirectly. Also, the governance, structure, and agenda of the international economy is highly influenced or set by industrial countries (the United States, western Europe, and Japan), which produce the bulk of the world income. Multinational corporations with a national home base are subject to national regulations and manage their affiliates from their home base. Open trade and investment are encouraged and agreed upon through multinational trade-regulating entities like the World Trade Organization, the International Monetary Fund, and the World Bank. Quantitative and qualitative changes and advances in communications and information technology facilitate intensification of economic exchange among national economies and promote awareness about new products and ideas that affect national tastes and preferences. Convergence of wages, productivity, and tastes across national economies progresses smoothly but it is constrained by the domestic configurations of supply and demand in different sectors of the national economies.

So far we have not attempted to provide our understanding of a proper definition or explanation of the meaning of globalization. However, it must be clear that intensification of trade and investments should not be confused with globalization. Here, we will provide a normative axiomatic meaning of globalization that can be a reference point for evaluation of secular trends and cycles toward a process of globalization of the economy. In a globalized economy, a system of international processes and transactions transforms the national economies into components of the system where national economic policies are the outcome of global processes. The distribution of power and global governance is concentrated in the hands of transnational governmental and nongovernmental institutions with a truly decentralized participation of the world citizens. The global economic system gains autonomy in a truly global market arena and production decisions are made locally or regionally based on the needs of the indigenous markets only constrained by natural impediments.

In the last stages of an international economy, national governments remove all barriers to free trade and capital movements and cede all those decisions to transnational institutions. With free movement of goods and capital, national trade, exchange rate, or monetary policies all become irrelevant and national governments will have no effective or meaningful control over these policies. Global monetary policy will be under the domain of a global central bank with the authority to manage the global money supply and its distribution. National currencies will cease to exist or will become a means of indirect taxation (quasi tax bill) in the hands of local authorities. A single global currency substitutes all national currencies, depriving national governments of national monetary policies to accommodate their fiscal activities. Fiscal policy without an accommodating monetary policy becomes limited in scope and purpose and will play a marginal role in macroeconomic policy or the redistribution and infrastructure policymaking at a local level. This brief description of an ideal type of global economy demonstrates that the passage of the international economy through secular and temporal cycles of openness and intensification of engagement should not be confused with a process of evolving into a truly globalized economy.

The metaphysical, sometimes vague, and confusing use of the term *globalization* by many authors and researchers compels one to attempt some clarification of its meaning and definition before any serious discussion of its related issues is attempted. We suggest that a dialectical approach be adopted when studying contributions to this volume. This approach to an understanding of globalization provides a dynamic view of all interconnections, contradictions, and syntheses of globalization. It entertains and embraces the ideal and material dialectics of the debate surrounding globalization. The significance of the approach is not in its claim to providing a more scientific reasoning, but rather in its illumination of different paths taken by different authors and their place in a dialectical journey of globalization debate. The approach suggested here sees globalization as a process of thesis, antithesis, and synthesis in the making. Unlike the metaphysical mode of inquiry, the dialectical approach does not view globalization and the resistance to it as cause-and-effect standings in a rigid antithesis mode. Rather, the dynamic interaction between the two goes beyond a metaphysical sphere and enters the realm of a dialectical mode with its own synthesis in the making.

ORGANIZATION OF THIS VOLUME

This volume contains a collection of chapters organized in two sections. The first discusses the meaning and economic consequences of globalization and the second considers the political, social, and cultural aspects of it. In the absence of a consistent and universally accepted theory of globalization, each author has provided a discussion of an issue of global magnitude and relevance. In this introductory chapter, Siamack Shojai and Robert Christopherson have provided a brief discussion of the meaning of globalization and have suggested the use of a dialectical approach to analysis of globalization.

In Chapter 2, Maryann K. Cusimano Love discusses the major pros and cons of globalization and argues that globalization is a virtuous vice. She suggests six approaches to harvest the virtues of globalization while managing its vices. She concludes that the challenge for policymakers is to harvest the fruits of globalization, while managing its vices effectively.

The rapid process of globalization during the past decade and the causes of globalization are examined by Dominick Salvatore in Chapter 3. He discusses international competitive positions of nations and the differential effects of globalization in labor markets across nations. He highlights the crucial importance of international competitiveness in the global economy.

In Chapter 4, Ann E. Davis examines globalized financial markets. She points out that since the demise of the Bretton Woods system and the growth of freely floating exchange rates, national currencies have become more stable as they gained greater worldwide acceptance. This she likens to a network externality. Davis discusses the competition among currencies to be dominant in world financial markets. This competition is particularly evident among the three leading currencies: the dollar, the yen, and the newly created euro. Further, Davis explores a paradox of globalization, where strong national governments are necessary for sound currencies, but the processes of global financial competition may well undermine strong financial institutions at the national level.

In Chapter 5, Della Lee Sue examines globalization and its impact on global income and wealth. Using a standard international trade model of comparative advantage, she discusses how countries specializing in the production of those goods in which they have a comparative advantage will increase production and, in turn, increase the incomes and wealth of workers in those industries. Thus, depending on the production process and the mobility of labor, globalization might well increase income and wealth inequality within a country. Increased inequality between countries will occur if the relative gain in income and wealth differs greatly across countries, due to the gains in specialization. Sue concludes by presenting empirical evidence supporting her theoretical model, that is, that income and wealth inequality has increased.

In Chapter 6, Spyros J. Vliamos identifies a number of events that have had a profound impact on the nature, the composition, and the organizational models of global economic activity. He discusses three events that make globalization a process, which leads to structural transformation of the world economy. He highlights the significance of considering economic issues surrounding globalization and the operation of the unified European economy in a proper political context set against European historical background and evolution. Vliamos concludes that in a Europe where politics remains predominantly national, this will limit the ability of Europe to play a central role in the global economy.

In Chapter 7, Maryann K. Cusimano Love addresses the issue of how rapid globalization during the past twenty years may affect sovereignty and the future of nation-states. She compares previous eras of global integration with the current period of globalization and concludes that state responses to globalization are changing the nation-state's function, form, and nature of control. State will remain as one less powerful player among many.

In Chapter 8, Vernon J. Vavrina presents the role of nongovernmental organizations (NGOs) and intergovernmental organizations (IGOs) in the process of globalization. He concludes that the system of sovereign nation-states will survive globalization for the foreseeable future. However, they will be in some jeopardy if they do not incorporate NGOs' viewpoints. Vavrian argues that NGOs will affect, but will not severely challenge, the nation-state system.

In contrast to Vavrina's chapter, in Chapter 9, Eve Sandberg studies the impact of globalization processes on NGOs. She suggests that NGOs are being pressured to globalize their governance structure to function more effectively and morally in a global setting. Also, professionalization of staffing in the NGOs and more collaboration between NGOs and IGOs are some other consequences of globalization.

In Chapter 10, Janet L. Rovenpor analyzes the global employment status and well-being of women. She reviews the literature on the types and levels of participation of women in the labor force in a select number of countries in the context of the impact of globalization on women's work. A careful and timely case study of the plight of women under the Taliban regime in Afghanistan leads her to conclude that socioeconomic background, educational opportunities, and local economic opportunities have a profound impact on accomplishments of women in a global economy. Rovenpor makes a strong argument that globalization is not gender blind.

In Chapter 11, Shawn Shieh examines how the process of globalization impacts the debate on universalism versus cultural relativism of human rights. He investigates whether globalization is creating a homogeneous global culture with a strong foundation for a universal moral code or is weakening the universalism position by promoting clashes of civilization. Shieh argues that globalization is tipping the balance toward the universalism position.

In Chapter 12, Hank Hilton studies three aspects of globalization and the environment. The impact of foreign direct investment, global trade, and e-commerce, and on pollution are discussed. He concludes that foreign direct investment and global trade have mixed effects on global pollution, but e-commerce tends to reduce global pollution.

In Chapter 13, Peter Lorenzi analyzes the growth and development of university-based business education and its relationship to global economic growth. He considers the role of business education during the past twenty-five years in the context of a global transformation from an industry- and science-driven society to one where information technology plays a leading role. Lorenzi suggests that global demand for business education will rise in the age of information technology.

In conclusion, this collection of chapters about globalization has raised some of the pressing issues regarding the globalization process. The diversity of the issues presented demonstrates that future researchers need to search for a comprehensive, coherent, and systematic framework or theory to analyze many diverse effects of globalization in a coherent way. Also, an attempt toward establishing a universally accepted definition of globalization and its measurements seems to be warranted.

REFERENCES

Albrow, Martin. 1990. *Globalization, Knowledge, and Society*. London: Sage.

Baker, Dean, Jerry Epstein, and Bob Pollin. 1998. *Globalization and Progressive Eco nomic Policy*. Cambridge: Cambridge University Press.

Cox, Robert W. 1994. Global Restructuring: Making Sense of the Changing International Political Economy. In *Political Economy and the Changing Global Order*, ed. Richard Stubbs and Geoffrey RD Underhill, 45–59. Toronto: St. Martin's.

Fukuyama, Francis. 1992. *The End of History and the Last Man*. Los Angeles: Avon Books.

Giddens, Anthony. 1990. *The Consequences of Modernity*. Cambridge: Polity.

Hirst, Paul, and Grahame Thompson. 1999. *Globalization in Question*. Cambridge: Polity.

Huntington, George. 1993. The Clash of Civilizations. *Foreign Affairs* 72 (3): 22–28.

Kanter, Rosabeth Moss. 1995. *Learning Organizations: Developing Cultures for Tomorrow's Workplace*. Portland, OR: Productivity.

Khor, Martin. 1995. *Globalization and the Need Coordinated Southern Policy Response*. New York: Cooperation South Journal.

Rodrik, Dani. 1998. *The Debate over Globalization: How to Move Forward by Looking Backward*. Cambridge, MA: Harvard University Press.

Rosenau, James N. 1997. *The Complexities and Contradictions of Globalization*. Philadelphia: Current History.

Sachs, Jeffrey, and Andrew Warner. 1995. *Economic Reform and the Process of Global Integration*. Brookings Papers on Economic Activity 1: 1–118.

Scholte, Jan Aart. 1997. *The Globalization of World Politics: An Introduction to International Relations*. Oxford: Oxford University Press.

Zevin, Robert. 1992. Are World Financial Markets More Open? If So, Why and with What Affects? In *Financial Openness and National Autonomy*, ed. Tariq Banuri and Juliet B Schor, 43–83. Oxford: Clarendon.

2 Globalization: A Virtuous Mount or a Contemptible Vice?

Maryann K. Cusimano Love

Polls indicate that 61 percent of Americans believe globalization should be promoted or maintained at current levels. However, 72 percent believe U.S. trade policymakers pay too little attention to the concerns of labor, and 60 percent believe that environmental considerations are given short shrift.[1] These findings underscore the concerns of this volume: is globalization a laudable or lamentable phenomenon? Some argue globalization is a means to bring peoples and cultures together; to route tyrannical governments; to easily and cheaply spread information, ideas, capital, and commerce; and to transfer more power than ever before to civic society and networked individuals.[2] Others see globalization as merely neoimperialism wearing Bill Gates's face and Mickey Mouse's ears, extending the web of global capitalism's exploitation of women, minorities, the poor, and developing regions; fouling ecosystems; displacing local cultures and traditions; mandating worship at the altar of rampant consumer capitalism; and deepening the "digital divide" between global haves and have-nots.[3] Is globalization a virtue or a vice? This chapter begins by cataloguing the major arguments and evidence offered by each camp, virtue and vice, and concludes with the assessment that policymakers need to give greater attention to the ethics of globalization. The main challenge for policymakers and citizens in the twenty-first century is how to harvest the virtues of globalization, while managing the vices. It is possible, but difficult.

THE VIRTUES OF GLOBALIZATION

Globalization increases connectivity among individuals, polities, and regional and functional sectors. This increase in connectivity leads globalization's proponents to argue that globalization increases information, transparency, and democracy, serving as a powerful engine of social, political, technological, and economic progress and development.

Information: The World Is a Mouse Click Away

The ready availability and cheap cost of information technologies, and the dependence of the globalized economy on information, now makes it more expensive to suppress information than to transmit it.[4] Globalization's advocates point to the cheap and easy spread of information and ideas as globalization's greatest benefit. Telemedicine increasingly allows individuals and groups in remote areas to have access to top-notch medical information and advice. Lives are saved and health improved as those wounded in Bosnia, a researcher with breast cancer stranded in the Arctic Circle, or a sailor alone on the high seas battling a life-threatening infection can get real-time medical consultations electronically. Many argue that access to information technologies such as the Internet levels the playing field internationally. An individual no longer needs a fancy degree or expensive education to literally have a world of information at their fingertips. Publishing houses can be bypassed as online publishing grows. And savvy Net researchers can now have access to up-to-date information that previously was available only to prestigious university libraries or well-paid research staffs.

Transparency and the Growth of Civil Society:
The World Is Watching

Globalization involves interlocking dynamics—the spread of open technologies and open, integrated economies helps to open societies, thus stimulating, reinforcing, intensifying, and speeding up globalization, making the sum of globalization more than its component parts. The advance of cheap and readily available information technologies and the connection of global economies through foreign direct investment means that embarrassing secrets are harder for regimes to keep. As information about Indonesia's economic difficulties became apparent, world financial markets responded by withdrawing their investments and downgrading Indonesia's bond ratings. While Indonesians at the time could not vote, world markets (or what Thomas Friedman refers to as "the electronic herd"[5]) could vote with their dollars in their lack of confidence in the regime. Abusers of human rights still exist, but they can no longer expect to go unnoticed, as handheld video cameras capture atrocities, and the

Internet and satellite technologies beam these pictures worldwide in real time. As one observer noted, "The information revolution is thus profoundly threatening to the power structures of the world, and with good reason. In Prague in 1988 the first protesters in the streets looked into CNN cameras and chanted at the riot police, 'The world sees you.' And it did. It was an anomaly of history that other Eastern Europeans watched the revolution on CNN relayed by a Russian satellite and mustered the courage to rebel against their own sovereigns."[6]

Knowing that the world is watching, individuals and nongovernmental organizations (NGOs) can pressure and shame regimes into action, or take action independent of governments. Cheap information technologies, and the easy flow of information, ideas, people, and capital across borders, has facilitated the rise in the number and effectiveness of NGOs worldwide. By some counts the number of NGOs has increased from 1,268 in 1960 to over 40,300 by 1997.[7] Not only are the numbers of these civic society organizations multiplying, from the Red Cross to Greenpeace, but they are increasingly active in negotiating international treaties and directly providing services. The NGO Doctors Without Borders won the 1999 Nobel Peace Prize for their work providing medical services to populations in war zones where governments would prefer to keep the outside world at bay. Jody Williams, a Canadian housewife, with her personal computer, e-mail, and Internet access, organized an international outcry because governments of the world had failed to ban land mines—lethal, low-cost weapons that continue killing and maiming civilians long after the wars are over. She and the coalition she built of one thousand NGOs, human rights groups, and arms control groups on six continents, single-handedly catapulted the land mine issue onto governments' agendas, and moved the rapid negotiation and entry into force of the Ottawa Convention.

Democracy: I'd Like to Buy the World a Vote

Proponents of globalization argue that open markets and open technologies are helping to spread democracy. This was the explicit assumption behind the Clinton administration's "Engagement and Enlargement" policy: engage in economic and political relations with states, enlarge the sphere of markets—capitalist economies—and democracy will follow. In essence, this is a theory of "trickle-down" democracy.[8] Create a middle and upper class of capitalist entrepreneurs, and people with economic and technological power and choice eventually will demand political power and choice.

The policy contains the assumption that free market economies are a Trojan horse: once a state liberalizes and privatizes its economy, open society values and dynamics are unleashed in ways that authoritarian leaders will ultimately be unable to contain or control. By this view, international trade and investment patterns are neither value-free nor value-neutral. Coca-Cola is a saboteur to authoritarian states, carrying a much more insidious political and cultural message than "A Coke and a smile." People get more from a McDonald's hamburger or Levi's jeans than a consumer product, and more from *Baywatch* or MTV than an entertainment product; they are buying into a values system that prioritizes individual rights, liberties, and freedoms. Free market advocates see the demise of Suharto in Indonesia as the eventual writing on the wall for the Chinese. Leaders of even authoritarian states, lured by the promise of foreign direct investments and trade, try to plug into global markets. Muommar Khadafy, Fidel Castro, the Iranian theocracy, and the communist regime in Vietnam are trying to attract international investment and tourism. Yet they soon find that these ties to global capital are ties that bind. In addition to wealth coming into the country, the state in the process loses some of its autonomy over internal affairs, market regulation, even labor and environmental standards. Further, global capitalism is self-perpetuating: once you liberalize economies and technologies, thereby empowering consumers and entrepreneurs and sowing the seeds of a middle-class, political liberalism cannot be forever forestalled.

By this view, it is no accident that the highly centralized states of the communist Soviet Union and eastern Europe, the apartheid regime in South Africa, the Suharto regime in Indonesia, and military regimes from Nigeria to Argentina, Brazil, and Chile came to their demise simultaneously, at the same time as the downsizing of the welfare state in Canada, the United Kingdom, Australia, and the United States. Globalization is revolutionary, and brings the end of big government, as power decentralizes to local governments in federated systems, and to NGOs, corporations, intergovernmental organizations (IGOs), and individuals. In a networked world, large, centralized bureaucracies are obsolete, and state institutions must adapt to globalization or become extinct. As a decentralized political form, federated democracies are on the rise the world over, even if democratization is neither assured nor complete.

Prosperity: Specialization Pays Off

Globalization lowers barriers to international trade, and proponents claim that in so doing it opens markets and opportunities for economic growth. Open markets and free trade allow countries to focus on the production of goods and services in which they have a comparative advantage. Specializing on your strengths for the export market, and importing goods that other states produce better or more cheaply, creates greater profits and efficiency than attempting to go it alone and produce all goods for the internal market self-sufficiently. Self-sufficiency produces a subsistence economy that is held back by some goods and services that are of inferior quality. Specialization allows all sectors of an economy to benefit from the higher quality and lower cost of goods that are someone else's strong suit. Trade has grown faster than production for the past fifty years, and the argument is that this benefits wealthy and poor states alike, "rising tide floats all boats." Twenty years ago only 2.9 billion people enjoyed market economies. Today, 5.7 billion people live in market economies. Simultaneously, the standard of living is slowly improving for many who live in market economies. For example, life expectancy has risen more in the past forty years than in the previous four thousand.[9] Globalization allows poor countries access to a slice of the greater disposable incomes and investment capital available in developed economies, which can then stimulate their own economic development more than if they were only reliant on internal capital and consumer flows. "In Korea, for example, between 1960 and 1996, exports grew from 3 percent of production to 32 percent, while imports grew from 13 to 36 percent. . . . The woman sewing a shirt in Bangladesh needs that income more than I [in the West] need another shirt. . . . It has also provided opportunities for Koreans, Chinese and Chileans, as well as Americans, to produce many more of some kinds of manufactures than they consume domestically. In India, a latecomer to globalization, computer-related services have been the hottest export industry of the decade."[10]

THE VICES OF GLOBALIZATION

Globalization's advocates note that information, transparency, and the growth of civil society, democracy, and the economy are the fruits of globalization's connectivity. Globalization's critics also note the intense connectivity that globalization brings, but see far more bitter fruit growing from the connection. Globalization produces an asymmetrical distribution of costs, benefits, and opportunities to participate in or govern the decision making concerning the process. These asymmetries, and where a state or individual stands in relation to the asymmetrical distribution, produce widely different attitudes about whether globalization is good or bad.

Asymmetries of Globalization

The benefits and costs of globalization are not spread equally. Capitalism is criticized for disparities between rich and poor in terms of income, political power and participation, and opportunities. In parallel, the worldwide spread and intensification of capitalism that globalization represents is criticized for exacerbating the excesses of capitalism, and exporting these problems worldwide. For example, "In 1960, before globalization, the most fortunate 20 percent of the planet's population were 30 times richer than the poorest 20 percent. In 1997, at the height of globalization, the most fortunate were 74 times richer than the world's poorest! And this gap grows each day. Today, if you add up the gross national products of all the world's underdeveloped countries (with their 600 million inhabitants) they still will not equal the total wealth of the three richest people in the world."[11]

Acknowledging the role of global population growth in contributing to a higher rate of poverty, still, 100 million more people now live in poverty than ten years ago.[12] Of the now 6 billion people on the planet, 3 billion live on less than $2 a day and 1.3 billion live on less than $1 per day.[13] Sixty countries are poorer than they were twenty years ago.[14] Wealth is only one indicator of globalization's asymmetries. Decisions concerning globalization are made in corporate boardrooms and state capitals located generally in Western and economically developed states. Environmental degradation from global production facilities fall disproportionately on the world's poorest communities, as some corporations exploit regions where environmental legislation or enforcement is weakest. Yet most foreign direct investment and collaborative corporate alliances go to developed states. "Controlling for the opening of both China and the former Soviet bloc, which attracted almost no investment before 1985, the share of foreign direct investment going to the developing world actually dropped" from 1985 to 1995.[15] Globalization's costs and benefits are unequally distributed.

Who's in Charge Here?
Accountability and Transparency in a Globalized World

Susan Strange argues that globalization has moved power from states to markets. Decisions that used to be made by governments are now being made in closed corporate boardrooms. Many functions that states used to fulfill, such as setting tax rates and spending money on large public works or social welfare projects, are now limited by market pressures.[16] Foreign direct investment decisions, which fuel globalization, are made in corporate boardrooms, not government offices. But who elects corporate chief executive officers? Beyond their direct responsibility to stockholders, and their indirect link to consumers who can vote with their pocketbooks against a corporation's products or policies, how are their activities transparent, accountable, or democratic?

This was the core complaint of the World Trade Organization (WTO) protestors in Seattle, Washington, whose demonstrations against the WTO turned violent. The WTO was created in 1995 to continue the work of opening and regulating trade and liberalizing markets begun by the General Agreement on Tariffs and Trade summits. One hundred thirty-five countries are members of the WTO; thirty-six others have observer status, and most of these have petitioned to become full members. Despite the wide membership in the WTO, critics claim that WTO negotiations are secret, as are the processes and players of their decision-making court, which can overrule specific member countries' actions or laws it judges to be in conflict with the WTO members' obligations to carry on free trade. For example, French attempts to keep out British beef were overruled, as were U.S. attempts to limit the sale of dirtier, more smog-inducing Venezuelan gasoline. In the gasoline example, the WTO ruled that the way the United States was implementing the U.S. Clean Air Act was preferential to U.S. oil refineries (which in certain circumstances were allowed to sell a dirtier quality gas) and discriminatory to Venezuela (which was not). This led to great protest that a nonelected, nontransparent body was overturning the clean air laws openly arrived at by a democratic process.

A recent study by the United Nations Development Programme acknowledges this problem.[17] The study notes that there is a jurisdictional gap, where no single country can solve issues like environmental degradation or terrorism alone. The issue cuts across lines of political power and sovereign jurisdiction. Different nations also have different incentives for addressing transsovereign problems because they will receive different benefits and have to pay different costs, creating a gap in incentives to solve problems. However, not all who are affected by global issues have a place at the table in deciding policy about transsovereign problems, creating a participation gap that the United Nations deems quite serious.

The Rise in Consumerism and the Loss of Local, Communal Values, Identity, and Sovereignty

"There is no such thing as globalization," according to skeptic Kenneth Waltz. "There is only Americanization."[18]

Globalization has been criticized for opening the floodgates to American goods and values (as many of these products have a comparative advantage, especially cultural products such as music, films, and entertainment goods and services). In besieging the world with MTV, *Baywatch*, Disney, and McDonald's, many argue that globalization has sounded the death knell for local traditions, tastes, authorities, and ways of life. The French lament English words creeping into their language, while decrying the decline in quality of truly French bread and wine; imports have diluted quality, and changing production techniques for the export market and foreign tastes further undermine the high quality of French products.

The critique goes deeper than a mere matter of taste, however, to questioning whether American products are a more subtle form of imperialism than colonialism, disrupting local beliefs and authorities such as church and state with worship of the market and excessive, unchecked consumerism. Pope John Paul II, a Pole and an ardent critic of communist rule, was scathingly critical of postcommunist Poland's consumerism. Had Poland abandoned its spiritual values, which had seen it through the world wars and was the source of Poland's successful opposition to the Soviet Union, in favor of the pursuit of money and consumer goods above all else? If globalization is Americanization, is it leading to a homogenization of world cultures, destroying local churches, authorities, and values, and leaving a swath of strip malls, dumps of discarded "Happy Meal" toys, and sex- and violence-filled music and videos in its wake? Americans tend to think of globalization as bringing the declaration of independence and bill of rights abroad. Some world citizens see globalization as a change agent, which brings the worst of American culture and values abroad, replacing their traditional value and culture.

COMMON GROUND

Critics and advocates alike acknowledge that globalization can lead to a loss in power or unilateral control by local political actors. However, they disagree over whether the fruits of that loss of local autonomy are increased protection of universal human rights and more open political participation and representation in democratic forms, or neocolonial, imperial impositions of Western values and political forms on traditional sources of authority. Likewise, both schools agree that globalization has a Trojan horse and demonstration effect of importing and promulgating Western values; they disagree over the desirability of these values. Finally, they disagree over whether information technologies and nested investment patterns open decisions to greater scrutiny by citizen and nonstate actors, or allow more behind-closed-doors bargaining among a few technologically and financially advanced actors.

Globalization is on the rise, but the benefits and liabilities of globalization are distributed asymmetrically, not equally. Globalization refers to the building of new political, economic, cultural, and technological infrastructures. Judgments about the worth of these new infrastructures will depend on how the highways are used, where they take you, whether you feel access to the new highways is fair, and how you feel about the destinations and processes of the old roadways that may fall into disuse or disrepair as the new highways are built.

A less popular but perhaps more realistic position is that globalization's infrastructures are neither inherently good nor evil. Terrorists and tourists alike can use them. The success of U.S. and Western foreign policies in opening markets, liberalizing trade, spreading new technologies, and promoting democracy has created the conditions in which transsovereign problems thrive. The Cali drug cartel uses the same infrastructure that Microsoft uses to get its product to market, attract consumers, and invest profits. Drug trafficking, nuclear proliferation, terrorism, international crime, environmental degradation, refugee flows, the spread of infectious disease—all of these transsovereign problems—use the same financial, communication, transportation, and political infrastructures of globalization as licit actors. These transsovereign problems are downsides of globalization; they transcend state borders in ways that no one nation-state can contain or control, and thus they are particularly difficult for polities to successfully address.[19] Our political institutions are still largely based on sovereignty, while global issues do not stop at sovereign borders. It is physically difficult to limit the flow of particular peoples and goods at a time when technological, market, and societal forces make such movement easier than ever before.

If globalization is neither inherently good nor evil, why are the debates over globalization so shrill and polarized? First, the effects are asymmetrical, the costs are high and real, and they fall, as many of capitalism's defects do, disproportionately on the world's poor and most vulnerable. To the Ford Motor Company worker in Brazil fired on Christmas day, it is no solace to point out that while she held the job she was earning more than her peers, and employment while it lasted was better than continued unemployment. The loss still smarts, more so because she had little say in her fate and because the jobless rate in Brazil is so high that she has few alternatives.[20]

Second, the process of globalization is distinct from its products. While the infrastructure produced by globalization may be used for either good or evil, the process involves profound social change, which like all social change creates winners and losers. While stable, established democracies may be less prone to go to war with one another, during the democratization process countries can be very vulnerable to military conflict and internal strife, as demonstrated by the coup in Pakistan. While liberal, privatized economies may outproduce their state-run counterparts, the process of economic liberalization and privatization is wrenching and fraught with dangers, especially in countries without established legal codes, as the Russian case shows. It is extremely difficult to change the major political, legal, and economic infrastructure simultaneously, while trying to run a country and respond to citizens' demands, yet this is precisely what many states are attempting to do. While new technologies may produce efficiencies in time and effort, changing over to new technologies changes social strata and reduces the profitability and stature of practitioners and producers of the old technologies. These social and educational adjustments take time, and displace workers, and those displaced from the old order are unlikely to be enamored of the new order.

Third, while the outcome of globalization may be intended (in part) to produce a more democratic, participatory, transparent, and accountable world, the process of globalization is often not democratic, participatory, transparent, or accountable. Corporations are responsible to their stockholders first, and are not directly responsible to the public at large. The International Monetary Fund and the World Bank are led by the governments of a few developed countries; even though the decisions of these IGOs and market leaders have global consequences, they are not representative of or directly accountable to the bulk of the world's population. While the outcomes of globalization may be greater political, economic, and technological openness, the processes of globalization, especially the decision-making process, is often closed.

Fourth, the debate over globalization is heated in part because the advocates of globalization oversell its benefits. No public policy is risk free and less expensive, but proponents of globalization often paint a win–win picture where all will easily benefit from the new economies, technologies, and their related political and social forms. Even if globalization produces more benefits than costs, it often cannot live up to unrealistically heightened expectations.

Finally, the debate is sharp and protracted because many attitudes were set long before the current intensified cycle of globalization. Long before e-cash, the Internet, global capital flows and extensive foreign direct investment, political scientists and publics debated the North versus South, or developed versus developing, divide on issues of postcolonial development. Prior to decolonization, the long-running debate between proponents of Tradition and proponents of Modernity echo many of the exact concerns of the globalization debate. Is change better, faster, more efficient, freeing, and more profitable, or are the old ways of doing things, the old tools, ways of dress, habits, norms, and authority structures more legitimate and holistic ways to tie individuals to each other and to the earth? Both the North versus South and the Tradition versus Modernity debates neatly parallel (if they do not exactly mirror) the battle lines between globalization and its critics. Poverty, environmental degradation, and injustice existed long before globalization. But globalization surely makes these problems, and the relative gains disparities between rich and poor, more readily apparent. Debates over globalization often import the heat but rarely bring to light these preceding debates.

If positions are often passionately held and long-standing, and if globalization's effects are asymmetrical, its processes wrenching and disruptive, and its infrastructure open to both licit as well as illicit actors, how can policymakers garner the virtues while reigning in the vices of globalization? First, even proglobalization leaders must acknowledge the problems and severe transition risks and costs of globalization. Taking off the rose-colored glasses is the first step toward seeing globalization's problems, and attending to the concerns of globalization's dispossessed.

Second, policymakers should proceed with an eye to how globalization policies (as well as other public policies) will affect the world's most vulnerable populations. Whether globalization alone can raise the plight of the world's poor, globalization policies should first do no harm. The mutually reinforcing and dynamic processes of globalization may be inevitable. The genie is out of the bottle, and the technology, information, and integration that has spread cannot be unlearned. However, the unequal effects of globalization are not inevitable, and can be softened or managed by concerted public policy efforts involving both public and private networks. International standards of worker, safety, health, and environmental codes are needed to ensure that globalization is not a race to the bottom. Legal protections are one way to do this. Capitalism works best when it plays by rules. Markets need law to profit, and societies need law to protect their weakest members. Solidarity with the poor makes good business sense as well as good moral sense. Developing, harmonizing, and enforcing laws to root out corruption and protect the poor, children, labor, and the environment creates a healthier, more stable and sustainable business environment, with more productive employees, more potential consumers, and less uncertainty and hidden costs. However, given that global problems cross sovereign jurisdictional borders, legal reform and harmonization are difficult and not always politically possible. For that reason, nonbinding international legal agreements (or "soft law") are on the rise in all issue sectors.[21] Soft law has stepped in to bridge the gap, rather than waiting with no agreements while states take their time negotiating. These voluntary regulatory guidelines can incorporate private firms, professional organizations, and NGOs, which are not usually party to negotiating international treaties. Soft law can serve as a precursor, until international treaties or legal harmonization can be achieved, or as a supplement, filling out broad formal accords with technical and specific detail. Protecting societies' most vulnerable can address many of the problems of globalization that critics raise, and is more realistic than trying to turn the clock back on globalization.

Third, law is not enough. The public sector is shrinking while the private sector is growing, and the private sector is increasingly the engine of globalization. Thus, reigning in globalization's vices cannot be done without cooperation between the public and private sectors. This may be difficult as governments are used to being in charge, and as the private sector may be suspicious or resentful of government intervention. Differences in culture, operating procedures, and organization also make public–private networks or partnerships difficult. But however difficult, such networks are necessary. Each brings unique resources, experiences, and understanding of the problems to the table that the other side needs to manage pressing global issues. As James D. Wolfensohn, president of the World Bank, put it, "[G]lobalization can be more than the unleashed forces of the global market. It can also be the unleashing of our combined effort and expertise to reach global solutions."[22] The World Bank is already working with over eighty global public–private networks on issues as diverse as malaria eradication and forestry management. The United Nations is also increasing its participation in global public–private networks. For such networks to work, stakeholders must inculcate a sense of mutual trust and responsibility and common purpose, and a recognition of interdependent short-term as well as long-term goals and costs. For example, insurance companies have recently become partners with NGOs and environmental groups concerned about global warming, as these companies realize that short-term profit orientations will create long-term costs to their industries. Likewise, many corporations working to increase international labor standards not only want to proactively self-regulate to avoid costly reactive government regulations, but also realize that healthy, rested, well-fed, and educated workers are more productive workers who produce greater profits and innovations for the company with fewer accidents and risks.

Fourth, the policies and processes of globalization in general need to be more transparent, accountable, and democratic. This means creating mechanisms for greater public participation and meaningful input by those affected by the outcomes of globalization. Globalization will trigger great backlash, and resurgent nationalism and local conflict and resistance if local populations are not brought on board in the decision-making and implementation process. There are riots in the streets when people feel excluded from the decision-making process, and political unrest disrupts business and increases costs. The principle of subsidiarity may shed some light on how to proceed. Subsidiarity is making decisions at the most local level possible. Corporations are already learning that local input into hiring, production, and marketing decisions can save billions. The United Nations and the World Bank are coming to the same conclusion, and are looking to lower the participation gap by increasing the roles of local civil society groups in their public–private partnership initiatives. Globalization is unsustainable in the long run without local support and legitimacy that comes through accountability, participation, and transparency.

Fifth, there is no need to believe that globalization is the latest showdown between God and Mannon, with the increasingly mobile and consumer-friendly money winning. Traditional institutions such as church and state may survive and thrive, as long as they adapt to new social and political circumstances. The proliferation of information creates a crisis of meaning, in which traditional institutions such as church and state may be better poised than ever to address the value void of materialism and consumerism. The growth of religious groups from Latin America to the formerly communist states shows that traditional sources of authority need not be set back by globalization. If anything, citizens may depend more on these traditional voices to talk back to globalization, bringing community values to help tame and channel global markets.

Finally, a little humility can go a long way. The greatest characteristics of democracy and capitalism may well be their openness to tinkering and peaceful change. Neither the market nor the ballot box guarantee wise choices, they merely allow midcourse corrections and revisions as previous choices do not work as intended. Globalization's increased and more intensive connectivity increases the opportunities for unintended consequences. Certainly no one intended Russian privatization and democratization to be marked by the rise in organized crime, or the greater openness of markets and borders in the Americas to facilitate drug trafficking or the terrorist attacks of September 11, 2001. Openness to globalization's shortcomings, and a humility about policymaking, can create a climate where midcourse corrections are embraced, not avoided.

The ethical concerns addressed here are not a luxury. For globalization to progress and be sustainable, ethical dimensions must be addressed. Globalization policies that ignore the views of local populations trigger political backlash, from protectionism and labor unrest at home to violent nationalist and terrorist movements abroad. When conservative Pat Buchanan, liberal Ralph Nader, and radical fundamentalists perceive some common ground, politicians should take note.

As UN Secretary-General Kofi Annan put it, "National markets are held together by shared values. In the face of economic transition and insecurity, people know that if the worst comes to the worst, they can rely on the expectation that certain minimum standards will prevail. But in the global market, people do not yet have that confidence. Until they do have it, the global economy will be fragile and vulnerable . . . unless those values [protection of human rights, labor, environment] are really seen to be taking hold, I fear we may find it increasingly difficult to make a persuasive case for the open global market."[23] Globalization did not happen by accident, but by a series of conscious public and private policy decisions, sustained over time and with public support. The same must be true for globalization to continue and spread. To harvest the virtues of globalization we must actively work to mitigate its vices.

NOTES

1. Steven Kull, *American Public Attitudes on Globalization* (College Park: Program on International Policy Attitudes, University of Maryland, 1999).

2. The White House, *The Engagement and Enlargement Strategy* (Washington, DC: The White House, May 1995).

3. Dani Rodrik, *Has Globalization Gone Too Far?* (Washington, DC: Institute for International Economics, 1997); Benjamin R. Barber, *Jihad vs. McWorld: How Globalism and Tribalism Are Reshaping the World* (New York: Ballantine Books, 1995); and Hans-Henrik Holm and Georg Sorensen, *Whose World Order?* (Boulder, CO: Westview, 1995).

4. Andrew L. Shapiro, "The Internet: Think Again," *Foreign Policy* (Summer 1999): 14–15.

5. Thomas L. Friedman, *The Lexus and the Olive Tree* (New York: Farrar, Straus, and Giroux, 1999).

6. Walter B. Wristen, "Bits, Bytes, and Diplomacy," *Foreign Affairs* (September/October 1997): 175–176.

7. Union of International Associations, ed., *Yearbook of International Organizations* (Brussels: K. G. Saur Verlag, 1997/1998), 1:app. 4.

8. Maryann K. Cusimano, *Unplugging the Cold War Machine: Rethinking U.S. Foreign Policy Organizations* (Thousand Oaks, CA: Sage, 2000).

9. James Wolfensohn, *Coalitions for Change: Address to the Board of Governors* (Washington, DC: World Bank, September 28, 1999), 3.

10. Bernard Wason, *The Silliness of Demonizing Trade* (New York: Century Fund, 1999).

11. Ignacio Ramonet, "Dueling Globalizations: Let Them Eat Big Macs," *Foreign Policy* (Fall 1999): 126.

12. Wolfensohn, *Coalitions for Change*, 3.

13. Ibid., 6.

14. Mark Malloch Brown, Foreword to *United Nations Development Program Human Development Report 1999* (New York: United Nations, 2000).

15. Wolfgang Reinicke, "Global Public Policy," *Foreign Affairs* (November/December 1997): 128.

16. Susan Strange, *The Retreat of the State: The Diffusion of Power in the World Economy* (Cambridge: Cambridge University Press, 1996), 189.

17. United Nations Development Programme, *Global Public Goods: International Cooperation in the 21st Century*, ed. Inge Kaul, Isabelle Grunberg, and Marc A. Stern (New York: Oxford University Press, 1999).

18. Kenneth Waltz, *Address on Realism, Globalization, and Comparative Politics* (Washington, DC: School of International Service, American University, November 30, 1999).

19. Maryann K. Cusimano, *Beyond Sovereignty: Issues for a Global Agenda* (New York: St. Martin's, 1999). Although many policymakers (and sometimes even scholars) use the term *transnational problems*, I instead use the more accurate term *transsovereign problems* because the term *nation* is *not* synonymous with the term *sovereign state*. A nation is a group with a common cultural, linguistic, ethnic, racial, or religious identity. A sovereign state, however, is an internationally recognized

unit of political authority over a given territory. National boundaries (where various ethnic or linguistic groups are located) often do not coincide with sovereign state boundaries. There are by some counts over 8,000 national groups, while there are only 185 sovereign states. While *transnational* is a common word, as present policy in Kosovo shows, there is a great deal of confusion about the relationship between nations and states, and as political scientists we want to clarify, not add to, the confusion. The terms *transstate*, *transborder*, or *global* are equally correct.

20. Thierry Linard de Gueterchin, S.J., *A Christmas Present for the Ford Workers in the ABC of Sao Paulo* (Washington, DC: Centro Cultural de Brasilia Global Economies and Culture Project, in conjunction with the Woodstock Theological Center, Georgetown University, April 6, 1999).

21. Dinah Shelton, *Commitment and Compliance: What Role for International "Soft Law?"* (Oxford: Oxford University Press, 2000).

22. Wolfensohn, *Coalitions for Change*, 6.

23. Kofi Annan, Secretary-General Proposes Global Compact on Human Rights, Labour, Environment, in Address to World Economic Forum in Davos (New York: UN Press Release, January 31, 1999).

3 International Competitiveness of Nations in a Globalized Economy

_____ *Dominick Salvatore*

The past decade has witnessed an increasingly rapid tendency toward globalization in the world economy. Rapid globalization has occurred in national tastes, in production, and in labor markets, and this has sharply increased international competitiveness of nations.

The first section of this chapter examines the rapid process of globalization that has taken place during the past decade in the world economy and the reasons for its occurrence. The second section provides some data on the international competitive position of nations and the reasons for the United States being in first place. The third section examines the differential effect of globalization and international competition on labor markets in the United States and in other leading industrial countries. The last part discusses the crucial importance of international competitiveness in the world today.

GLOBALIZATION OF THE ECONOMY

The tremendous improvement in telecommunications and transportation during the past decade has led to a strong cross-fertilization of cultures and convergence of tastes around the world. Tastes in the United States affect tastes around the world and tastes abroad strongly influence tastes in the United States. Coca-Cola has 40 percent of the U.S. market and an incredible 33 percent of the world's soft drink market, and today you can buy a McDonald's hamburger in most major cities of the world. As tastes become global, firms are responding more and more with truly global products. For example, in 1990, Gillette introduced its new Sensor

Razor at the same time in most nations of the world and used the same advertisement (except for language) in nineteen countries in Europe and North America. By 1999, Gillette had sold over 400 million of its razors and more than 7 billion cartridges. In 1994, Ford spent more than $6 billion to create its "global car" conceived and produced in the United States and Europe and sold under the names Ford Contour and Mercury Mystique in the United States and Mondeo in the rest of the world. The list of global products is likely to grow rapidly in the future and we are likely to move closer and closer to a truly global supermarket.

In his 1983 article "The Globalization of Markets" in the *Harvard Business Review*, Theodore Levitt asserted that consumers from New York to Frankfurt to Tokyo want similar products and that success for producers in the future would require more and more standardized products and pricing around the world. In fact, in country after country, we are seeing the emergence of a middle-class consumer lifestyle based on a taste for comfort, convenience, and speed. In the food business, this means packaged, fast-to-prepare, and ready-to-eat products. Market researchers have discovered that similarities in living styles among middle-class people all over the world are much greater than we once thought and are growing with rising incomes and educational levels. Many small national differences in taste do, of course, remain; for example, Nestlé markets more than two hundred blends of Nescafé coffee to cater to differences in tastes in different markets. But the converging trend in tastes around the world is unmistakable and is likely to lead to more and more global products. This is true not only for foods and inexpensive consumer products but also for automobiles, portable computers, phones, and many other durable products.

Globalization has also occurred in the production of goods and services with the rapid rise of global corporations. These are companies that are run by an international team of managers, have research and production facilities in many countries, use parts and components from the cheapest source around the world, and sell their products, finance their operation, and are owned by stockholders throughout the world. In fact, more and more corporations operate today on the belief that their very survival requires that they become one of a handful of global corporations in their sector. This is true in automobiles, steel, aircrafts, computers, telecommunications, consumer electronics, chemicals, drugs, and many other products. Nestlé, the largest Swiss company and the world's second largest food company has production facilities in fifty-nine countries, and America's Gillette has production facilities in twenty-two countries. Ford has component factories in twenty-six different industrial sites around the world, assembly plants in six countries, and employs more people abroad (201,000) than in the United States (188,000). One important form that globalization in production often takes in today's corporation is in foreign "sourcing" of inputs. There is practically no major product today that does not have some foreign inputs. Foreign sourcing is often not a matter of choice for corporations to earn higher profits, but simply a requirement for them to remain competitive. Firms that do not look abroad for less expensive inputs face loss of competitiveness in world markets and even in the domestic market. This is the reason that $625 of the $860 total cost of producing an IBM PC was incurred for parts and components manufactured by IBM outside the United States or purchased from foreign producers during the mid-1980s. Such low-cost offshore purchase of inputs is likely to continue to expand rapidly in the future and is being fostered by joint ventures, licensing arrangements, and other nonequity collaborative arrangements. Indeed, this represents one of the most dynamic aspects of the global business environment today.

Foreign sourcing can be regarded as manufacturing's new *international* economies of scale in today's global economy. Just as companies were forced to rationalize operations within each country in the 1980s, they now face the challenge of integrating their operations for their entire system of manufacturing around the world to take advantage of the new international economies of scale. What is important is for the firm to focus on those components that are indispensable to the company's competitive position over subsequent product generations and "outsource" other components for which outside suppliers have a distinctive production advantage. Indeed, globalization in production has proceeded so far that it is now difficult to determine the nationality of many products. For example, should a Honda Accord produced in Ohio be considered American? What about a Chrysler minivan produced in Canada? What about now that Chrysler has been acquired by Daimler-Benz (Mercedes)? Is a Kentucky Toyota or Mazda that uses nearly 50 percent of imported Japanese parts American? It is clearly becoming more and more difficult to define what is American, and opinions differ widely. One could legitimately even ask if this question is relevant in a world growing more and more interdependent and globalized. Today, the ideal corporation is strongly decentralized to allow local units to develop products that fit into local cultures, and yet at its very core is very centralized to coordinate activities around the globe.

Even more dramatic has been the globalization of labor markets around the world. Services and production activities, which were previously done in the United States and other industrial countries, are now often done at lower cost in developing countries. And this is the case not only for low-skilled assembly-line jobs but also for jobs requiring high computer and engineering skills. Most Americans have only now come to fully realize that there is a truly competitive labor force in the world today willing and able to do their job at a much lower cost. If anything, this trend is likely to accelerate in the future.

Even service industries are not immune to global job competition. For example, more than thirty-five hundred workers on the island of Jamaica, connected to the United States by satellite dishes, make airline reservations, process tickets, answer calls to toll-free numbers, and do data entry for U.S. airlines at a much lower cost than could be done in the United States. Nor are highly skilled and professional people spared from global competition. A few years ago, Texas Instruments set up an impressive software programming operation in Bangalore, a city of four million people in southern India. Other American multinationals soon followed. Motorola, IBM, AT&T, and many other high-tech firms are now doing even a great deal of basic research abroad. American workers are beginning to raise strong objections to the transfer of skilled jobs abroad. Of course, many European and Japanese firms are setting up production and research facilities in the United States and employing many American professionals. In the future, more and more work will simply be done in places best equipped to do the job most economically. Try to restrict the flow of work abroad to protect jobs in the United States, and the company risks loosing international competitiveness or ends up moving all of its operations abroad.

GLOBALIZATION AND THE INTERNATIONAL COMPETITIVENESS OF NATIONS

During the 1970s and 1980s, the United States lost relative competitiveness in one industry after another with respect to Japan and, in some industries, even with respect to Europe and the newly industrializing economies of Asia. Since the late 1980s and early 1990s, however, the United States has recaptured most of the lost competitiveness ground and in 1994 it was ranked once again as the most competitive economy in the world, displacing Japan, which had occupied that position since 1985. The United States was judged the most competitive economy in the world in each subsequent year up to the year 2000. Indeed, during the past year it has increased its lead over the other G-7 (most important) industrial nations.

The Institute for Management Development in Lousanne (2000) assigned a competitive index of 100 to the United States, 64.4 to Germany (this means that Germany was about 35 percent less efficient on an overall level with respect to the United States), 63.4 to Canada, 59.3 to the United Kingdom, 57.3 to Japan, 54.3 to France, and 34.7 to Italy. To be sure, in the ranking, between the United States and Germany there were six other nations (Singapore, Finland, the Netherlands, Switzerland, Luxembourg, and Ireland), but these were very small nations and cannot be compared to large industrial nations (the G-7 countries). In any event, most of the competition that the United States faces as a country comes from the other G-7 countries rather than from these small countries. Out of the forty-six countries that were ranked, Japan came in seventeenth in the year 2000.

Competitiveness was defined as the ability of a country or company to generate more wealth for its people than its competitors in world markets. Eight factors were used in measuring the relative productivity of each nation: (1) domestic economic strength (measured by the degree of competition in the economy); (2) internationalization (measured by the degree by which the nation participates in international trade and investments); (3) government (given by the degree by which government policies are conducive to competitiveness); (4) finance (given by the performance of capital markets and the quality of financial services); (5) infrastructure (extent to which resources and systems are adequate to serve the basic needs of business); (6) management (extent to which enterprises are managed in an innovative and profitable manner); (7) science and technology (scientific and technological capacity); and (8) people (availability and qualifications of human resources). The United States ranked first among the G-7 countries in seven out of the eight factors. It ranked second only in factor 3 (government) after Canada.

Measuring international competitiveness, however, is an ambitious and difficult undertaking and there are only a handful of such comprehensive studies. Although useful, the competitiveness study discussed above faces a number of serious shortcomings. One is the grouping and measuring of international competitiveness of developed and developing countries and of large and small countries together. It is well-known, however, that developed and developing countries, on the one hand, and large and small countries, on the other hand, have very different industrial structures and face different competitiveness problems. Using the same method of measuring the international competitiveness for all types of countries, thus, may not be appropriate and the results may not be very informative or, at least, may be difficult to interpret.

Another serious shortcoming with the above competitiveness measure is that the correlation between real per capita income and standard of living of the various nations may not be very high. For example, the United Kingdom has a higher competitiveness index, higher than Japan's even though its real per capita income is more than one-quarter lower than Japan's. Similarly, the United Kingdom has a competitiveness index much higher than Italy even though their real per capita income is practically the same. The questions that naturally arise are, If Italy is so much less competitive than the United Kingdom, how can it have an equal real per capita income? Where is Italy's high per capita income and standard of living coming from? In economics, we like to think that productivity determines per capita income and the standard of living and it is disconcerting to see such a blatant variance between expectations and reality. As a result, these overall international competitiveness figures must be taken with a grain of salt. Furthermore, a nation may score low on its overall competitiveness and still have some sectors in which it is very productive and efficient. Nevertheless, and to the extent that entrepreneurs and managers rely on these overall competitiveness measures in deciding whether to invest in a nation or in another, these overall competitiveness measures are important.

RELATIVE LABOR AND CAPITAL PRODUCTIVITY IN THE UNITED STATES, JAPAN, AND GERMANY

Table 1 shows labor productivity in terms of value added per hour worked in various industries in Japan and Germany relative to the United States in 1990. Taking the labor productivity in the United States as 100, we can see from the table that Japan's labor was more productive than U.S. labor by 47 percent in steel, 24 percent in auto parts, 19 percent in metalworking, 16 percent in automobiles, and 15 percent in consumer electronics. On the other hand, U.S. labor was more productive than Japanese labor in computers and general merchandising retailing (beer, soaps and detergents, and especially food). For all industries together, Japanese labor was, on the average, only 83 percent as productive as U.S. labor. Table 1 also shows that German labor was as productive as U.S.

TABLE 1
Productivity of Japanese and German Labor Relative to U.S. Labor, with U.S. Index = 100

Industry	Japanese	German
Steel	147	100
Auto Parts	124	76
Metalworking	119	100
Automobiles	116	66
Consumer Electronics	115	76
Computers	95	89
Telecommunications	77	52
General Merchandising Retailing	44	96
All Industries	83	79

Source: Elaboration on McKinsey Global Institute (1993).

labor only in steel and metalworking and less productive in all other industries, especially in beer production. Overall, German labor was only 79 percent as productive as U.S. labor.

In a more recent study—of productivity of German and French industry relative to U.S. industry—the McKinsey Global Institute (1997) found that German and French productivity increased over the past decade but at a slower rate than U.S. productivity and so it is now further behind U.S. industry today than it was a decade ago. Overall, McKinsey found that German industry is 30 percent less efficient and French industry is 40 percent less efficient than U.S. industry. In general, the higher U.S. labor productivity is not due to bigger firms, more automation, or better managers (although these factors might be determinant in some specific industries), but is the result of greater competition and much more flexible labor practices in the United States than abroad. Specifically, the higher U.S. productivity depends on the ability of U.S. managers to introduce new and improved products much faster than abroad and the ability of U.S. engineers to invent new and more efficient ways of making products and designing products that are easy to make.

Furthermore, despite the fact that the United States has in recent years been saving and investing less than Japan, Germany, and France (and, for that matter, less than most other nations), it seems to have gotten more mileage out of its investments. In fact, the McKinsey Global Institute (1996) found that Germany and Japan use their physical capital only about two-thirds as efficiently as the United States. McKinsey looked at the entire economy and five industries in-depth: telecommunications, utilities, auto manufacturing, food processing, and retailing. It found that Germany uses excessive capital for the job at hand. For example, the phone cables for Deutsche Telekom are built to withstand being run over by a tank, even though the cables are underground. Such "gold-plating" of equipment is expensive and wasteful. Japan keeps massive electrical generating capacity idle most of the time in order to meet peak demand on hot summer days, while the United States avoids this great capital waste by creative time-of-day and summer electricity pricing schemes that discourage usage at peak times. Such higher capital productivity translates into higher financial returns for U.S. savers—9.1 percent compared with 7.4 percent in Germany and 7.1 percent in Japan. This higher U.S. capital productivity more than makes up for its lower savings rate than Germany and Japan.

Since the 1970s, the United States has moved faster than Japan, Germany, and France and other nations in deregulating (that is, in removing government regulations and controls of economic activities) airlines, telecommunications, trucking, banking, and other sectors of the economy. For example, cutthroat competition makes American airlines about one-third more productive than the larger regulated or government-run foreign airlines. General merchandise retailing is twice as efficient in the United States as in Japan, and so is American telecommunications in relation to German telecommunications. Most American firms today face much stiffer competition from domestic and foreign firms than their European and Japanese counterparts. Stiff competition makes most American firms lean and mean—and generally more efficient than foreign firms.

A second reason for higher productivity of U.S. than Japanese and European labor is the much higher degree of computerization in the United States than Japan or Europe. The United States has sixty-three computers per one hundred employed workers to Japan's seventeen and even fewer in Europe. Labor flexibility is still another reason for the larger productivity of U.S. labor. While labor practices abroad are often constrained by unions, social policies, and regulation, U.S. firms are much freer to hire, fire, reorganize, and use labor and other resources where they are most productive. This makes life difficult for U.S. workers who can lose their jobs when caught in a competitive squeeze, but it also enhances firm efficiency and labor productivity. Coupled with adequate job creation, this higher labor productivity is responsible for the higher gross domestic product (GDP) per capita and standard of living in the United States than abroad.

THE IMPORTANCE OF INTERNATIONAL COMPETITIVENESS FOR A NATION

In a 1994 article, Paul Krugman stated that international competitiveness is an irrelevant and dangerous concept because nations simply do not compete with each other the way corporations do, and that increases in productivity rather than international competitiveness are all that matter for increasing the standard of living of a nation. In trying to prove his point, Krugman points out that U.S. trade represents only about 10–15 percent of U.S. GDP (and so international trade cannot significantly effect the standard of living, at least in the United States), international trade is not a zero-sum game (so that all nations can gain from international trade), and that concern with international competitiveness can lead governments to the wrong policies (such as trade restrictions and industrial policies).

All of these statements are true, but Krugman's conclusion that because international trade is only 10–15 percent of U.S. GDP, it cannot significantly affect the U.S. standard of living, simply does not follow. The reason is that if a nation's corporations innovate and increase productivity at a lower rate than foreign corporations, the nation may be relegated to exporting products that are technologically less advanced and this may compromise its future growth. For example, the U.S. superiority in software makes possible faster productivity growth in the United States both directly (because productivity growth is faster in the software industry than in many other industries) and indirectly (by increasing the productivity of many other sectors, such as automobiles, which make great use of computer software in design and production). Thus, international competitiveness is crucial to the nation's standard of living.

Pointing out, as Krugman does, that some high-tech sectors artificially protected by trade policies and/or encouraged by industrial policies have grown less rapidly than some low-tech sectors, such as cigarettes and beer production, misses the point. This only proves that wrong policies can be costly. Productivity growth and international competitiveness must be encouraged not by protectionist or industrial policies by improving the factors affecting international competitiveness discussed in the previous section. A country's future prosperity depends on its growth in productivity and this can certainly be influenced by government policies. Nations compete in the sense that they choose policies that promote productivity. As pointed out by John Dunning (1995) and Michael Porter (1990), international competitiveness does matter.

That industrial policies and protectionism only provide temporary benefits to the targeted or protected industries but slows down the growth of productivity and standards of living in the long run, is clearly evidenced by the competitiveness situation in Europe vis-à-vis the United States and Japan today. Aside from banking and the space industry (and, maybe, the chemical industry), there is practically no other industry in Europe that can stand up to U.S. and Japanese competition. This is the case for the steel industry, the automobile industry, the commercial aircraft industry, the airline industry, the computer industry, and many others. Without the billions of dollars that some of these industries receive in subsidies or for repeated restructuring and trade protection, and without alliances with U.S. or Japanese firms, most European firms in these industries would be unable to compete with U.S. and Japanese firms. Seven of the top ten computers firms (including the top five) in Europe are American, one is Japanese, and only two are European. In software, America has an undisputed lead. In telecommunications, online services, biotech, and aircraft the United States also has a big lead over Europe. In automobiles, Japan has an undisputed lead and even U.S. automakers are much more efficient than Europeans. To be sure, European automobiles are of high quality, but command a much higher price than Japanese automobiles and a higher price than even American automobiles.

Although Europe has been able to keep wages and standards of living relatively high and rising during the past two decades, the rate of unemployment is nearly double the U.S. rate and three times higher than the unemployment rate in Japan. And while the United States, with a smaller population than Europe, has created more than thirty million jobs during the past thirty years, employment has stagnated in Europe. The United States has also been much more successful than European countries in meeting the growing competition from newly industrializing and other emerging economies in Asia (see Rausch, 1995).

The restructuring and downsizing that rapid technological change and increasing international competition required has resulted in average wages and salaries not rising very much in real terms in the United States during the past decade, however, millions of new jobs have been created. In Europe, on the other hand, real wages and salaries grew but few new jobs were created, and this left Europe less able to compete on the world market than the United States and Japan. It is true that Japan has also been very protectionistic and made extensive use of industrial policies in the past, but Japan fostered intense competition at home, while Europe did not. The result has been that Japanese firms have become highly competitive while European firms have not. Being unable to fire workers when not needed, firms have tended to increase output by increasing capital per worker rather than by hiring more labor and this has made the return to capital lower and the wage of labor higher in Europe than in the United States.

REFERENCES

Dunning, John H. 1995. Think Again Professor Krugman: Competitiveness Does Matter. *International Executive* 37 (4): 315–324.

Institute for Management Development. 2000. *The World Competitiveness Yearbook.* Lousanne, Switzerland: Institute for Management Development.

Levitt, Theodore. 1983. The Globalization of Markets. *Harvard Business Review* (May–June): 92–102.

Krugman, Paul. 1994. Competitiveness: A Dangerous Obsession. *Foreign Affairs* (March–April): 28–44.

McKinsey Global Institute. 1993. *Manufacturing Productivity.* Washington, DC: McKinsey Global Institute.

———. 1996. *Capital Productivity.* Washington, DC: McKinsey Global Institute.

———. 1997. *Removing Barriers to Growth and Employment in France and Germany.* Washington, DC: McKinsey Global Institute.

Porter, Michael. 1990. *The Comparative Advantage of Nations.* New York: Free Press.

Rausch, Lawrence M. 1995. *Asia's New High-Tech Competitors.* Washington, DC: National Science Foundation.

4 Globalized Financial Markets

Ann E. Davis

This chapter will review major theories about the role of money in the economy. A particular area of emphasis is the role of money as a control device. According to this argument, money is not a "veil" and it is not "neutral," contrary to much theory in the mainstream. Rather it is used as a means of disciplining labor, financing government, and supporting government spending. While not part of the usual approach to analysis of money, these aspects help provide insights into the role of government, supported by its ability to issue currency and to protect the value of the currency. There is widespread agreement in the economics literature that a fundamental threshold has been crossed in the nature of globalization since the early 1970s.

For journalist Thomas L. Friedman, the new system is ten years old.[1] He suggests that there have been three periods of globalization, the first from the mid-1800s to the late 1920s, the second from 1945 to 1989, and the third since the fall of the Berlin Wall. What is new in the past ten years is partly scale, as reflected in daily trading volume of foreign exchange, as well as the number of countries involved. What is also new is the worldwide consensus on the free market system, a point made by Daniel Yergin and Joseph Stanislaw (1998) as well.

Former U.S. Treasury Secretary Lawrence H. Summers stated in his Richard T. Ely Lecture at the Allied Social Science Association meetings in Boston in January 2000:

Recent years have witnessed a sea change in the global financial system, as the flow of private capital from industrial to developing countries has mushroomed from $174 billion in the 1980s to $1.3 trillion during the 1990s. In 1990, one emerging-market economy issued sovereign Eurobonds. By 1998, 40 or so emerging-market economies had issued them over the course of the 1990s. And the incidence of major financial accidents [sic] has risen sharply, to the point where in the fall of 1998 we experienced what many regarded as the worst financial crisis of the last 50 years following Russia's default, leading many to question the premise that an integrated global financial system is desirable. (2000, 2)

MEASURES OF GLOBALIZATION

According to some, the relevant measure of globalization is the type and the volatility of capital flows (see, for example, Pugel and Lindert [2000]). Net long-term capital flows to developing countries remained relatively stable in the 1980s, beginning with $83 billion in 1980 and returning to that same level in 1989, after a decline of 20 percent by 1986. Then from 1990 to 1997 the total tripled, from $101 billion to $338 billion, declining again in 1998 by nearly 20 percent to $275 billion. Over the period from 1980 to 1998, the share of official capital went from 42 percent of the total long-term financial flows in 1980 to a high of 70 percent in 1986 to a low of 10 percent in 1996. The share of private debt went from one-half in 1980 to one-third in 1996 to 20 percent in 1998. Net inflows of short-term capital have been even more variable. From $20 billion in 1990, the total tripled to $60 billion in 1995, before falling to $5 billion in 1998, only 25 percent of the 1990 level (Pugel and Lindert, 2000, 606).

From other points of view, the relevant measure of globalization of finance is the relative size of currency trading relative to central bank reserves. Daily turnover of foreign exchange increased from $18.3 billion in 1977 to $1.2 trillion in 1995. Over that same period, the ratio of global official foreign exchange reserves to daily trading volume went from 14.5 to 1.0. The ratio of annual global foreign exchange volume to annual world exports went from 3.51 in 1977 to 64.06 in 1995 (Felix, 1998, 172). These measures reveal the extent to which exchange rates are beyond control of central banks, and trading of foreign exchange is conducted for speculative as opposed to trade-related purposes. As Friedman (1999) puts it simply, "*No one is in charge*" of the "Electronic Herd," his term for the "often anonymous stock, bond and currency traders and multinational investors, connected by screens and networks" (112–113; italics in original). Kenneth Rogoff (1999, 28) presents a point of view similar to that of Friedman. Not only is the amount of funds available to the International Monetary Fund (IMF) small relative to global output, but having a larger amount accessible to the "lender of last resort" may also lead to problems of moral hazard, and would therefore be undesirable.

To others, the measure of globalization of finance is the magnitude of cross-border capital flows relative to gross domestic product. For example, the share of private capital flows to the "crisis countries in Asia" (Indonesia, Korea, Malaysia, the Phillippines, and Thailand) went from over 5 percent of gross domestic product in 1979 to a negative 8 percent in 1997, the year of the Asian crisis (Little and Olivei, 1999).

For still others it is the interdependence between advanced and emerging economies in the same global financial system, and the increased potential for contagion. The good news in the article by Bong-Chan Kho, Dong Lee, and Rene M. Stulz (2000) is that only exposed banks were affected by the crises in the emerging markets in the 1990s and the collapse of "Long Term Capital Management," the hedge fund. The evidence in their article makes clear, nonetheless, that "a subset of banks could lose 29% of their equity capitalization in six trading days," still a phenomenal impact on the U.S. financial system, relative to past years. As noted by another recent contribution, "[T]he liquidity crisis that did occur forced the Federal Reserve to relax U.S. monetary policy and to coordinate the rescue of the hedge fund Long Term Capital Management" (Calvo and Mendoza, 2000, 59). As former Treasury Secretary Robert Rubin is reported to have said, "I can't imagine that twenty or twenty-five years ago my predecessors would have been worried about an economic crisis in Thailand or Indonesia, or even Korea" (Friedman, 1999, 249; also see Kho, Lee, and Stulz, 2000, 28).

Globalization of finance is different, then, from the globalization of trade and even investment. The exchange of currencies for the purposes of arbitrage, unrelated to trade in goods and services, is a new phenomenon, partly facilitated by technology and communications, as well as the integration of countries into a single global system, the relative freeing of exchange rates since 1973, and the elimination of capital controls since the 1980s (Kaminsky and Reinhart, 1999). The whole system is anchored by a set of institutions that have replaced or been significantly restructured since the end of Bretton Woods and the General Agreement on Tariffs and Trade, now centered on the World Trade Organization and the International Monetary Fund, with a global consensus in support of the ideological hegemony of free market system capitalism.

THE MONEY MYSTIQUE

This globalization of finance has occurred, however, with a lack of theoretical consensus on the nature of money. According to Richard Cooper, "One factor that has inhibited serious resolution of exchange rate choices is the continuing use by the economic profession of an extraordinarily primitive theory of money in its theorizing, and its insistence on separating monetary and real factors in analyzing economies" (1999, 106). There are various heuristic definitions of money within the economics literature:

1. *Neoclassical:* Money is a veil, and the economy is driven by "real" production and profit motives. The interest rate is set by intertemporal time preferences, not the supply and demand for money.

2. *Keynes:* The quantity of money matters in interest rate determination and incentives to invest. The supply and demand for money determines the interest rate, not the rate of time preference. Keynes's innovation was to include the asset demand for money, and to consider that money has its own rate of return, relative to other financial assets.

3. *Marx:* The belief that money has "value" is a characteristic of "commodity fetishism"; the appearance that money has its own value is a façade, an illusion that obscures the origin of profit in exploitation of labor. The power of money to expand value is based on the ability to hire and command labor in production and to sell the product for a price higher than the wages paid to the workers. Money has to be continually reinvested in production to have "self-expanding value," $M - M'$. Profit and rates of return are actually produced by labor and obscured in the process of exchange between labor, money, and commodities. The particular commodities that serve as money are arbitrary, but symbolize the purchasing power, the command of labor, and the access to the myriad pleasures that can be purchased as commodities in the capitalist marketplace.

But even these three diverse views do not encompass all the relevant dimensions of money. For example, according to Pedrou Pou (1999), what makes the globalization of the past twenty-five years unique is the presence of "fiat money," which has only existed since the end of the Bretton Woods arrangement: "Until very recently the dominant monetary arrangement was one that relied either directly or indirectly on monies backed by gold. . . . Indeed, we have become so accustomed to the use of fiat money, and to its main property, namely an independent monetary policy, that we sometimes miss the point that *fiat money is a very recent innovation, one that is only 25 years old.* It was not really until the collapse of the Bretton Woods arrangement in 1973 that true fiat money appeared" (244; italics in original). This view would place gold in a different category than fiat money, such as paper money or even electronic transfers. What this view misses is that even the use of gold as money is embedded in an institutional framework, typically of a nation-state, which "backs" the designation of any particular object as money, as legal tender. Arguably what money also represents is the power of the state to enforce contracts, including creditor/debtor, payment of taxes to the government, and labor contracts.

As Friedman (1999) puts it, "Sustainable globalization requires a stable power structure. . . . The hidden hand of the market will never work without a hidden fist. Markets function and flourish only when property rights are secure and can be enforced, which, in turn, requires a political framework protected and backed by military power. . . . And the hidden fist that keeps the world safe for Silicon Valley's technologies to flourish is called the U.S. Army, Air Force, Navy, and Marine Corps. And these fighting forces and institutions are paid for by American taxpayer dollars" (464).

What Rogoff (1999) sees as an important set of "imperfections in international capital markets" is the difficulty in "enforcing contracts across borders" (24). According to Pou (1999), "[M]ost emerging economies have attempted to develop their own fiat money, but have not succeeded," a fact that he believes *"lies at the core of the problems of the international financial architecture, at least with respect to emerging countries"* (246; italics in original).

Perhaps the difficulties of production of money involve not just the selection of the "optimal currency area," as in Robert Mundell's analysis. which includes such considerations as openness to trade, labor mobility, symmetry of shocks, and the presence of compensating fiscal transfers (Little and Olivei, 1999, 66). Additional considerations may also include the power of the nation-state to enforce contracts domestically and to promote national interests in international bargaining arenas. The size and competitiveness of the economy is an additional consideration that affects the international demand for the currency. In this view, the liquidity of a currency is analogous to a network externality represented by the issuing nation's international economic power, the credibility of control of inflation (and, hence, labor contracts), and the strength of its military.

THE ORIGIN OF MONEY

The history of the production of money in the context of nation-states has been reviewed by Benjamin Cohen (1998). As he points out, only at the Peace of Westphalia (1648) did nation-states agree to recognize the territorial sovereignty of each other. The power to issue money is one of the powers of the sovereign state, but it was not until the mid-nineteenth century that most nations had achieved a single unified national currency. For example, in 1844 the Bank Charter Act established the Bank of England and the national currency system. The dollar was not recognized in the United States as the country's sole legal tender until 1861 (Cohen, 1998, 33–34). The Federal Reserve Act was only passed in 1913, consolidating a single national financial system. Some of the actions necessary to establish a national currency were the declaration of the dollar as acceptable in payment of debt and taxes, and the prohibition of the use of any other currency, to prevent currency substitution.

Although the power to determine and manage the national currency is the assumed role of national governments (Polanyi, 1944, 202–203), the actual period in which this norm was in effect was only from 1870 to 1970. This period ended with the demise of the Bretton Woods system in 1971, an international system of stabilization exchange rates among the currencies of the major capitalist countries.

The authority to issue currency gives governments four important powers (Cohen, 1998, 35–46): (1) symbol of political unity, (2) seigniorage, (3) macroeconomic management, and (4) monetary insulation. To elaborate each point:

1. Often coins and currency are engraved with important national symbols.
2. Seigniorage refers to the power to control real assets by the issuing authority. The government will issue the currency, at a certain cost, and gain access to real resources that are probably more valuable than the production cost of the currency. This is a once-for-all gain. A second gain is the ability to allow the currency value to depreciate, in reference to the real assets, giving the government a form of "inflation tax."
3. Control over the money supply by the government allows influence of the rate of investment through the effect on interest rates, as well as the exchange rate.
4. Monetary insulation prevents control by foreign governments. For example, the country of Panama uses the U.S. dollar as its currency. While this is a strategy to assure stability and liquidity, it can be difficult during strained relationships with the United States. In the 1980s, the Reagan administration froze Panamanian assets in the United States and prohibited all dollar transfers to Panama, as a method to sanction Commander General Noriega for drug trafficking. The overall economy suffered severe consequences, including a contraction of 20 percent. (See also LeBaron and McCulloch [2000].)

If the power of nations is based on taxation and control of the military, a national currency is essential in order to lay claim to these real resources.

MONEY AS A DISCIPLINARY DEVICE

- Inflation and income distribution (contract money supply, raise interest rates to raise unemployment rate to lower wages to modify inflation; Baker, Epstein, and Pollin [1998]).
- Cash nexus for traditional societies.

- Cash nexus for less developed countries.
- Seignorage for natural resources for less developed countries (Amin, 1978).

Does the specific currency matter? In most theoretical economic discussions, the particular currency in question does not matter, especially in the neoclassical school of thought. But there are contexts for which it does matter. In the case of national sovereignty, the particular currency in circulation does matter, according to whether it is legal tender in that nation or not. Each national government, with control over the supply of its own domestic currency, can have significant control over its real value in terms of purchasing power, whereas in exchange with the currencies of other nations, there are more factors beyond its control.

Since the breakdown of the Bretton Woods system, and the presence of freely floating exchange rates, some currencies are more stable than others. Cohen (1998) argues that there is now a system of competition among currencies to become dominant.

Currencies become more attractive as they are used more widely. This is like a network externality. The more a currency is used, the broader the market for it, the less likely that any particular trader will affect its price, and the more likely that there will be a buyer for every seller, and vice versa. This increases the liquidity and the stability of the currency, in a type of first-mover advantage (Cohen, 1998, 154). Currencies of countries with large, stable economies and substantial military power are also more influential. Often rules of international finance must be enforced or even imposed on other countries, giving a country with military power some extra leverage. This was true of the relative economic and military power of England when the pound sterling was the dominant international currency, and the United States when the dollar was the key international currency (Block, 1977). Before the issuance of the euro, the key currencies were the dollar, the deutsche mark, and the yen (Cohen, 1998, 60–62).

Nations may actually compete to promote their currencies (Cohen, 1998, 138–142). For example, the U.S. government is explicitly concerned with the market share of its currency (Cohen, 1998, 153). Competition among "the big three" currencies—the euro, the yen, and the dollar—may complicate international coordination needed in any international financial crisis, like the Asian crisis in the summer of 1997 (Cohen, 1998, 156–164).

The related advantages to a country for having a powerful currency (Cohen, 1998, 119–130) include:

1. *Symbol:* A strong international currency has become a matter of national pride.
2. *International Seigniorage:* For example, if the U.S. dollar is in demand for international trading purposes, the United States can import products, pay

with dollars, and have those dollars traded internationally, without ever being "redeemed" for goods and services produced in the United States. This increases the real standard of living in the United States (Cohen, 1998, 123). This factor also helps account for the continual U.S. balance of payments deficit (Block, 1997). Also, if U.S. dollars are held as international reserve currency, rather than in bonds or stocks, there is no interest of dividend payment that the United States must pay. Also, foreign direct investments in key currencies, such as dollars, are more welcome in other countries, facilitating the international transactions of U.S. multinational corporations. This preference for dollars may also extend to the U.S.-based investment banks and the development of New York as a world finance capital. And to the extent to which foreign demand for the dollar as an international currency increases its value, U.S. citizens can purchase more goods produced overseas, because of the dollar's greater relative purchasing power.

3. *Macromanagement:* The wider the use of a currency, the easier the international adjustment of balance of payments imbalances. For example, the United States routinely runs a trade deficit in goods and services. However, other countries prefer to accumulate dollars for use as reserve currency because the dollar is a key currency and they have more confidence in financial assets denominated in dollars, which can help balance the capital account.

4. *Political Insulation:* Large powerful countries with key currencies can influence the terms in which other countries gain access to their currency, giving them more leverage, and potential coercive power. They can often set the international financial rules in their favor, as a result. An example is the dominant role of the United States in the IMF.

With governments competing to achieve dominance in an international currency hierarchy, the balance of power may shift to the private currency traders, who have the market power to choose among competing currencies (Cohen, 1998, 130). In a context in which governments try to please "the markets," there is some concern about a "crisis of legitimacy" (Cohen, 1998, 147–149), in which democratically elected governments are subject to the choices of those with economic and financial power. (For example, dollarization may provide a more stable currency, but increase the risk of political and economic coercion from abroad. Anonymous market actors or foreign central banks substitute for the country's own elected government [Cohen, 1998, 165–166].)

FINANCIAL INSTABILITY HYPOTHESIS VERSUS EFFICIENT MARKET HYPOTHESIS

Despite conventional wisdom in strong support of international capital flows (Cooper, 1999, 112), there have been recent extensive examinations that raise the question about whether capital flows can be destabilizing in the wake of the 1997–1998 Asian crisis (see Rogoff, 1999, 21–23; Madrick, 2000a, 2000b).[2] There are various explanations of the increasing frequency of international financial crises (Aizenman, 1999, 3; Kaminsky and Reinhart, 1999, 475–480; Mishkin, 1999, 6–10; Pou, 1999, 246–247; Gilpin, 2000, 150–160).

Quoting John Maynard Keynes and Hyman P. Minsky, some see international finance as inherently unstable (Bhagwati, 1998; Gilpin, 2000, 137–138). David Felix (1998) argues that the traditional positive relationship between the development of the domestic financial sector and economic growth has been reversed since the end of the Bretton Woods era: "Higher volatility [since the early 1970s] increases liquidity and other risks of investing long term, tilting private investors toward investments with faster payoffs. It has led nonfinancial corporations to raise the investment share devoted to purchases of existing firms and buybacks of their stock and to lower the share devoted to constructing new capacity" (181–182).

Ross Levine's recent review of the literature (1997) affirms the orthodox relationship between the development of the domestic financial sector and economic growth, but explicitly does *not* take into account "the relationship between international finance and growth" (690). Michael Klein and Giovanni Olivei (1999) suggest that institutional change must occur before the desirable impact of international capital flows can be experienced. Levine's review (1997) also stresses the importance of the institutional development of the financial sector, including the full range of financial instruments and intermediaries, not just money and banks, as well as "a country's legal system and political institutions" (690). This research suggests a sequencing of reforms, in which the development of the institutions of finance, if not also political democracy, precedes liberalization of the capital account.

In a recent discussion of the efficacy of capital controls, Sebastian Edwards (1999) puts the issue succinctly:

During the 1990s, a number of authors argued that a successful sequencing required establishing a sound banking system—including effective prudential regulations—before restrictions on capital mobility were lifted. McKinnon (1991) and McKinnon and Pill (1995) argued that, because of the moral hazard associated with the financial sector, capital account liberalization should wait until the end of the reform episode. In the aftermath of the Mexican and east Asian crisis, economists have become particularly aware of the need to put in place, very early on in the reform process, a modern banking supervisory system. As Calvo (1998) has pointed out, the problem is that poorly regulated banks will intermediate the inflows of capital in an inefficient or even corrupt way, increasing the probability of a systemic financial crisis (see also Dornbusch, 1998; Kaminsky and Reinhart, 1999). (67)

This suggests that currency convertibility or liberalized financial markets are not per se sufficient conditions or vehicles for reform. Access to international finance may represent an incentive to develop the appropriate institutions, whether characterized by democracy, or information transparency, enforcing the rational allocation of capital, or establishing a coercive power to enforce contracts, property, labor, and finances.

Symbol of wealth and power does not translate into actual wealth and power, especially if challenged by a different organizing principle (for example, the Islamic Jihad).

GOLDEN STRAITJACKET AND BACKLASH

International capital flows sometimes seem to bring with them freedom and sometimes coercion. Friedman (1999) uses the term *Golden Straitjacket* to express the discipline required of a country that participates in the global financial marketplace:

To fit into the Golden Straitjacket a country must either adopt, or be seen as moving toward, the following golden rules: making the private sector the primary engine of its economic growth, maintaining a low rate of inflation and price stability, shrinking the size of its state bureaucracy, maintaining as close to a balanced budget as possible, if not a surplus, eliminating and lowering tariffs on imported goods, removing restrictions on foreign investment, getting rid of quotas and domestic monopolies, increasing exports, privatizing state-owned industries and utilities, deregulating capital markets, making its currency convertible, opening its industries, stock and bond markets to direct foreign ownership and investment, deregulating its economy to promote as much domestic competition as possible, eliminating government corruption, subsidies and kickbacks as much as possible, opening its banking and telecommunications systems to private ownership and competition and allowing its citizens to choose from an array of competing pension options and foreign-run pension and mutual funds. . . . As your country puts on the Golden Straitjacket, two things tend to happen: your economy grows and your politics shrinks. (105)

On the one hand, a strong nation-state seems required to support an accountable financial system, to enforce property rights, and to establish credible systems for the allocation of capital. On the other hand, it seems that a strong state is incompatible with a global financial system because the conditions and policies for managing a domestic economy are prescribed by international lending institutions, multinational corporations, currency traders, and global financial intermediaries. This possible contradiction between states and markets has been noted in the literature (see, for example, Kuttner, 1991; Schwartz, 1994; Ohmae, 1995; Greider, 1997).

"Dollarization" is only a more recent symbol of this potential relinquishment of national autonomy and sovereignty to a global financial system (Chang and Velasco, 2000; LeBaron and McCulloch, 2000). Howard Wachtel (1990) quotes a leading multinational banker about the "tension between the bounded political geography of government and the unbounded economic geography of supranational private enterprises" (246; see also 192): "This is a 'new system . . . not built by politicians or economists . . . which in turn has allowed [the] creation of a new international monetary system,' says Walter Wriston who, as chairman of Citicorp during the period, was in on the creation. 'This state of affairs does not sit too well with many sovereign governments because they correctly perceive [it] as an attack on the very nature of sovereign power'" (246).

Wachtel (1990) also sees the process of international competition for financial investment among governments as a form of tax and regulatory competition, a race to the bottom. The regulation of international banking is more like a "cat and mouse chase between the regulators and the regulated" (97). The stateless supranational banks are "like children who run away from home because they do not want to submit themselves to [their parents'] authority but return when they become hungry and want a meal" (101). Wachtel contends that the resulting international economy is characterized by global debt, high interest rates, and austerity, as countries compete for favorable business climates for foreign investment. IMF conditionality imposes conditions on debtor countries (128), much like Friedman's Golden Straitjacket (1999). The deregulation and loss of fiscal authority by national governments, in turn, weakens the capacity of the public sector, lowering public confidence and feeding arguments in favor of free market ideology and the private sector (Wachtel, 1990, 183): "Rather than the crisis of the welfare state causing inadequate growth, the supranationalism promotes a global austerity that leads to government's inability to fund the growing claims on the welfare state. The public complaint, therefore is misplaced. It is directed at government and not at the unregulated supranationalism" (ibid.). That is, Wachtel sees international financial competition as serving to weaken and undermine the strength of individual nation-states.

An alternate picture is presented by Edward Kane (2000), who sees international competition as rewarding effective financial supervision. He agrees with Wachtel in identifying a type of "regulatory arbitrage" in which there is a tendency for "private capital and loan-making opportunities to flow to markets and institutions that offer their customers the best deals" (17). He also acknowledges a political dimension to effective banking that requires, in his view, "public standing, coercive authority, and disciplinary power" (19). While pointing out that information asymmetries and principal-agent problems may limit effective competition in international banking regulation (18), Kane is nonetheless optimistic about the salutary effects of such competition:

Each new crisis constitutes an exit cost that society pays to shrink the domain of a high-cost or inequitable regulator. Crises are triggered by efforts to avoid the inefficiencies and inequities that political maneuvering tends to produce when a government enjoys monopoly power in its domestic "onshore" market for regulatory services. By squeezing the equilibrium rents that short-sighted or corruptible officials can extract in individual countries, offshore regulatory competition has the salutary effect of creating pressure to discipline inefficient regulators and perhaps even to improve public-service contracting in the longer run. (20)

On the other hand, John Eatwell and Lance Taylor (2000) argue that the "systemic risk" of financial markets is a form of market externality (17), so competition within markets will not be effective. For example, the Asian crisis affected countries that were otherwise sound in fiscal and financial policies when "contagion" was imported from the international capital markets. They argue for a "World Financial Authority" to bridge the externalities and to supersede the economic competition among individual nations.[3]

From a longer-term historical perspective, Karl Polanyi (1944) also sees an incompatibility of states and markets. In the early period of globalization based on the gold standard, he attributes the stability of the one hundred years peace, from 1815 to 1914, to the influence of the market. The self-regulating market was the integrating mechanism and provided the reward for keeping the peace, in terms of trade, finance, and wealth creation. He warns, however, that the fiction of a self-regulating market itself was responsible for the forces of protection that brought this period to an end (145–149): "Our thesis is that the idea of a self-adjusting market [is] a stark utopia. Such an institution could not exist for any length of time without annihilating the human and natural substance of society. . . . Inevitably, society took measures to protect itself, but whatever measures it took impaired the self-regulation of the market, disorganized industrial life, and thus endangered society in yet another way" (3–4). Polanyi argues that the self-regulating market cannot exist without a strong state. As he put it, "[T]he liberal state was itself a creation of the self-regulating market" (3); "*laissez-faire* itself was enforced by the state" and the associated increase in "elaborate administrative mechanisms (139, italics in original; see also 140–141).

Ultimately, the attempt to maintain a sound currency in the 1920s required "no less a sacrifice than that of free markets and free governments" (233). For Polanyi, the requirements of maintaining a free market in land, labor, and money were so severe, extracting large human and environmental costs, that the attempt to do so undermined every other institution than the currency itself: "The 1920s saw the prestige of economic liberalism at its height. . . . [S]tabilization of currencies became the focal point in the political thought of people and governments. . . . The repayment of foreign loans and the return to stable currencies were recognized as the touchstones of rationality in politics. . . . The thirties lived to see the absolutes of the twenties called into question" (142).

The paradox of globalization might be that the enforcement powers of national governments are required for sound currencies. At the same time, the processes of global financial competition also undermine strong, accountable financial institutions at the national level. If global finance is the sole focus, there may be no national institutions left in place to support the domestic infrastructure necessary to support that global finance.

CONCLUSIONS

A complete theoretical understanding of the nature of money would include its role as a symbol of a complex of legal and economic institutions in a particular country. The concrete characteristics of that symbol represent the political, military, and economic power of the nation that issues it, and, in turn, a strong currency helps reinforce the power of that nation-state. It is a paradox, however, that the global exchange of these financial symbols cannot reproduce per se the institutional structures necessary for accountable financial systems in each country where the symbols may be traded. As a consequence, global trade in national currencies may serve to undermine the global financial system, without explicit attention to the establishment and maintenance of national political and financial institutions. Even currency substitution, such as dollarization, is not sufficient per se to install the necessary financial infrastructure for an adopting country.

The benefits and potential dangers of global finance are the subject of a large literature, with increasingly diverse points of view. It is clear that the globalization of finance is an integrating device of diverse national economies, although disagreements remain about the impact on long-run growth and stability. To some analysts, the policy implication is a sequencing of reforms in which political and financial institution building at the national level precedes the integration of global financial markets. Others express doubts as to the long-term viability of complete international financial integration, without strong regulations and safeguards, pointing to recent instability as well as long-term historical trends.

NOTES

1. Friedman, (1999, xvi–xvii). See also Pou (1999, 243–244). For a different view of whether the current level of globalization is unprecedented, see Bordo, Eichengreen, and Irwin (1999).

2. Jeff Madrick (2000a, 2000b) has argued that recently published books are beginning to question the acceptance of the efficient market hypothesis, in a new challenge to this orthodoxy. See also Shiller (2000) and Shleifer (2000). For information about the instability of capital markets, see Keynes (1964, ch. 12).

3. For alternative models of global governance in the era of globalization of finance, see Palley (1998) and Rodrik (2000).

REFERENCES

Aizenman, Joshua. 1999, October. Capital Controls and Financial Crises. Working Paper 7398. Washington, DC: National Bureau of Economic Research.

Amin, Samir. 1978. *Unequal Exchange and the Law of Value*, trans. Brian Perace. New York: Monthly Review.

Baker, Dean, Jerry Epstein, and Bob Pollin. 1998. *Globalization and Progressive Economic Policy*. Cambridge: Cambridge University Press.

Bhagwati, Jagdish. 1998. The Capital Myth: The Difference between Trade in Widgets and Dollars. *Foreign Affairs* 77 (3): 7–12.

Block, Fred L. 1977. *The Origins of International Economic Disorder*. Berkeley and Los Angeles: University of California Press.

Bordo, Michael, Barry Eichengreen, and Douglas Irwin. 1999, June. *Is Globalization Today Really Different than Globalization a Hundred Years Ago?* Working Paper 7195. Washington, DC: National Bureau of Economic Research.

Calvo, Guillermo, and Enrique G. Mendoza. 2000. Capital Market Crises and Economic Collapse in Emerging Markets: An Informational-Frictions Approach. *American Economic Review* 90 (2): 59–64

Chang, Roberto, and Andres Velasco. 2000. Exchange Rate Policy for Developing Countries. *American Economic Review* 90 (2): 71–75.

Cohen, Benjamin J. 1998. *The Geography of Money*. Ithaca, NY: Cornell University Press.

Cooper, Richard N. 1999, June. Exchange Rate Choices. In *Rethinking the International Monetary System*, Conference Series No. 43, ed. Jane Sneddon Little and Giovani P. Olivei, 99–123. Boston: Federal Reserve Bank of Boston.

Eatwell, John, and Lance Taylor. 2000. *Global Finance at Risk*. New York: New Press.

Edwards, Sebastian. 1999. How Efffective Are Capital Controls? *Journal of Economic Perspectives* 13 (4): 65–84.

Felix, David. 1998. Asia and the Crisis of Financial Globalization. In *Globalization and Progressive Economic Policy*, ed. Dean Baker, Jerry Epstein, and Bob Pollin, 163–191. Cambridge: Cambridge University Press.

Friedman, Thomas L. 1999. *The Lexus and the Olive Tree*. New York: Anchor.

Gilpin, Robert. 2000. *The Challenge of Global Capitalism*. Princeton, NJ: Princeton University Press.

Greider, William. 1997. *One World, Ready or Not: The Manic Logic of Global Capitalism*. New York: Simon and Schuster.

Kaminsky, Graciela, and Carmen Reinhart. 1999. The Twin Crises: The Causes of Banking and Balance-of-Payments Problems. *American Economic Review* 98 (3): 473–500.

Kane, Edward J. 2000, January. Capital Movements, Banking Insolvency, and Silent Runs in the Asian Financial Crisis. Working Paper 7514. Washington, DC: National Bureau of Economic Research.

Keynes, John Maynard. 1964. *The General Theory of Employment, Interest, and Money.* New York: Harcourt Brace.

Kho, Bong-Chan, Dong Lee, and Rene M. Stulz. 2000. U.S. Banks, Crises, and Bailouts: From Mexico to LTCM. *American Economic Review* 90 (2): 28–31.

Klein, Michael, and Giovanni Olivei. 1999, October. Capital Account Liberalization, Financial Depth, and Economic Growth. Working Paper 7384. Washington, DC: National Bureau of Economic Research.

Kuttner, Robert. 1991. *The End of Laissez-Faire.* New York: Knopf.

LeBaron, Blake, and Rachel McCulloch. 2000. Floating, Fixed, or Super-Fixed? Dollarization Joins the Menu of Exchange-Rate Options. *American Economic Review* 90 (2): 32–37.

Levine, Ross. 1997. Financial Development and Economic Growth: Views and Agenda. *Journal of Economic Literature* 35 (2): 688–726.

Little, Jane Sneddon, and Giovanni P. Olivei. 1999, June. Why the Interest in Reform? In *Rethinking the International Monetary System,* Conference Series No. 43, ed. Jane Sneddon Little and Giovanni P. Olivei, 41–97. Boston: Federal Reserve Bank of Boston.

Madrick, Jeff. 2000a. All Too Human. *New York Review of Books* 47 (13): 38–41.

———. 2000b. Market Messes Happen, and Inefficiencies Have Consequences. *New York Times,* August 3, economic scene, p. C2.

Mishkin, Frederic S. 1999. Global Financial Instability: Framework, Events, Issues. *Journal of Economic Perspectives* 13 (4): 5–20.

Ohmae, Kenichi. 1995. *The End of the Nation State: The Rise of Regional Economies.* New York: Free Press.

Palley, Thomas. 1998. *Plenty of Nothing.* Princeton, NJ: Princeton University Press.

Polanyi, Karl. 1944. *The Great Transformation: The Political and Economic Origins of Our Time.* Boston: Beacon Press.

Pou, Pedro. 1999, June. Is Globalization Really to Blame? *Rethinking the International Monetary System,* Conference Series No. 43, ed. Jane Sneddon Little and Giovanni P. Olivei, 243–250. Boston: Federal Reserve Bank of Boston.

Pugel, Thomas A., and Peter H. Lindert. 2000. *International Economics.* New York: Irwin/McGraw-Hill.

Rodrik, Dani. 2000. How Far Will International Economic Integration Go? *Journal of Economic Perspectives* 14 (1): 177–186.

Rogoff, Kenneth. 1999. International Institutions for Reducing Global Financial Instability. *Journal of Economic Perspectives* 13 (4): 21–42.

Schwartz, Herman M. 1994. *States versus Markets: History, Geography, and the Development of the International Political Economy.* New York: St. Martin's.

Shiller, Robert J. 2000. *Irrational Exuberance.* Princeton, NJ: Princeton University Press.

Shleifer, Andrei. 2000. *Inefficient Markets.* Oxford: Oxford University Press.

Summers, Lawrence H. 2000. International Financial Crises: Causes, Prevention, and Cures. *American Economic Review* 90 (2): 1–16.

Wachtel, Howard M. 1990. *The Money Mandarins: The Making of a Supranational Economic Order*. New York: Sharpe.

Yergin, Daniel, and Joseph Stanislaw. 1998. *Commanding Heights*. New York: Simon and Schuster.

5 Globalization and Its Impact on Global Income and Wealth Distribution

Della Lee Sue

For centuries, globalization has been on the move. Our history books are packed with tales of explorations by adventurous voyagers who were encouraged by various kings and queens to seek new trade routes or acquire new territory in the fifteenth and sixteenth centuries. They were followed in time by technological progress, international conflicts, and domestic disruptions. As globalization has evolved, so has interest in its ramifications on society. In particular, how has globalization affected the distribution of income and wealth in our society?

WHAT IS GLOBALIZATION?

To assess the effect of globalization on the distribution of income and wealth in our society, it is necessary to clearly define what is meant by *globalization*. Because it is not a new concept, it is a term that has been appropriately applied and reapplied to many situations, each time implying something different. In a general economic sense, globalization refers to the economic activity that occurs between people who live in different countries. More specifically, globalization as we know it currently can be expressed in the following various forms:

- *Exports and Imports:* Exports refers to the market value of goods and services produced in a country that are sold in another country; imports refers to the market value of goods and services that a country purchases from another country.

- *Foreign Direct Investment:* Foreign direct investment refers to business spending by firms in a country other than their home country; typically, the purpose is for a firm to setup and maintain business operations in another country.
- *Capital Market Flows:* Capital market flows refer to the flow of savings funds across international borders; their attraction is that they allow a wider diversification of asset portfolios.

Data obtained from the World Bank indicates that globalization has been increasing. From 1987 to 1997, exports and imports as a proportion of gross domestic product increased from 27 percent to 39 percent among developed countries. During the same time period, the ratio increased from 10 percent to 17 percent for developing countries. Foreign direct investment more than tripled throughout the world in the ten years from 1988 to 1998. The flow of financial investment funds between countries has been less stable than the trends in either international trade or foreign direct investment, and flows have been concentrated between particular countries. Nonetheless, capital market flows have been increasing on average over time.

The process of globalization has been occurring for centuries and there is no reason to suggest that it will not continue into the future. In 1947, the General Agreement on Tariffs and Trade (GATT) was established; it is an organization that is dedicated to promoting international commerce. Since its establishment GATT negotiations have successfully reduced tariffs for all member nations (which include most non-communist countries) under the most-favored-nation principle, in which any tariff concession that is extended by one country to another country is extended to all participating countries. In April 1994, member countries signed a trade agreement (the "Uruguay Round") that lowered import tariffs by 40 percent on average and, most importantly, established new rules that make it harder for national governments to restrict their country's foreign commerce. If globalization is here to stay and continue, one question that arises is, To what extent does globalization affect the distribution of income and wealth?

GLOBAL INCOME AND WEALTH DISTRIBUTION

To address the impact of globalization on the distribution of global income and wealth, the meaning and implications of such a distribution needs to be clarified. The distribution of income (or wealth) involves looking at what percentage of a society's income (or wealth) is received by various percentages of the population within that society. This allocation provides information on how equally income (or wealth) is divided among members of society, and consequently allows one to measure the inequality of income (or wealth).

There are three aspects to global income (or wealth) inequality: (1) inequality within a country, (2) inequality between countries, and (3) world inequality. Inequality within a country can be measured by using Lurenz curve methodology, which involves correlating various percentiles of the population with their share of income (or wealth). Inequality between countries generally involves a comparison of average income (or gross domestic product) per capita among the countries and possibly the difference between countries' growth rates. World inequality combines the first two aspects.

Globalization implies trade between two or more countries. Countries trade with one another because there are mutual benefits to trading. The benefits to trading are expressed in the law of comparative advantage, a fundamental principle in economics that was developed in the early nineteenth century by the British economist David Ricardo (1817). A country has a comparative advantage in the activity in which its opportunity cost is lower than the forgone cost of another country.

Because resources are scarce, each country would do well to specialize in the production of the good in which it has a comparative advantage and trade with the other country. Specialization and trade will allow both countries to consume more of each good than would be possible without trade. The law of comparative advantage is not limited to two countries. In fact, more generally, there would be an increase in world production if all countries specialize in the production of those goods in which they have a comparative advantage and then trade with other countries.

But what effect would this have on income and wealth distribution within each country? Going back to the example of two countries and two goods, in the absence of trade, each country would probably produce both goods that would involve the use of various factor inputs (for example, labor, capital, and land). In exchange for their contribution to production, the factor inputs would be paid returns that equal the value of their marginal product. In each country, the relative price of each good would reflect the opportunity cost of producing the good domestically.

In the presence of free trade, the market for a particular good in each country combines into a world market for that good. As implied by the law of comparative advantage, goods would flow from the country in which the good's relative price is lower to the country in which its relative price is higher. As a result, the new world price for the good will converge to a relative price that is somewhere between the two domestic prices for that particular good in the absence of trade. The exporting country of a particular good can now obtain a higher price for the exported good and pay a lower price for its imports.

The change in relative prices of the goods that results from trade will be accompanied by a change in production. As each country becomes more specialized in the production of the good in which it has a comparative advantage, each country will increase its production of exported goods and decrease its production of imported goods. Since the demand for inputs is a derived demand, the increase in production of the exported good will lead to an increase in the demand for factors of production used in the production of the exported good. If the market for factors of production is competitive such that inputs receive compensation that reflects the value of their marginal product, then the compensation to inputs used to produce the exported good will increase for two reasons. One is that the productivity of these inputs is increasing due to specialization and the other is that the price of the good being produced is increasing because of trade.

On the other hand, the factors of production that were used to produce the imported good will no longer be needed in the import country. There will be a decrease in demand for these factors by the producers who are no longer producing the good that is now being imported. As a result, the compensation to these factors of production will fall.

Therefore, as specialization takes place in the presence of trade, the production of the exported good increases along with the compensation paid to its factor inputs. At the same time, the production of the imported good decreases in the home country along with the compensation that is paid to its factor inputs. This adjustment process implies that there will be an increase in inequality in the distribution of income and wealth within each country as some factors benefit while others lose.

Some of the increase in income and wealth inequality might be temporary if the factor inputs from the good that is now being imported can adjust and be absorbed by the producers of the good that is now being exported. This transitional adjustment is more likely to occur among particular types of factors such as labor, land, or capital. For example, those individuals who were employed in the production of the good now being imported might be able to find employment with producers who are now increasing their production of the good that is now being exported. Nonetheless, the mobility between industries for different types of factors might be more limited. For example, if the production of the good being exported is capital-intensive while the production of the good being imported is labor-intensive, absorption of the unemployed labor by the growing industry is unlikely and the increase in inequality in the distribution of income and wealth would become more permanent.

If one allows for the mobility of factor inputs across geographic trade boundaries, then factors will have the incentive to migrate to areas where their compensation is larger because the demand for these inputs is greater.

If this were to occur, the disparity between employment opportunities and consequently income and wealth would become smaller within each country. As a result, there would be a decrease in inequality in the distribution of income and wealth within each country.

In summary, an increase in trade will tend to increase inequality in the distribution of income and wealth within a country. This increase in inequality can be mitigated and even reversed if the factors of production that are displaced are able to migrate to the production of the good to which they are better suited.

Now what can be expected to happen to the distribution of income and wealth between countries when they trade with each other? The answer to this question lies in distinguishing between specialization in production and trading goods. The motivation for two countries to trade with each other is that they can each increase total production by specializing in the good in which they have a comparative advantage. Since each country is now producing a smaller variety of goods, trading allows the countries to increase the diversity of goods available in each country. The increase in each country's income or wealth is due to the advantages gained from specialization, not from the act of trading.

The effect of globalization on the distribution of income and wealth between countries becomes apparent. A country that experiences a larger relative increase in income and wealth will benefit more from specialization in comparison with other countries. Thus, if the benefit from specialization varies from one country to another, then an increase in globalization will increase the inequality in the distribution of income and wealth between countries.

WHAT DOES THE EMPIRICAL EVIDENCE INDICATE?

Empirical studies of the distribution of income and wealth are numerous. In general, the focus of the studies is on measuring inequality in the distribution of income and wealth for a particular country and tracking changes in inequality over time. Fewer studies compare changes in inequality between countries.

There are two standard statistical measures of inequality. The most common measure is the Gini coefficient, which ranges between 0 and 1. If total income (wealth) within a society were equally distributed among all members of the society, then the Gini coefficient would equal 0. At the other extreme, if one member of society received the totality of income generated within a specified time period, then the Gini coefficient would equal 1. Thus, a higher value for the Gini coefficient implies a greater degree of income (wealth) inequality. When looking at the distribution of income (wealth) over time, a series of Gini coefficients can be converted into a Gini index to measure changes in inequality over time.

Alternatively, the Theil T-statistic provides a measure of the change in earnings inequality within a country as well as a comparison of degrees of change between countries. In a study of inequality by James K. Galbraith and Lu Jiaqing (1999), they used the Theil T-statistic to create a chain-linked index of earnings dispersion that was updated annually to reflect changes in the structure of employment as well as changes in relative earnings per capita.

In general, research efforts indicate that inequality has been increasing over time, both within countries and between countries. In a study of the distribution of income in the United States, Brian Motley (1997) found that inequality has been increasing since 1968 but noted that the inequality does not appear to be accelerating. In measuring inequality within a country, the data used is usually median family income. It is important to bear in mind that using only money income excludes noncash benefits that are provided by employers or governments. Employer-provided noncash benefits have been growing in availability and importance. Including these benefits in a measure of inequality tends to increase the dispersion between low-income households and middle-income households but it decreases the disparity between middle-income households and upper-income households, implying a small net effect overall. On the other hand, cash benefits from the governments have also been increasing, and to the extent that these benefits are directed disproportionately to lower-income households, including them in a measure of inequality would lower the degree of inequality indicated by the calculations.

Barry Bluestone (1995) found similar results: the degree of inequality has been increasing in the United States and the United Kingdom since mid-1970. After World War II, wages and income not only grew rapidly but also became more equally distributed across the labor force. After 1973, inequality increased, in part due to wage dispersion and also due to a change in labor force participation by demographic groups. The number of two-earner households has increased and women have been working more continuously. At the same time, there has also been an increase in the number of single-parent households. The former has raised income among middle- and upper-income households while the latter has increased the number of low-income households.

These results were confirmed in a study by Peter Gottschalk and Timothy M. Smeeding (1997) in which Gini coefficients for the Organization for Economic Cooperation and Development countries were calculated using household disposable income data. While the United States and the United Kingdom were leaders in income inequality along with Sweden, almost all industrialized countries have been experiencing some increase in earnings inequality. Exceptions are France and Spain where the change in the Gini coefficient has been minimal, at best.

In their study of industrial earnings inequality for numerous countries, Galbraith and Jiaqing (1999) looked at trends in inequality from 1970 to 1995. Decreases and increases in inequality vary from country to country although most countries have been experiencing an increase in inequality since the early 1980s which has continued to increase into the 1990s. The authors note that the data used in calculating the Theil T-statistic is restricted to the manufacturing sector, omitting the public sector and agriculture. However, since the manufacturing sector is more apt to experience technological change, fluctuations in aggregate demand, and trade variations, inequality within the manufacturing sector is a reasonable measure of inequality within a country as a whole. A major advantage of using the Theil T-statistic rather than the more common Gini coefficient is that hourly wages are used in the calculation. Gini coefficients typically measure household or personal income inequality, not annual earnings or hourly wages. However, globalization is more likely to affect wages or earnings.

Increases in inequality are not limited to developed countries. Branko Milanovic (1998a, 1998b) measured the change in income inequality and in overall inequality in former Soviet bloc economies as they made the transition from a planned economy to a market economy. His findings indicate that inequality within each of these countries increased faster and more dramatically than for other countries.

In measuring inequality between countries, Milanovic (1999) derives the distribution of individuals' income for two years and estimates the degree of inequality between countries based on data from household surveys. After adjusting for differences in purchasing power parity between countries, he found that inequality between countries has been increasing, as evidenced by the rising differences in mean incomes between countries. The studies by Milanovic assert that world income inequality is high primarily due to inequality between countries and less so to inequality within countries.

Although most studies indicate an increase in inequality in the distribution of income and wealth between countries, some evidence points to a positive effect of globalization. A study by Albert F. Ades and Edward L. Glaeser (1999), found that among poor countries, those that are more open to trade have been experiencing higher growth rates than countries that are closed to trade. Furthermore, the growth rates of the more open poor countries have, in some cases, been slightly higher than the growth rates of rich countries.

A recent study has been developed by A. T. Kearney (PR Newswire, 2000), a management consulting subsidiary of EDS, which is a global information technology services company, and its Global Business Policy Council. Their Globalization Ledger focuses specifically on the extent and impact of economic globalization among a sample of thirty-four developed and emerging markets between 1978 and 1997. The economics included in the study account for more than 75 percent of the world's economic output gross domestic product and more than two-thirds of the world population. Although globalization appears to increase income inequality within a country, the benefits are not limited to the wealthy. Economic growth that is attributable to globalization has substantially reduced the percentage of the world's population that is living in poverty. This presents a glimmer of hope that the increase in income and wealth inequality could be overshadowed by increases in overall economic growth and reductions in poverty with further developments in globalization.

However, the increase in the gap between the incomes of the different countries is also discussed in a study by Lant Pritchett (1996). Using purchasing-power-adjusted measures of income for a variety of countries, Pritchett found that the ratio between the average per capita income of the richest country (that is, the United States) and the average per capita income of the poorest countries has increased dramatically over time. Their data extends back to 1870 and the observed divergence in incomes between countries continues presently. Projecting into the future, Pritchett discusses the prognosis for developing countries to catch up and possibly overtake the per capita income of the United States or, more generally, high-income countries. A majority of developing countries have had historically negative income growth rates and, at best, growth rates that are still much lower than the average growth rate of the high-income countries. For these countries, it is expected that they will never be able to catch up to the high-income countries. For those developing countries whose recent growth rates are similar and, in a few cases, higher than the average for high-income countries, the amount of time needed for them to catch up is measured in centuries.

In defense of globalization and its purported impact on the distribution of income and wealth, it is necessary to question the role of history, economic growth, price and wage controls, welfare programs, and education policies that potentially widen the distribution of income, independent of globalization. As mentioned earlier in this chapter, the distribution of income and wealth could become less unequal if factor resources are allowed to migrate across geographic trade boundaries, motivated by greater compensation for that resource. In a historical recount of economic development, Bruce R. Scott (2001) highlights the obstacles that have stood in the way of economic performance. His thoughts reinforce the sentiments expressed by Frances Stewart and Albert Berry (2000) in an essay that examines the effect of liberalization on income inequality. Some of these obstacles to equality are social or political policies, especially the protectionism immigration barriers that the richer countries have constructed. The poor countries are in a precarious situation that renders them at a perpetual disadvantage because their governments often lack the qualitative resources and administrative techniques necessary to propel their economies over the hurdles. In short, the widening distribution of income and wealth may not necessarily be the result of globalization but rather in spite of it.

Given that globalization is likely to continue escalating and to the extent that globalization accompanies an increase in inequality in the distribution of income and wealth, our expectation is that the disparity in income and wealth is only going to widen in the future.

REFERENCES

Ades, Alberto F., and Edward L. Glaeser. 1999. Evidence on Growth, Increasing Returns, and the Extent of the Market. *Quarterly Journal of Economics* 114 (3): 1025–1046.

Bluestone, Barry. 1995. The Inequality Express. *American Prospect* (Winter): 81–93.

Galbraith, James K., and Lu Jiaqing. 1999. Measuring the Evolution of Inequality in the Global Economy. Paper presented at the Levy Institute Conference on the Macro Dynamics of Inequality, The Jerome Levy Economic Institute of Bard College, New York, October 28–29.

Gottschalk, Peter, and Timothy M. Smeeding. 1997. Cross-National Comparisons of Earnings and Income Inequality. *Journal of Economic Literature* 35 (2): 633–687.

Milanovic, Branko. 1998a. *Explaining the Increase in Inequality during the Transition*. Washington, DC: Development Economics Research Group, World Bank.

———. 1998b. *Income, Inequality, and Poverty during the Transition from Planned to Market Economy*. Washington, DC: World Bank.

———. 1999. *True World Income Distribution, 1988 and 1993: First Calculations, Based on Household Surveys Alone*. Washington, DC: Poverty and Human Resources, Development Research Group, World Bank.

Motley, Brian. 1997, January 31. Inequality in the United States. In *Economic Letter*, 1–3. San Francisco: Federal Reserve Bank of San Francisco.

PR Newswire. 2000, April 5. *New A. T. Kearney Study Finds Globalization Linked with Economic and Income Growth, Reduction in Poverty—and Also with Wider Income Gap, Worsening Air Pollution*. Washington, DC: PR Newswire.

Pritchett, Lant. 1996, June. Forget Convergence: Divergence Past, Present, and Future. In *Finance and Development*, 40–43. New York: International Monetary Fund and the International Bank for Reconstruction and Development/ World Bank.

Ricardo, David. 1817. *The Principles of Political Economy and Taxation*. London: Janus.

Scott, Bruce R. 2001. The Great Divide in the Global Village. *Foreign Affairs* 80 (1): 160–177.

Stewart, Frances, and Albert Berry. 2000. Globalization, Liberalization, and Inequality: Real Causes, Expectations, and Experience. *Challenge* (January). Available online: www.findarticles.com/m1093/1_43/issue.jhtml.

6 European Integration and Globalization: From European Regionalism to Globalization

Spyros J. Vliamos

GLOBALIZATION: CONCEPTS AND EVENTS

Since the mid-1970s, the world economy has entered a new period of prevailing new rules and characteristics concerning the operation of economic agents. This new period has been characterized by some "magnificent changes" such as international trade, the movement of labor and services, and, of course, the flow of capital that have rendered economies more open and interlinked. In addition, consumption models are becoming increasingly more international and economic development depends more on exports and on the introduction of technology and knowledge now than before. This caused the term _domestic market_ to have a weaker meaning in the mainstream of economic thinking. This process had several very important repercussions, not only for the application of economic policy but also for the economic theory itself, in the sense that the exercise of national economic policies is becoming rather ineffective. The set of these rules has been called "globalization." Thus, globalization refers to the multiplicity of linkages and interconnections between the states and societies, which make up the present world system. It describes the process by which events, decisions, and activities in one part of the world come to have significant consequences for individuals and communities in quite distant parts of the globe (McGrew, 1992).

Based on this, a number of events have been identified (Dunning, 2000) that had a profound impact on the nature, composition, and organizational modes of global economic activity:

1. *The liberalization of both internal and cross-border markets.* Since the early 1980s barriers to trade (either institutional or monetary) have dramatically fallen, resulting in a growing openness of countries to the rest of the world. We have witnessed a sharp increase in the share of trade and foreign direct investment to gross national product in the great majority of countries and a spectacular expansion of cross-border financial flows coupled with further international financial integration. Finally, movement of labor (migration, employment of foreigners, and so on), aided by liberalization or deregulation of markets, complete the picture of the degree of openness of the economies.

2. *The emergence of new players in the world economy.* Indeed, several developing economies emerged as major players on the world economic scene. These emerging economies (better called "newly industrializing economies") increased their share in the world's gross national product. It has been pointed out (Dunning and Narula, 1996) that as they move along their development paths, their economic structure tends to move closer to that of their more advanced industrialized counterparts. However, the more knowledge-intensive, asset-augmenting activities tend to still remain very heavily concentrated in developing economies.

3. *The increasing importance of all forms of intellectual capital.* Over the past three centuries the main source of wealth in market economies has switched from natural to intangible assets, mainly intellectual capital (knowledge and information of all kinds). Given the rapid growth of the latter (OECD, 1997), this implies that intangible assets are now eminently increased and mobile with considerable consequences to the spatial distribution of economic activity.

4. *The growth of cooperative ventures.* In recent years, a variety of interorganizational cooperative agreements either complemented or replaced the hierarchical form of governance of both private and public organizations. These alliances may take several forms and usually aim to increase the efficiency of existing asset deployment (facilitating economies of scale and better use of managerial and marketing capabilities).

Therefore, the occurrence of these events makes globalization a process that leads to the structural transformation of the world economy. It has been said that it is a discontinuity in the process of internationalization, in the sense that it creates new and deeper cross-border relationships and dependencies (Dunning, 2000, 14).

EUROPEAN INTEGRATION: A GLOBALIZATION-BASED CONCEPT

Even if globalization did not exist, the creators of the European Union (EU) would have invented it. True, the whole process of European integration can be considered as being the "general rehearsal" to globalization, a process that started more than twenty-five years before the latter became commonly noticed. And as it will be seen in the next section (which draws heavily from Tsoukalis [1997, ch. 2]), the road to European integration bears all the characteristics mentioned above concerning the features of globalization. This concept can be considered therefore as providing an after-the-event theoretical support to the European integration process. However, as usually happens in magnificent changes, this process has always been characterized by fits and starts, due to frequent changes of the economic and political climate in the world economies and in Europe in particular. European integration has been and continues to be largely about economics; but economics with wider political ramifications. Thus, in this chapter the study of economic issues will be placed in its proper political context, set against their historical background and evolution, to facilitate a better understanding of the interaction of globalization and the operation of the *unified* European economy.

From European Regionalism to European Monetary Union: The Evolution of an Idea

The period after World War II has been characterized as being a period of efforts toward national economic integration and international disintegration, implying the application of autarkic economic policies based on a high degree of protectionism (Myrdal, 1956). In particular, European economies emerged with severe economic and social problems and most of them reached the 1936 production levels only at the end of 1949. The period after 1949, the so-called reconstruction period, was characterized in turn by high economic growth, leading though to large balance of payments deficits, and rapid expansion of intra-European trade. This lasted for almost thirty years without any major interruption.

During this reconstruction period the foundations of European regionalism (that is, the regional economic cooperation) were established and it was the United States that helped Europe promote its economic and political integration. True, the well-known Marshall Plan—a U.S. initiative for large bilateral aid to Europe—provided western European economies the means to finance their development and therefore their balance of payments deficits, through the creation of two organizations: the Organization for European Economic Cooperation, which was later transformed to the Organization for Economic Cooperation and Development (OECD), and the European Payments Union. Indeed, these two organizations significantly contributed to the development of intra-European trade and the European economic recovery in general. But still, even after the creation of the two organizations, the recovery of the European economies has been achieved through protectionism. European governments continued, therefore, an extensive system of trade controls implying a discrimination against American exporters.[1]

However, the disastrous experience of the previous years forced European governments to reverse this trend. But the prevailing Keynesian ideas, at the time, dictated policies toward the manipulation of the aggregate demand and a decisive role of national governments in controlling the economy, which led to not adopting more laissez-faire attitudes. Therefore, they could not comply with the liberal vision held by the United States. As has been rightly put forward, American power and money were largely unsuccessful in shaping the European economic order according to Washington's preferences.

Thus, in May 1950, a new attempt for the cooperation of Europe was launched through a French initiative, the so-called Schuman Plan, which led to the signing of the Treaty of Paris and the establishment of the European Coal and Steel Community, comprised of six western European countries (the Federal Republic of Germany, the Benelux countries, Italy, and France); Britain decided to abstain due to different interests and priorities. As is widely accepted today, this plan laid the foundations of Franco-German reconciliation, providing the cornerstone and the main driving force for regional integration. However, the economic system set up by the Treaty of Paris has been characterized as "regulated competition" and clearly it was very different from the liberal order dreamed of by postwar U.S. administrations.

The Treaty of Paris was clearly an attempt to develop an atmosphere of cooperation in two strategic (for economic and defense purposes) sectors of the European economy. However, the evolution of the European economies in the 1950s led Europeans to put new plans forward and look for ways of extending their cooperation in other sectors of the economy as well, for example, agriculture, transportation, commerce, and so on. Therefore, a new treaty signed in 1957, the well-known Treaty of Rome, created two new communities: the European Economic Community and the European Atomic Energy Community, with the former being by far the most important and far reaching in terms of scope and instruments among the three communities that constitute what was generally referred to as the European Community. In Article 2 of the treaty, it is stipulated that the treaty provides for the "harmonious development of economic activities" and for "the continuous and balanced expansion." It reflected the increased (some say too much) confidence of the European governments to market mechanisms, a result of the successful performance of their economies during the previous years. Therefore, it pointed toward a more liberal economic approach through the creation of a common market, that is, an economic area within which there would be a common external tariff (establishment of a customs union) and free movement of goods, services, persons, and capital, using as weapons the progressive elimination of tariffs and quantitative restrictions, the launching of a new competition policy, along the lines of the U.S. competition policy, the negative attitude on state aids, and the suppression of any form of discrimination based on nationality. The provisions of this treaty being vague and kept at a very general level were severely criticized for their lack of correspondence between objectives and instruments. Besides, there were two newly established institutions—the European Investment Bank and the European Social Fund—designed only for the Mezzogiorno (the southern part of Italy), while there was virtually no provision for establishing policy instruments for other regions.

However, the creation of a common market was, by itself, a very ambitious objective. National differences in macroeconomic policies, along with different perceptions among policymakers concerning the control over fiscal and monetary policy, designed to guarantee that full employment should be exercised within national frontiers, forced the signatories of the treaty to be very cautious concerning the concept of common market. True, the liberalization of capital movements could only take place "to the extent necessary to ensure the proper functioning of the common market." Greater mobility of capital across national frontiers would undermine the effectiveness of national monetary instruments. Thus, even in that way there had been a hesitant reference to the importance of macroeconomic policies and in particular monetary policy. So one can trace some references to macroeconomic objectives and especially to balance of payments problems, treating the exchange rate as a matter of common concern. Therefore, the need for the coordination of economic policies was stressed without any reference as to how this might be achieved. Only specific provisions were made regarding monetary policy.[2]

Monetary policy was considered by the authors of the Treaty of Rome as being an important macroeconomic policy for "the progressive stability and the proper functioning of the common market." This led to the creation of the Monetary Committee, which would mainly decide on capital mobility rules and address exchange rate problems, without any intention of setting up a regional currency bloc. After all, during the 1950s the Bretton Woods system provided the undisputed international framework and the U.S. dollar the undisputed international currency (or monetary standard). However, in the late 1960s the United States proved unable (or unwilling) to secure monetary stability, and this led to discussions in Europe concerning closer regional cooperation and coordination of policies concerning monetary targets, so as to secure exchange rate stability. Thus, the international monetary turmoil of 1968–1969 revealed the inability of the six member states to insulate themselves from monetary instability. As a result, some European common policies, such as the Common Agricultural Policy, were put in danger, leading to The Hague summit of 1969, which was held to discuss the creation of a European Monetary Union (EMU), as an immediate goal, which would replace the Customs Union.

However, disagreements arose very soon concerning the adopted priorities and strategies during the transition period aimed at achieving this goal mainly through the harmonization of national economic policies. The most important disagreement was between the economists and the monetarists. Their crucial difference regarding the ultimate objective was whether the European Community would move toward economic policy coordination or monetary integration. What the economists (Federal Republic of Germany, the Netherlands, and Italy) targeted was the convergence of the inflation rates of other countries to that of their own through policy coordination. On the contrary, monetarists (France, Belgium, and Luxemborg) insisted on the importance of an exchange rate discipline, which would pass the balance of payments adjustment burden to surplus countries and thus leave them with the choice of either financing the deficits of others or accepting a higher rate of inflation. There was certainly a degree of confusion on both sides and some double-talk.

Finally, even with those disagreements, an EMU was proposed in October 1970 by the Werner report (after the name of the German finance minister). In this plan, the creation of the union would be achieved in three stages within an overall period of ten years, leading to the establishment of a single currency (European Currency Unit). The creation of EMU would require the transfer of a wide range of decision-making powers from the national to the European Community level, such as decisions on monetary policy. Concerning fiscal policy, the report argued that an agreement would need to be reached on budget aggregates and on the method of financing deficits or utilizing surpluses.

European Monetary Union: Highlights of Globalization

Monetary union has had a long history, going back almost thirty years, starting with the early plans on economic union. A new treaty on European union was signed in Maastricht, Netherlands, in February 1992, setting the necessary preconditions to be fulfilled by the member-states before the adoption of the single currency. EMU constitutes the most important and concrete part of the Maastricht Treaty. It should be noted that this treaty was accepted with skepticism and little applause from European societies and international markets alike. The lack of enthusiasm was due to the prevailing turmoil in the exchange markets in the early 1990s. The volatility of exchange rates was caused by slow growth rates in European economies, which in turn led to the withdrawal of certain currencies from the

European Monetary System and the widening of the margins of fluctuations (to 15 percent) for those remaining in the system. Consequently, a paradox emerged: instead of having a system of irrevocable fixed exchange rates that would lead to a single currency, a more flexible exchange rate mechanism was created, not a promising situation for the final goal.

However, EMU must not be treated as being simply a narrow economic issue but rather a major political one, as it touches the very heart of national sovereignty. After all, monetary union is a fact that brings together some of the oldest and most advanced industrialized economies of the world and this is something that challenges both economists and economic theories. Money must rather be seen as an instrument of wider political objectives and application of high politics, than as a means through which markets and other economic variables operate and produce wealth, prosperity, and happiness. That is why the whole process leading to the creation of the EMU has been characterized as "being a long and bumpy road leading to narrow gates" (Tsoukalis, 1997, 172).

The return to higher rates of growth of the European economies and the subsequent exchange rate stability, coupled with the creation of the European Monetary Institute in 1994, brought monetary integration issues back to the table. As such, a number of important decisions were made at the European Council meeting in Madrid in December 1995, which reassured the real willingness of the EU to proceed with the monetary integration and the changeover to the single currency (the euro).[3]

There has been considerable literature concerning the economics of the EMU, the merits and demerits of the system[4] (European Commission, 1995; Kenen, 1995), and criticism of the convergence criteria.[5] Although, in economic terms, the latter could be viewed at best as a very rough indicator of the stability orientation of countries to be admitted into the final stage, they have been characterized as mechanistic, some of them arbitrary and, perhaps, also superfluous (Tsoukalis, 1997, 175) and not referring to any real economic variables. For example, the convergence criteria are based on the assumption that there is no real trade-off between price stability, on the one hand, and growth and employment, on the other hand (except for short-run periods).

GLOBALIZATION AND EUROPEAN INTEGRATION: INTERACTING CONCEPTS

The advent of the euro will give Europe a key role to play in economic and monetary matters. For this to happen, it will be necessary for the EU to define the relationship between international financial institutions and the arrangements for external representation in this field. The external potential of the single market should be developed on a solid base. Both the strength and the experience of the internal market can be used to promote the EU's interests and presence internationally, for example, in areas such as aeronautics and satellites but also in financial services, intellectual property, and competition policy.

Economic and social cohesion was introduced in the single European Act, paving the way for the 1988 reform of the structural funds. The Treaty on European Union turned cohesion into one of the three pillars of the European construction alongside economic and monetary union and the single market. Finally, the "Amsterdam Resolution" on growth and employment enshrines the priority to be given to fighting unemployment.

There is no doubt that economic and social cohesion remains a political priority. These processes bear all the features brought by what I have defined above as globalization. Trade barriers have fallen and this has promoted an increase in the share of trade to gross national product. There is greater mobility of labor and the emergence of new European market economies with economic structures similar to that of more advanced industrialized countries. Intellectual capital (knowledge and information) has spread; and several cooperative agreements have complemented and/or replaced the hierarchical form of governance in both private and public organizations.

In fact, the prospect of enlargement involving new countries with widely differing levels of development makes cohesion still more essential. Solidarity is necessary in the era of globalization and therefore European solidarity is becoming more important than ever in achieving the major goal of reducing disparities in levels of development, as explicitly set by Article 130a of the Treaty on European Union. It makes a vital contribution to the stability of the EU and the promotion of a high level of employment. The structural funds aim at fostering competitive development and sustainable and job-creating growth throughout the EU and the promotion of a skilled, trained, and adaptable workforce.

The priority given to economic and social cohesion has been translated into comprehensive programs implemented in partnership with member-states and regions, both for regions where development is lagging behind (Objectives 1 and 6), and for declining industrial areas (Objective 2) and rural areas (Objective 5[b]). A substantial effort is also being devoted to employment and industrial change (Objectives 3 and 4). The first Cohesion Report drawn up under Article 130b of the treaty showed the need for and the relevance of the European Community structural support system and allowed for lessons to be learned for the future. It also demonstrated that the member-states and regions that lag behind and are eligible under Objective 1 have made progress toward real convergence, not least as a result of assistance from the structural funds and the cohesion fund. However, despite significant successes, there is still much left to be done, particularly regarding employment: unemployment has not fallen significantly and is growing not only in many less-developed regions where disparities are widening but also in the more prosperous parts of the EU. The effort to support both the balanced development of the EU and the development of human resources throughout it will therefore have to continue over the next period of the financial perspective.

Furthermore, the international environment must not be seen as a threat to the EU, but rather as a positive challenge and factor for development. The EU, the biggest trader on the world stage, has a strong interest in consolidating the new World Trade Organization (WTO) structures and in promoting further international trade liberalization beyond that which is already programmed. The alternative to a multilateral approach is likely to be a risk of less advantageous conditions of access and competition. It is also essential that the dismantling of trade barriers be accompanied by the development of competition policy principles within the WTO framework. Taking into account the new forms of international trade, it will be necessary to make full use of the new opportunities offered by Article 113, as amended by the Treaty of Amsterdam, for conducting international commercial negotiations in the field of services and intellectual property. In this way, the enlarged EU will be able to act more decisively and more cohesively in international organizations such as the WTO or the OECD.

CONCLUSIONS

This chapter has focused on the complex process of European economic integration within a globalized world. However, European integration has been and continues to be largely about economics with wider political ramifications. This is true not only in the case of the internal market, but also in the case of the EMU. Although the analysis of the political integration process lies beyond the scope of this chapter, a few comments could be added. For example, despite the progress as far as economic integration is concerned, there is no significant progress in terms of political integration. Even worse, the gap between economic and political integration has been growing wider. *Politics remains predominantly national.* Further enlargement and the challenges of the knowledge economy require stronger and more efficient institutions and a political system that rests on a solid popular basis. Therefore, bridging the gap between economic and political integration is an important precondition to the establishment of the new democratic Europe, which will play a central role in the globalized world today.

NOTES

1. As Loukas Tsoukalis (1997) points out, "[T]he granting of Marshall aid and the creation of the two organizations meant that the American Administration appeared ready to accept, albeit reluctantly, that the principle of multilateralism would have to be put in cold storage. Multilateralism had been one of the main planks of US policy with respect to the new postwar economic order" (9).

2. In 1960, western Europe was divided again by the creation of another initiative, mainly led by the United Kingdom: the European Free Trade Association. According to the authors of this treaty, the seven member countries that had decided, essentially for political reasons, to stay away from the European Economic Community (Austria, Denmark, Norway, Portugal, Sweden, Switzerland, and the United Kingdom) kept their independence in the conduct of external trade policies, and had no intention of extending cooperation beyond trade.

3. According to this decision, the euro and those national currencies participating in the final stage of EMU coexisted, with conversion rates established by law, until July 2002 when the euro became the only legal tender. Banknotes and coins in euro circulated by January 1, 2002.

4. The most important of them being (a) elimination of risks in currency conversion and savings in other transaction costs, and (b) achievements in price stability stemming from the irrevocable fixity of the exchange rates and the fact that a strong single new currency could become an international means of payment that would secure relative price stability. However, these benefits of the single currency must be weighed against the loss of two policy instruments: an independent monetary policy and the option of changing the exchange rate. By losing these, a country, which suffers from "asymmetric demand shocks," that affects it differently from the rest of the single-currency area, is no longer able to respond by exercising its national monetary policy or devaluing its currency. But, on the other hand, are countries able to conduct independent monetary policies in an increasingly interdependent world economy? Key advances made in telecommunication technologies and financial market innovation and deregulation, as well as the diversification of currency portfolios, have all weakened the old grasp of national authorities on domestic monetary control. Indeed, this trend would appear to make a case for a greater degree of international control to be applied.

5. These consisted of the basis through which qualified majority in the European Council would decide admission to the final stage of EMU, and they are (a) public debt should not exceed 60 percent of gross national product, (b) budget deficit should not be more than 3 percent of gross national product, (c) national inflation rates should not exceed the average of the lowest three inflation rates of other member-states plus 1.5 percent, (d) national interest rates should not exceed the average of the lowest three interest rates of ten-year bonds of other member-states plus 1.5 percent, and (e) existence of stability of exchange rate of the country, for a two-year period prior to the year of accession.

REFERENCES

Dunning, J. H. 2000. Regions, Globalization, and the Knowledge Economy: The Issues Stated. In *Regions, Globalization, and the Knowledge-Based Economy*, ed. J. H. Dunning, 7–41. Oxford: Oxford University Press.

Dunning, J. H., and R., Narula, eds. 1996. *Foreign Direct Investment and Governments*. London: Routledge.

European Commission. 1995. The Impact of Exchange Rate Movements on Trade within the Single Market. Reports and Studies No. 4. *European Economy*. Brussels: Office for Official Publications of the European Commission.

Kenen, P. 1995. *Economic and Monetary Union: Moving beyond Maastricht*. London: Cambridge University Press.

McGrew, A. G. 1992. Conceptualizing Global Politics. In *Global Politics: Globalization and the Nation States*, ed. A. G. McGrew and P. G. Lewis, 1–28. Cambridge: Polity.

Myrdal, G. 1956. *An International Economy*. London: Routledge and Kegan Paul.

OECD. 1997. *Internationalization of Industrial R&D: Patterns and Trends*. Paris: Group of National Experts on Science and Technology Indicators, OECD.

Tsoukalis, L. (1997) *The New European Economy Revisited*. London: Oxford University Press.

Part II

Political, Social, and Cultural Consequences of Globalization

7

The Changing Role of Nation-States and Their Sovereignty

Maryann K. Cusimano Love

Globalization has dramatically increased over the past twenty years. Markets and pressing public policy problems, and attempts to solve these problems, are no longer limited by geography. As markets, problems, and governance are no longer exclusively tied to territorial borders, states increasingly work with (and contract out to) nonstate actors. In doing so, the function, form, and nature of state control changes. What do these changes mean for sovereignty and the future of nation-states?

GEOGRAPHY ISN'T EVERYTHING

One of the defining features of globalization is that markets are no longer geographically delimited. Investment, supply, production, assembly, delivery, and marketing abide by the logic of corporate lines of organization, not geographic or state lines of organization. Companies such as Disney and Nike are engaged in so many partnering, joint venture, and buyout arrangements that it can be misleading to call them American companies. These companies are organized to integrate their far-flung global operations. Markets are no longer tied to territory.

Many argue that this is the key difference between the current period of globalization and the period of economic interdependence that preceded and facilitated it. Interdependence was primarily state-driven whereas globalization is primarily driven by nonstate actors.[1] For example, economic interdependence was pushed by the United States in Europe and Asia following World War II to efficiently rebuild war-devastated markets by relying on principles of comparative advantage, and to create deep and difficult-to-reverse cooperative dynamics among polities previously prone to internecine warfare. French and German cooperation in the steel sector, for example, was a prerequisite to receiving Marshall Fund reconstruction aid. While interdependence was marked by increasingly interconnected markets and societies, facilitated by advanced transportation and communication technologies (like the current period of globalization), interdependence began primarily fueled by states. With the exponential rise in foreign direct investment (FDI) in the 1980s and 1990s (FDI has increased over 700 percent since 1980),[2] and with the greatest rise in transborder economic activities occurring entirely within corporations, nonstate actors are the drivers of the current period of globalization. The economic, social, and political integration produced are manifested in deep structures of intracorporation foreign direct investment patterns rather than in surface structures of more easily reversible state-to-state trade.

Some discount the importance of this new era of globalization, arguing that it is nothing new and, also, that it is not very important since states have created the infrastructure of globalization, and presumably can revoke it anytime they wish.[3] Centuries ago, Christopher Columbus and the colonizers, the British East India Company, and Dutch and Florentine traders opened up international trade routes and created contact and interaction among previously disparate cultures, polities, and peoples. Changes in transportation and communication technologies have revolutionized world affairs before, allowing the colonization of the less-developed world by countries that had access to sailing ships, gunpowder, and printing presses. This contact created transsovereign problems such as environmental degradation and the spread of infectious disease, as is occurring today.[4]

However, the current era of globalization differs from the past in a number of ways. First, previous colonizers and trading companies if not direct agents of the crown at least worked closely with state authorities. Nonstate actors that would not cooperate with sovereign authorities had less autonomy of action, as the Jesuit order discovered in 1773 when they were banned when their missionary work ran afoul of state colonial plans. Expansion of trade routes went hand in hand with the expansion of sovereign political control over territory. Sovereignty began in Europe, codified by the Treaty of Westphalia in 1648 ending the Thirty Years War. This form of political organization, granting exclusive jurisdiction over territory, helped solidify the gains of merchant classes and undermine the control of the church. With colonization, Europeans exported not only their products but this form of political organization. Whether by conquest or imitation, the history of colonialism is also the history of the spread of sovereignty and the demise of other forms of political organization—empire, city-state, tribe, clan. At the end of World War II, the cost of holding on to colonial territories rose at the same time as European resources fell, and rapid decolonization ensued.

In a few decades Europeans lost control over territories they had taken centuries to acquire. Decolonization was marked by an expansion of sovereign states, however, not by the end of this European form of political organization, as might have been imagined. Sovereignty was too entrenched and too attractive to emerging polities to be discarded, with its promise of exclusive control over territory and internal affairs. Leaders of newly independent territories wanted recognition by other nation-states as autonomous sovereign states; the newly independent territories did not seek to revert to previous organizational forms, or to organize as empires, city-states, urban leagues, or tribes.

While the previous era of global integration was marked by the expansion of sovereignty, the current period of globalization is marked by the shrinking of sovereignty (as will be discussed at greater length in the rest of this chapter). Now, foreign direct investment (not merely trade) is the means of integrating across the globe, and FDI follows corporate direction not sovereign flags. Global economic activity is not associated with a division of territory into exclusive political units, as occurred in the colonizing period. Instead, in the current globalization period, economic activity integrates across geography, making sovereign borders less important and more permeable.

The second way the current period of globalization differs from its predecessors is that three interlocking dynamics—the spread of open societies, open economies, and open technologies—stimulate, reinforce, and speed up globalization, making the sum of globalization equal more than its component parts. The current period of globalization thus differs from previous ones in intensity and speed. The size of the Internet doubles every ninety days, and the processing capacity of computer chips doubles every eighteen months. This is not merely a quantitative change but a qualitative one, because the rate of change is faster than the ability of governments to respond. Sovereign states had centuries to respond to the challenges of colonization, and they had decades to respond to decolonization. In contrast, during the Asian financial crisis, many governments had only hours to formulate a response to market and currency fluctuations, and the governmental response was not as pivotal as the private sector response. As the current wave of democratization sweeps the globe, the problem of the speed of change becomes even more apparent. While democratic governments have many positive attributes, speed and efficiency are hardly their defining hallmarks. The argument is not that states are unimportant (or entirely unable to adapt) in the current era of globalization. They are drivers on the highway of globalization, but they are no longer the only or the largest trucks on the road. The private sector has greatly increased in size, power, and speed, while the public sector has shrunk (often in response to demands by the private sector) and can be slower to change. Thus, the new infrastructures of globalization are being built with the resources and around the operating needs of users, which are no longer exclusively states. States are a player, but now they increasingly find themselves responding to rather than leading globalization.[5]

As globalization has increased so have transsovereign problems, such as drug trafficking, international crime and terrorism, environmental degradation, refugee flows, and the spread of disease. These problems are the unintended consequences of globalization. It is physically difficult to limit the flow of particular peoples and goods at a time when technological, market, and societal forces make such movement easier than ever before. Not only are transsovereign problems the underside of globalization, but they are resistant to unilateral efforts by states to solve them alone. As markets, technologies, and societies are increasingly open and networked, important public policy issues do not stop at geographic borders. Strong and weak nation-states alike are decreasingly able to exclusively control their own territories or effectively respond alone to transsovereign problems. Important public policy problems are no longer geographically bound, nor responsive to territorial states alone. States increasingly must act in concert with other states, nongovernmental organizations (NGOs), intergovernmental organizations (IGOs), and corporations to manage global problems.[6]

Governance is no longer tied to geography either. Attempts to manage these transsovereign problems has led to the rise of global public policy networks, which integrate the activities of state, corporate, and civil society actors in managing issues from money laundering to malaria eradication. Currently, the World Bank finances over eighty such public–private networks.[7] Even powerful states, such as the United States, increasingly are turning to public–private networks to help manage issues from cybercrime to nuclear proliferation.[8] It may be less surprising to see the emergence of public–private networks in social and economic issue areas, where the arm of liberal, capitalist states reaches the least and where nonstate actors have been traditionally strong. However, more surprising is the emergence of public–private networks in issue areas relating to security and control over territory, where the claims and reach of sovereign actors have traditionally been strongest. Public–private networks have been emerging less as a concerted or theoretically informed alternative to sovereignty, and more as a practical response to problems that sovereign actors have not been able to manage alone. Adopting a "whatever works" approach, states and state bureaucracies have been actively experimenting with new organizational forms.

THE STATE CHANGES

In innovating new responses to intractable global issues, states are changing. Globalization, and state responses to globalization, are changing the nation-state's function, form, and nature of control.

Function

Susan Strange discusses ten important functions claimed by states that now are either on the decline, that nonstate actors fulfill, or that no one does anymore.[9] First, the state is responsible for defending national territory against foreign invasion, but in developed countries the threat of foreign invasion is declining and minimal, thereby eroding this source of state authority. Second, the state is responsible for maintaining the value of the currency, but inflation in one country can spread to others, thereby showing that this responsibility is now a more collective one.

Third, the state used to choose the appropriate form of capitalist development, but open economies now allow market pressures from the International Monetary Fund (IMF), the World Bank, and private investors to limit state choice and force convergence on a narrow range of development models (what Paul Krugman calls the "Washington Consensus"[10]). Fourth, the state used to be responsible for correcting the booms and busts of market economies through state spending to infuse money into public works or other state enterprises. President Franklin Delano Roosevelt combated the Great Depression in the 1930s in the United States by initiating large public works projects, building national parks, the Hoover Dam, highways, and bridges in order to put people back to work and get the economy moving again. But this option is no longer open to governments, given the market pressures to keep government spending at a minimum. Fifth, states used to provide a social safety net for those least able to survive in a market economy, by providing assistance to the very old or young, sick, disabled, or unemployed. Today, market pressures are leading states to cut back on their social welfare benefits and protective regulations. Sixth, states used to have the ability to set tax rates appropriately in order to pay for whatever government public works or social benefits spending the state wanted to engage in. Today, all states are pressured by international market forces to keep tax rates to a minimum, thereby limiting state autonomy and authority in its ability to raise funds.

Seventh, states used to have great autonomy in control over foreign trade, especially imports. Today, government intervention in trade flows can only impact the margins, because most of the decisions concerning trade flows are the "aggregate result of multiple corporate decisions."[11] Strong international market forces pressure governments to reduce obstacles to cross-border trade.

Eighth, governments used to take responsibility for building the economic infrastructure of the state, "from ports and roads to posts and telegraphs. . . . Even where governments, as in the United States, looked to private enterprise to find the necessary capital, they never hesitated in revising the laws on landed property so that landowners could not easily obstruct the infrastructural investment."[12] Today, public utilities are being privatized, and the key infrastructure needed in modern economies is communications technology, most of which does not depend on government's control over territory, which diminishes governments' ability to bargain with private interests. Most infrastructure development decisions are being made in corporate boardrooms, not state offices. Eastern European states are being integrated into the modern telecommunications grid not by governments, primarily, but by private corporations who recognize the profit margins open to the corporation that gets there first. Microsoft is computerizing Russia, not the Russian state. States may have built the infrastructure of highways, but firms and private actors are building and extending the information superhighways.

Ninth, states used to be able to create or allow public or private monopolies to dominate the local market, often as part of the government's economic development strategies. Today, competition in the world market requires an increasingly competitive local market. International market pressures now impose greater costs on state governments that try to maintain monopolies.

Finally, states used to entertain one "special kind of monopoly—that of the legitimate use of violence against the citizen or any group of citizens."[13] Now, international market forces and technological advances make the means of violence more readily available to nonstate actors (for example, al Qaida). Strong and weak states alike are losing their monopolies on the use of force. The attack on the World Trade Center on September 11, 2001, and the chemical attack on the Japanese subway on March 20, 1995, show that it is not only weak states, such as Colombia, or states in transition, such as Russia, that face challenges from nonstate actors who possess increasingly destructive firepower.

From these examples, Strange concludes that the functions states used to perform in society and the economy are shrinking, and what were once functions exclusively performed by states are now being shared with other actors (such as private firms, IGOs, and NGOs) or are not being performed at all.[14] States continue to exist, but no longer fulfill the functions they once did. The result is "a ramshackle assembly of conflicting sources of authority." As citizens come to rely on actors other than states for performing key functions, loyalty to, identity with, and authority of sovereign states becomes diffuse as well.[15]

Scholar William Zartman has his own list of state functions. In discussing failed or weak states that are collapsing, he lists five basic functions states perform: the state as the decision-making center of government; the state as a symbol of identity; the state as controller of territory and guarantor of security; the state as authoritative, legitimate political institution; and the state as a system of socioeconomic organization, the target of citizen demands for providing supplies or services.[16]

Although Zartman offers this list as a litmus test for when weak states are failing because basic state functions are no longer being performed, many of these functions correspond with Strange's and others' observations of things all states (weak and strong) used to do but no longer fulfill. States are no longer the sole decision-making center; firms and multinational corporations (MNCs) and IGOs and NGOs increasingly make decisions over matters that used to be handled by states. Economic decisions increasingly take place in corporate boardrooms, on the floors of international stock exchanges, and in the conference rooms of the IMF, and states increasingly react to rather than generate these key decisions.

Concerning transsovereign problems, states no longer can unilaterally control territory or borders, or secure territory from external threats. Alternative institutions, be they MNCs, NGOs, IGOs, or other nonstate actors, are increasingly the target of citizen demands for services or supplies that citizens do not believe the state can supply. It is interesting that few people protested the U.S. government at the signing of the World Trade Organization (WTO), but tens of thousands of protesters turned out in the streets of Seattle, Washington, to protest the WTO's operations. Triggering protests is one sign that the WTO, a nonstate actor, is increasingly the direct target of citizen demands. Finally, states are being challenged as the symbol of identity and as authoritative, legitimate political institution, as citizens increasingly place their loyalties elsewhere, in firms, professions, civic groups, ethnic ties, and so forth. If the sovereign state is no longer performing the basic functions associated with sovereign states, at what point does sovereignty cease as traditionally conceived?

Form

Early in the twentieth century, in the heyday of sovereign states, nation-states were organized as hierarchical bureaucracies, and big government was the common feature across very divergent regime types, from the fascist states to the Soviet bloc to military regimes to the democratic socialism of Britain or Roosevelt's United States. Now states around the world are moving away from strong, centralized, highly bureaucratic state forms to more network-oriented, decentralized organizational forms.[17] New organizational forms are emerging, such as many different types of public private networks, on a variety of issue areas. In addition, multilateral organizational forms are increasing in number, size, function, and importance, from the World Trade Organization to an expanded, more activist North Atlantic Treaty Organization.

Globalization goes hand in hand with government decentralization, as measured by the amount of money and decision-making power that goes to the local government level as opposed to the central government. This phenomenon has been labeled "glocalization."[18] A preliminary study of twelve states over the past twenty years showed a correlation between indicators of open societies, open economies, and open technologies and government decentralization. States that increased in openness over the time period also increased in government decentralization. States that stayed closed in the same time period did not experience government decentralization. Correlation is not causation, and so open economy, technology, and society forces and government decentralization might be caused by some third factor (the IMF, for example, as international investors pressure states both to decentralize governments and to privatize markets). But initial evidence does show that there are "simultaneous trends in globalization and decentralization";[19] decentralization and open society, open market, open technology forces go together.

By this view it is not an accident that the highly centralized states of the communist Soviet Union and eastern Europe, the apartheid state of South Africa, the military regimes in Argentina, and the social-welfare states of the United Kingdom and the United States are undergoing decentralization simultaneously. As President Bill Clinton put it, the era of big government is dead, but not just in the United States. The president was referring to the end of welfare, as we knew it, and reforms, which have downsized the federal government to the smallest it has been since the Kennedy administration. Big government is being downsized all over the planet, and power is increasingly moving to local governments in federated systems, and to nonstate actors, such as private firms and NGOs. Sometimes the central state government retains authority over certain functions, but no longer performs the functions themselves, as when states turn the operation of prisons or schools over to private actors or to local governments:

When a country's political, economic, and development activities become globalized, the national government may no longer be the dominant entity; transnational cooperations emerge at all levels of government (national and subnational) and among all types of organizations (public organizations, multinational organizations, and NGOs). Linkages between global and local socioeconomic, political, and administrative organizations are webs of organized networks and human interactions. Global changes occurring today are creating new, complex, and decentralized systems of networks that are radically different from the old centralized systems of governance which controlled the process of international activities and decision making. Global changes influence the functions and actions of local administrators. And as local administrators become more conscious of global information, they become prepared to take innovative actions without the supervision of the national government.[20]

Network forms are increasingly used to manage transsovereign problems that states are unable to contain or control unilaterally. But in adopting network forms, states must change their forms away from highly centralized bureaucracies, and this changes their functions as well. In networking with the private sector, with nonstate actors, with other states and multilateral organizations, states function primarily as facilitators, organizers, forums, and clearinghouses for information. They cannot unilaterally command or control the network process; in fact, the network will fail utterly if states attempt to assert that role.

New forms of organizing are also evident in international law. "Hard law," consisting of treaties, conventions, or customary international law, used to be the main form of regulating world politics, and only nation-states could negotiate treaties or conventions. Hard international law was primarily agreements among nation-states, prefaced on the common legal assumption of sovereignty. Today, nonstate actors are increasingly parties to hard law. In addition, "soft law" is growing in number, importance, variety, effectiveness, and issue area.[21]

Nature of Control

The nature of state control is also changing. Territory no longer excludes. State domain is still primarily territorial, but territory is less important for economic and social relations in an information-based, mobile economy, and states no longer maintain exclusive control over even this traditional geographic domain. As the means of organizing politically (according to a territorial logic) become less linked to the economic and social means of organizing (where territory no longer delimits relations), the state becomes decoupled from some of its main sources of legitimacy and power.

The intent of state control is also changing. Sovereignty came about in part because nation-states could better provide security and rationalize markets for their citizens. Nation-states no longer can provide either. In a nuclear age, even the strongest states cannot safeguard their citizens from attack. And in a globalized age, market borders do not coincide with state borders, and states have less autonomy in influencing markets.

State control is also changing in the exclusivity of its reach. States traditionally try to exclude other actors. This was one strong factor that contributed to the rise of sovereignty as the accepted political form—the ability of elites within sovereign states to exclude those who did not organize as sovereign states. Sovereignty's exclusion of multiple, intersecting authorities and jurisdictions was its big advancement from the feudal age. Today, however, the logic of globalization is inclusive, tying together a variety of types of actors across a variety of functional areas, issue areas, and geographic areas. States are learning that they must be more inclusive, entering into cooperative arrangements with a variety of diverse groups. Because states cannot solve transsovereign problems alone, they are forced out of their exclusive stance to work in a more integrated, coordinated, and regular fashion with other actors. Thus, the United States works with IGOs such as the UN Commission on Human Rights, NGOs such as CARE, as well as private firms such as Booz Allen to stabilize Bosnia. A private firm, Military Professional Resources, Inc. (not part of the U.S. government), trained the Croatian army in 1995, which helped bring the Serbs to the peace table.[22] As states share, contract, or abdicate powers and functions to other actors, the state no longer claims exclusivity in either theory or practice. If the main advantages of sovereignty were centralization and rationalization of security and the economy, and if the main innovations of sovereign control were exclusivity and one-to-one attachment to territory, and if these conditions no longer hold, what does that mean for sovereignty?

THE SHIP OF THESEUS

At what point do we have a new ship of state? The situation is analogous to a famous puzzle in the study of philosophy, the ship of Theseus. There are three different ways the ship of Theseus problem is discussed. The first stems from its origins in Greek mythology. Theseus sailed away to fight a heroic battle, but after slaying the Minotaur he forgot to change the sails to indicate the victory to his father. Sailing in the same old sails unwittingly brought about tragedy, as his father did not realize the battle had been won because the changed situation was not immediately apparent by viewing his son's ship. In a fit of despair Theseus's father committed suicide, throwing himself from a cliff into the sea. The analogy here relates to the rate of institutional change not being able to keep pace with global changes. Are we heading for disaster by traveling with our old sails on new seas?

The more pressing analogy, however, concerns the other two ways in which the ship of Theseus problem is discussed, questioning the nature of change and identity. If the planks of a ship are removed one by one over intervals of time, and each time an old plank is removed it is replaced by a new plank, is it a new vessel or not, and at what point did it reach critical mass to call it something new?

This is the question we now face in considering the sovereign state. The primary innovation of the sovereign state was its connection of authority to territory, but territory is no longer as important as it was, and states no longer maintain exclusive authority, even over territory. If sovereignty is no longer about territory or exclusivity, what is it about? Sovereignty has changed in form, function, intent, and extent. If characteristics at the heart of sovereignty are removed, is what remains still properly called sovereignty? How many planks must be pulled for us to recognize it as something different?

The difference between the case of sovereignty and the changes that occurred to the ship of Theseus was that the ship's planks were replaced exactly, in the same manner and fulfilling the same functions. The planks were not altered to turn the ship into a biplane, cruise liner, or a tugboat. But in the case of sovereignty, some facelift changes have occurred. Such changes might be correlated to the changes in form, from the strong centralized, bureaucratic governments of the twentieth century to the decentralized, capitalist, more networked regimes of the century's end. But the changes discussed in this chapter are not just changes in sovereignty's face or outward appearance, but changes in its very nature. Unlike the ship of Theseus, the ship of state is changing the very defining functions it performs and how it performs those functions. If sovereignty is as sovereignty does, and what sovereignty does is changing, is what sovereignty is changing is its very existence?

The final analogy with the ship of Theseus concerns the nature of change. Some philosophers argue for foundationalism, that sound principles need to be laid out first for new concepts to be built and based on. But Otto Neurath argues that we seldom have the luxury of changing our ideas in a pristine vacuum, starting from scratch. Instead he argues that "we are like sailors who must rebuild their ship on the open sea, never able to dismantle it in drydock and to reconstruct it there out of the best materials."[23] Certainly this is the nature of the changes now occurring to sovereignty. The ship's wheel is being replaced while the ship is still in operation; new planks are added and old ones are jettisoned while we are underway. New nonstate actors are cropping up and assuming functions that states used to perform, and new policies toward transsovereign problems are sprouting, utilizing nonstate sectors at the same time that state responses are being fine-tuned. We are not dry-docked awaiting the emergence of a new ship of political organization, but we must go forward while we are in the midst of major construction.

SPRUYT'S EQUATION

It is instructive to remember scholar Hendrik Spruyt's story of the emergence of the sovereign state over 350 years ago. Prior to the Treaty of Westphalia in 1648, there were overlapping jurisdictions of political authority with no clear hierarchy or pecking order among them. In this feudal system, claims to authority were diffuse, decentralized, and based on personal ties, not territory. Taxes and military service could be required of a person from several different authorities within the same territory.[24] Secular and spiritual authority were intertwined. People were the primary object of rule, not territory, and "rule was per definition spiritual,"[25] not spatial.

There were many reasons why the feudal system declined and the sovereign state emerged. According to Spruyt, the rise of long-distance trade in the late Middle Ages created both a new merchant class of elites and a need for a new political system that could better accommodate the mercantilist economic system. The Church was against the exchange and lending of money and the taking of oaths, but currency and contracts were crucial to long-distance trade. Trade also required more precise and consistent measurements of time, weights, jurisdiction, and property:

The result of this economic dynamism was that a social group, the town dwellers, came into existence with new sources of revenue and power, which did not fit the old feudal order. This new social group had various incentives to search for political allies who were willing to change the existing order. The new trading and commercial classes of the towns could not settle into the straightjacket of the feudal order, and the towns became a chief agent in its final disruption. . . . Business activity could not be organized according to the . . . system of personal bonds. . . . The necessity to have circumscribed areas of clear jurisdiction, and the desire to substantiate private property combined with the necessity of more formalized interaction which could exist independent of the specific actors, renewed interest in Roman law. There was the attraction—especially felt by merchants—of more convenient and rational procedures.[26]

The rise of a new economic system with its own needs, however, was not enough to bring about the rise of the sovereign state. The currency of other ideas, from the Protestant Reformation to the Scientific Revolution, aided the development of the concept of sovereignty and challenged the authority and legitimacy of the Church in Rome. Roman ideas of property rights were on the rise, which stressed exclusive control over territory.[27] Ideas of individual autonomy and freedom from outside interference, later captured by Immanuel Kant, were important in the development of sovereignty.[28]

Besides conceptual changes, sovereignty also emerged because of changes in practical political balances. Sovereign states were more effective and efficient in waging war[29] and in conducting trade than were feudal forms. Elites that benefited from the new form of organization sought to delegitimize actors that were not like them (that were not organized as sovereign states) by excluding them from the international system.

There were other forms of political organization, which competed with the sovereign state to be the successor to the feudal system: the city-state, the urban league, the empire. Spruyt believes that the sovereign state eventually won out because states were better able to extract resources and rationalize their economies than other forms of political organization; states were more efficient and effective than medieval forms of organization, especially in being able to "speak with one voice" and make external commitments necessary to the new trading system; and social choice and institutional mimicry meant that sovereign states selected out and delegitimized other actors who were not sovereign states.[30]

Out of these changes came the eventual acceptance of the sovereign state. Authority was now based on exclusive jurisdiction over territory. Identity became based on geography; you were where you lived, a citizen of French territory, not primarily a member of the Holy Roman Empire or the community of Christians or the Celtic or Norman clans. Thus, sovereignty emerged when the economy changed; new elites were created that benefited from the new economic system and needed a new form of political organization to better accommodate them and their economic practices; ideas changed; new organizational forms emerged and competed; and after centuries of flux the sovereign state eventually won out.

There are a number of parallels today. The economy has changed. The new economic system is based on information, technology, and services, and is less dependent on the control of territory. Production, capital, and labor are mobile, not fixed. Players who make use of modern information, communication, transportation, and financial technologies reap the benefits of increasingly open borders and economies. Political systems that make room for the new economic system reap the profit in foreign direct investment, and so regime types as distinct as the Chinese communist system, the Australian parliamentary system, and the Iranian theocracy are all simultaneously reforming to make themselves more attractive to investors' capital and technology flows.

New elites are emerging who profit from the new economic system. Typified by George Soros, Bill Gates, and Ted Turner, these business investors increasingly follow no flag. They are passionate about expanding technologies and markets, and they are frustrated by what they see as anachronistic state barriers to investment and trade flows. The international business information classes attend the same schools, fly the same airlines, vacation at the same resorts, eat at the same restaurants, and watch the same movies and television shows. These elites mobilize (independent of national identities) to try to make states facilitate market dynamics. Political scientist Samuel Huntington calls it the "Davos culture," after the annual World Economic Summit that meets in that Swiss luxury resort.[31] Sociologist Peter Berger calls it the "yuppie internationale," typified by the scene in a Buddhist temple in Hong Kong of "a middle aged man wearing a dark business suit over stocking feet. He was burning incense and at the same time talking on his cellular phone."[32] Even though clearly there are many economically underprivileged around the world who do not partake of this lifestyle, Berger argues that the values of this new elite percolate into the rest of society as people mimic the behavior of the elites and as they strive to better their economic situations to one day rise into the wealthier classes.

Ideas are changing (including ideas of authority, identity, and organization), facilitated by the new information technologies and changes in the economy. Never before in human history have we been able to spread ideas so quickly and widely. Modern communication technologies allow a wider and wider swath of the planet to be tuned in to the same advertisements, the same television shows, and, thereby, to some of the same ideas about consumerism and personal freedoms. Identity is becoming less tied to territory. If identity and authority do not stem from geography, what is our new church, our new religion? In the Middle Ages, identity came from Christendom, the church, while authority stemmed from spiritual connections. In the modern era, identity was tied up with the nation-state; authority flowed from geography.

Now authority and identity are increasingly contested. As Richard Rosecrance describes it, "Today and for the foreseeable future, the only international civilization worthy of the name is the governing economic culture of the world market."[33] Benjamin Barber refers to this popular, consumer market culture as "McWorld."[34] As market values permeate various cultures, certain ideas emerge as prized: the value of change, mobility, flexibility, adaptability, speed, and information. As capitalism becomes our creed with technology as our guide, distinct national and religious cultures are becoming permeated with common market values. Ideas of organization become based on markets and technologies: the computer, the Internet, and the marketplace are diffuse, decentralized, loosely connected networks with a few central organizing parameters but heavy weights to the activities of individual entrepreneurs. Perhaps, as in Spruyt's analysis of the late

Middle Ages, ideas drawn from the new economic system are helping shape new ideas of political organization.

Finally, Spruyt acknowledges that new forms of political organization are beginning to emerge, as evidenced by the European Union and the increasing roles and profile of IGOs. Thus, even if, as Spruyt maintains, the sovereign state is still supreme, three out of four of his indicators of fundamental change are with us: change in economy, elites, and ideas are in evidence. No one form of political organization has unseated or dissolved the sovereign state. But new forms have emerged, such as public–private networks, which are chipping away at functions previously performed by the state, and which are changing the role of the state.

THE SPEED OF CHANGE

If the sovereign state is changing and new forms of political organization are emerging, will change take centuries this time around? In Spruyt's story of the emergence of sovereignty, competing political forms coexisted for centuries before feudalism receded and the sovereign state emerged as the standard. He and other theorists imply that it will take a similarly long time before current changes in economic or social structures mount a fundamental challenge to the sovereign state system, in part because those who benefit from the existing state system will fight to keep it around. But the end of feudalism and the rise of sovereignty took place in an era when the modes of transportation and communication were horseback and slow-moving ships. Might change occur more quickly in an era of jet planes, the Internet, faxes, e-mail, personal computers, and cell phones?

Strange argues that the sovereign state's authority over society and economy is eroding and becoming more diffuse, but she also believes that the rate of change is different than it used to be:

What is new and unusual is that all—or nearly all—states should undergo substantial change of roughly the same kind within the same short period of twenty or thirty years. The last time that anything like this happened was in Europe when states based on a feudal system of agricultural production geared to local subsistence, gave way to states based on a capitalist system of industrial production for the market. The process of change was spread over two or three centuries at the very least and in parts of eastern and southern Europe is only now taking shape. In the latter part of the twentieth century, the shift has not been confined to Europe and has taken place with bewildering rapidity.[35]

Ideas are spread instantaneously in an era of satellite television and Internet connections. In an era of globalization, change is disseminated much more quickly than in an era of Gutenberg printing presses and wooden ships.

Stephen Krasner introduces the idea of "punctuated equilibrium" from evolutionary biology to draw the analogy that institutional change may occur rapidly over a limited period of time in unexpected ways. Rather than the Darwinian idea of change as slow, steady, continuous, and gradual, punctuated equilibrium stresses that change is "usually accomplished rapidly when a stable structure is stressed beyond its buffering capacity to resist and absorb. These evolutionary shifts can be quirky and unpredictable as the potentials for complexity are vast."[36] One question this raises is if the rate of external change vastly supersedes the institution's ability to respond, will sovereign institutions be stressed beyond their ability to evolve and adapt?

Krasner emphasizes that changes can occur rapidly when threshold effects are reached, and structures developed for one reason may later be put to very different uses. So even though Krasner concludes that the sovereign state "will not be dislodged easily, regardless of changed circumstances in the material environment," he acknowledges that in evolution, surprises are possible.[37]

CONCLUSION

States remain as one less powerful player among many. The state derives most of its power from the past, from accumulated deference and institutional inertia and advantage, rather than from proactive dynamism in being well poised to single-handedly address pressing public policy issues of the future. To accrue the benefits of name-brand recognition (because of the power, accepted nature, and institutional credibility of the words *sovereignty* and *nation-states*), future forms of political organization may keep these titles, but they may be far different in form, function, and the nature of control from their predecessors. The irony of globalization is that forces that states either unleashed or abetted are now undermining sovereignty in ways states could neither foresee nor forestall. States will weather the storm, but will become increasingly enmeshed in a network of other actors that are not functionally or organizationally equivalent. States become enmeshed in these networks as they attempt to respond to pressing public policy problems that they are incapable of responding to alone. In an effort to satisfy citizen demands and not be branded as irrelevant or impotent to solve pressing problems, states join with others, but in the very act of joining with others, they are forced to mutate in ways that change and undermine the nature of sovereignty.

Neorealism posits that states are the primary unit of international politics, and because these units are functionally equivalent, unit level factors drop out, allowing theorists to focus attention only on the structure of the international system, its polarity, and the distribution of capabilities among states. In contrast, studies of globalization reveal that states are no longer the only important units in world politics. If nonstate actors such as corporations and NGOs can frequently command the resources, autonomy, and legal standing once the sole preserve of states, and can increasingly restrict or impact on state policy (rather than the other way around), then there are now a variety of types of unit actors, and units are no longer functionally equivalent. If units are not functionally equivalent, then the study of unit-level behavior becomes a more important object of theoretical analysis, since the important action of the system cannot merely be derived or assumed by the structure of the system. The state's loss of monopoly has practical and important ramifications for both theorists and practitioners of world politics.

Finally, we are left with Thomas Jefferson's challenge. When he assumed the office of U.S. president, the country's navy had been sold off after the Revolutionary War in an effort to make some money for the new government. Barbary pirates were plundering U.S. Merchant Marine ships, and because the pirates could hit and hide before the U.S. ships could adequately respond, Jefferson was in a quandary. It was thought at the time that presidents could not authorize any commitment of troops without the explicit, advance consent of Congress, as only Congress had the power to declare war. But as long as U.S. institutions remained reactive to the Barbary pirates, U.S. ships were sitting ducks to a rapidly changing, flexible, and fast threat. Authority was not located where it was needed, and institutions were outpaced by rapidly adaptive threats. Jefferson eventually created new institutions and responses: the U.S. Navy, and the precedent of presidents authorizing the use of force.

Today, we face Jefferson's same challenge. Authority is located in territory, not where it is needed, and sovereign institutions are often unable to adequately respond to the rapidly adaptive threats and problems of globalization. Like Jefferson, we are engaging in institutional experimentation and innovation to meet changing circumstances, but unlike Jefferson we do not have available the simple option of increasing state capacity and institutions for military response. State military institutions are ill-poised to meet the challenges of globalization. States today must move authority where it is needed and create new institutions, but these efforts further empower public–private networks and nonstate actors, making states increasingly just one actor among many. Yet we have no other choice but to evolve new forms of political authority, often as seat-of-the-pants responses to emerging situations. As Jefferson noted, "Laws and institutions must go hand in hand with the progress of the human mind."

NOTES

1. Wolfgang Reinicke, *Global Public Policy: Governing without Government?* (Washington, DC: Brookings Institution, 1998).

2. Ibid., 19.

3. Emma Rothschild, "Globalization and the Return of History," *Foreign Policy* (Summer 1999): 106–116.

4. Dennis Pirages and Paul Runci, "Ecological Interdependence and the Spread of Infectious Disease," in *Beyond Sovereignty: Issues for a Global Agenda*, ed. Maryann K. Cusimano (New York: St. Martin's, 1999), 173–194.

5. In terms of capacity, the private sector (including both the profit and non-profit components) may be better poised to lead the current and future period of globalization. For example, when the barriers to integration were state-imposed tariffs, taxes, and customs duties, states were an important player in advancing globalization. But now that state borders are increasingly permeable and the re-maining obstacles to the globalization of finance and trade are primarily nontariff barriers, the expertise and information of the private sector is increasingly needed to develop consensual common standards and processes.

6. Maryann K. Cusimano, *Beyond Sovereignty: Issues for a Global Agenda* (New York: St. Martin's, 1999).

7. Motoo Kusakabe, "Key Note Address to the Workshop on Global Public Policy Networks" (paper presented at the Workshop on Networks to Address Transnational Development Challenges, World Bank, Washington, DC, November 7, 1999).

8. Maryann K. Cusimano, *Unplugging the Cold War Machine* (Thousand Oaks, CA: Sage, 2000).

9. Susan Strange, *The Retreat of the State: The Diffusion of Power in the World Economy* (Cambridge: Cambridge University Press, 1996), 189.

10. Paul Krugman, "Dutch Tulips and Emerging Markets," *Foreign Affairs* (July/August 1995): 28–44.

11. Strange, *The Retreat of the State*, 78.

12. Ibid., 79.

13. Ibid., 81.

14. Ibid., 77, 82.

15. Ibid., 77, 199.

16. I. William Zartman, *Collapsed States* (Boulder, CO: Lynn Rienner, 1995), 5.

17. Cusimano, *Unplugging the Cold War Machine*.

18. Jane Nelson, "Creating an Enabling Policy Environment" (remarks at the Carnegie Endowment for International Peace conference on "International Business: The Public Role of Private Interest," Washington, DC, May 20, 1999).

19. Jong S. Jun and Deil S. Wright, *Globalization and Decentralization: Institutional Contexts, Policy Issues, and Intergovernmental Relations in Japan and the US* (Washington, DC: Georgetown University Press, 1996), 1.

20. Ibid., 3–4.

21. Dinah Shelton, *Commitment and Compliance: What Role for International "Soft Law?"* (Oxford: Oxford University Press, 2000).

22. Colonel Bruce D. Grant, "U.S. Military Expertise for Sale: Private Military Consultants as a Tool of Foreign Policy" (third-place paper in the 1998 Chairman of the Joint Chiefs of Staff Strategy Essay Competition; Washington, DC: U.S. Army War College, 1998), 7.

23. Otto Neurath quoted in A. J. Ayer, ed., *Logical Positivism* (Glencoe, IL: Free Press, 1959), 109.

24. F. H. Hinsley, *Sovereignty* (London: C. A. Watts, 1966).

25. Hendrik Spruyt, *The Sovereign State and Its Competitors* (Princeton, NJ: Princeton University Press, 1994), 47.

26. Ibid., 62, 75.

27. Friedrich Kratochwil, "Sovereignty as Dominium: Is There a Right of Humanitarian Intervention?" in *Beyond Westphalia: State Sovereignty and International Intervention*, ed. Gene M. Lyons and Michael Mastanduno (Baltimore, MD: Johns Hopkins University Press, 1995), 21–42.

28. Nicholas Onuf, "Intervention for the Common Good," in *Beyond Westphalia: State Sovereignty and International Intervention*, ed. Gene M. Lyons and Michael Mastanduno (Baltimore, MD: Johns Hopkins University Press, 1995), 43.

29. Charles Tilly, *The Formation of National States in Western Europe* (Princeton, NJ: Princeton University Press, 1975).

30. Spruyt, *The Sovereign State and Its Competitors*.

31. Samuel Huntington, *The Clash of Civilizations and the Remaking of World Order* (New York: Simon and Schuster, 1996).

32. Peter L. Berger, "Four Faces of Global Culture," *National Interest* (Fall 1997): 24.

33. Richard Rosecrance, "The Rise of the Virtual State," *Foreign Affairs* (July/August 1996): 59–60.

34. Benjamin Barber, *Jihad vs. McWorld* (New York: Ballantine Books, 1996).

35. Strange, *The Retreat of the State*, 87.

36. Stephen Krasner, "Sovereignty: An Institutional Perspective," *Comparative Political Studies* 21 (April 1988): 79.

37. Ibid., 80.

8 The Role of Nongovernmental Organizations and Intergovernmental Organizations in the Process of Globalization

Vernon J. Vavrina

Globalization, the buzzword of the new millennium, will have a profound future impact on intergovernmental organizations (IGOs)[1] and nongovernmental organizations (NGOs).[2] Both of the latter, in turn, will shape the former. However, globalization is a term with a variety of meanings. John Pennell, of the Academy for Educational Development, defines globalization as "an economically-driven process whereby the politics, economics, and culture of one country . . . penetrate other countries. Globalization is also seen as a force that can unite economic forces (e.g., as in regional economic blocs) while at the same time causing social resistance to these forces. It is also seen as a force that can undermine state autonomy and power" (Pennell, 1997).

Perhaps, Robert O. Keohane and Joseph S. Nye Jr. (2000) offer the clearest definition: "Globalization and deglobalization refer to the increase or decline of globalism," a state of the world "involving networks of interdependence at multi-continental distances" (105). Hence, for these two political scientists, globalization implies that globalism is actually increasing. In contrast, globalism, with its economic, military, environmental, and social/cultural forms, may either increase or decrease. "Globalization is the process by which globalism becomes increasingly thick" involving many intensive relationships, large continuous long-distance flows that affect the lives of many (ibid.). It refers to large-scale shrinkage of distances. Contemporary globalization for Keohane and Nye is marked by "magnitude, complexity and speed" (ibid.).

It is important to be precise about what is meant by globalization in order to understand and evaluate the role of IGOs and NGOs in its process. Interestingly, how academics perceive the phenomenon may be a function of their disciplines. David Newman, chair of the Department of Politics and Government at Ben-Gurion University in Negev, Israel, observes that economists tend to talk of borderless worlds, global markets, and worldwide flows of information. Political scientists, sociologists, and geographers, in contrast, are apt not to see "the emergence of a single, undifferentiated global space" (2000, 23). For many of them, the walls are not tumbling down. Newman warns "we should not be naïve or deterministic in automatically assuming that a globalized world is a world without borders" (ibid.). Globalization "may not necessarily affect every region, country, or society in the same way" (Pennell, 1997). In addition, cross-border activity does not have to be admirable. Recently, there has been a "rise of intolerant, violent, racist and sexist groups organizing across national boundaries" (Naidoo, 2000, 35).

Kenneth N. Waltz (1999) sees globalization as a made-in-America fad of the 1990s.[3] He notes that what he found to be true in his research in the 1970s is true today; namely, that the world is less interdependent than is usually supposed. "Many globalizers underestimate the extent to which the new looks like the old" (695). Indeed, there is a history of globalization dating back at least to the eighteenth century (Rothschild, 1999, 107). Francis Fukuyama (1999) believes that "in many respects, globalization is still superficial"—its real layer being restricted to capital markets. Trade is still predominantly regional and most companies are predominantly national. Despite the economic pressures, Fukuyama argues that societies are maintaining their individual characteristics. For him, cultural homogeneity is not resulting from globalization. In the year 2000, the expansive reach of the English language cannot be denied; but some scholars believe it will eventually wane in influence as the importance of regional languages increases (for example, Fishman, 1998). Others see regionalism, not globalism, as the greatest threat to the authority of European nation-states (for example, Newhouse, 1997). Still others have identified an interesting paradox: the enormous new increase in the capacity to produce and distribute news from abroad has been met by a corresponding decrease in its consumption (for example, Moisy, 1997).

Many writers and activists vehemently disagree with the aforementioned authors. Typical is the response of the International Forum on Globalization, a nonprofit alliance founded in 1994. Most of its members view the process of globalization as "the most extreme restructuring of the planet's social, economic and political arrangements since the Industrial Revolution, bringing with it profound effects on human life and the natural world" (International Forum on Globalization, 2000). Spokeswomen for the Women's Environment and Development Organization (1998) bemoan that women are the "shock absorbers" for structural change: "Women in economies in transition . . . pay a disproportionate share of the costs of economic globalization while being excluded from its benefits. An abhorrent aspect of the global economy is the prostitution of women in a sex industry that spans the world." Some lawyers, highlighting the genesis of the 1997 Ottawa Convention on Land Mines, assert that the information age will transform international law as well as the very systems and assumptions that undergird it. IGOs and NGOs will take on decision-making roles theretofore the exclusive domains of states (Gamble and Ku, 2000).

However one conceives of globalization and its consequences, it is clear that the phenomenon in myriad ways impacts, and is impacted by, organizations. The latter must deal with multitudinous issues: migration, international news, drug trafficking, transnational corruption, child labor, women's rights, Third World debt, economic and political integration, and so forth.

The Union of International Associations, a Brussels-based transnational actor, uses "a legalistic criterion to distinguish between intergovernmental organizations (IGOs) and international nongovernmental organizations (NGOs). This criterion defines IGOs as organizations established by intergovernmental treaty, as specified in a United Nations Economic and Social Council (ECOSOC) resolution of 1950, regardless of the character of their membership" (Skjelsbaek, 1971, 72). ECOSOC is authorized to enter into consultative relationships with private organizations, the NGOs (Bennett, 1988). Growth in the number of NGOs, as well as IGOs, has been astounding. Thirty-seven IGOs and 176 INGOs existed in 1909. Eighty years later the numbers had climbed to some 300 IGOs and 4,624 INGOs (Held, 1997; Magstadt and Schotten, 1999). Numbers fluctuate but are still impressive.[4] NGOs and INGOs, in particular, have greatly augmented activity levels. Some NGOs have gained significant name recognition such as environmental giant Greenpeace, the International Campaign to Ban Landmines, and Jubilee 2000, which calls for Third World debt cancellation.

But, the capabilities of various IGOs and NGOs differ drastically. At the same time, the World Trade Organization (WTO) is criticized for having too much power, the International Labor Organization (ILO) is said not to have enough (Naim, 2000). Human rights activists in China lament the dearth of independent NGOs and trade unions there. They contrast the unhappy Chinese situation with that of Indonesia where many independent NGOs exist to organize workers (*Multinational Monitor*, 2000).

GLOBALIZATION AND NONGOVERNMENTAL ORGANIZATIONS

Globalization has won the attention of a whole host of nonstate actors. For example, Pope John Paul II has preached that globalization must include solidarity. Its unexpected possibilities for growth have been accompanied by the marginalization of the masses. The pontiff pleads for a calm, respectful dialogue among various cultures and religions. In addition, the leader of the Catholic Church urgently calls for debt forgiveness for the poorest, and sharing the fruits of economic expansion (*America*, 2000).

Peter Sutherland, chair of the Overseas Development Council, believes the effects of globalization have been overwhelmingly good. Millions of jobs have been created at the same time there has been an enormous increase in international investment. He agrees with the pope that the foremost challenge is to ensure the fruits of globalization extend to all countries. Like other commentators, he laments that sub-Saharan Africa has been left out of the picture (Sutherland, 1998). Manhattan contains more telephone connections than the entire poverty-stricken region.

In November 1999, the Turning Point Project bought full-page advertisements in the *New York Times* warning readers of global monoculture, the results of economic globalization, and World Trade Organization rules. Thus, a coalition of more than fifty nonprofit organizations, such as the Sierra Club and the Institute for Policy Studies, called out "democratic, localized, ecologically sound alternatives" to the status quo (Turning Point Project, 1999; c.f. Swerdlow et al., 1999).

Many NGOs criticize current IGOs, like the WTO, for lacking democracy, accountability, and transparency. Governments and international bureaucrats counter by claiming that most global NGOs, as well as their constituent parts, are self-appointed, not elected, nor accountable to well-defined constituencies (Naidoo, 2000; Naim, 2000). Furthermore, a certain degree of secrecy is said to be essential in the treaty-making process (Gamble and Ku, 2000).

Lori Wallach, director of Public Citizen's Global Trade Watch, is credited with spearheading the anti-WTO protests in Seattle, Washington, in late 1999. She was the driving force behind the "No New Round Turnaround" campaign—a successful (at least in the short term) effort to thwart a new "Millennium Round" of WTO talks designed to augment the WTO's power vis-à-vis agriculture and trade in services. A "WTO: Fix it or Nix It" campaign is now in the works (Naim, 2000).

Seattle's violence, which Wallach blames on inept Seattle police and anarchists from Eugene, Oregon, showed the extent to which certain elements of the public have become alarmed about globalization forces. Therefore, one might claim that 1999 became the "Year of Globalization."

Wallach and her colleagues had suffered their share of past defeats. They were unable to force Congress to defeat the North American Free Trade Agreement in 1993. Similarly, they could not prevent the 1994 Uruguay Round of the General Agreement on Tariffs and Trade that led to the creation of the WTO. Wallach's global coalition, which today is comprised of over twenty-five country-based campaigns, finally achieved a major success in 1997 when "fast-track" trade authority for the president was shelved. If passed, this would have forced Congress to vote without amendments on trade agreements negotiated by the executive. Another victory for Wallach and her colleagues was the Organization for Economic Cooperation and Development's tabling of the Multilateral Agreement on Investment (MAI), a kind of proposed world constitution on investment rules (*Public Citizen*, 1997).

Some content new technologies strengthen the capacities of NGOs to influence policy (Cutter, Spero, and Tyson, 2000). They point to Seattle as a star example. Certainly, NGOs, such as Amnesty International, Oxfam, Christian Aid, Friends of the Earth, and the Institute for War and Peace Research, are increasingly availing themselves of computer-mediated communication (Rodgers, 1998). Wallach and her colleagues, for instance, made liberal use of the Internet in the No New Round Turnaround campaign. Nevertheless, she explains that the major planning and organization for Seattle was done person to person (see Naim, 2000, 33). The World Wide Web was also instrumental in scuttling MAI (Kobrin, 1998). Opponents used the Web to leak a draft agreement that, in turn, led to considerable erosion of support for MAI.

Despite being a fantastic tool for many professionals, the Internet, it may be contended, "represents in no way the miraculous advent of the much heralded 'global village'" (Moisy, 1997, 78). Andrew L. Shapiro (1999) cites evidence that many people may actually use their new power over information "to reinforce existing political beliefs rather than challenge themselves." He adds that "citizens might feel less of a connection with, and less of an obligation toward, one another" (25). Another problem is the Net's promotion of information overload.

Over the past twenty years, globalization has enabled developing countries to possess chemical plants, biological research equipment, and missile technology (Libicki, 1999). Surely, modern technology is not an unmixed blessing. Saudi Arabian officials have tweaked computer codes to filter out material they deem objectionable. Iran, in turn, has tinkered with codes to make chat rooms unavailable to more than two individuals at one time. Human rights NGOs, which of necessity must protect the identities of both victims and witnesses, will be dealt a harsh blow if governments outlaw strong encryption techniques (Shapiro, 1999).

It is not so much the speed of modern telecommunications that is important, but rather the lower costs they entail (Keohane and Nye, 2000). This, of course, is beneficial to any given NGO. However, the technology is likewise available to others who are at odds with a particular NGOs objectives. On globalization, as in everything else, NGOs disagree. The International Confederation of Free Trade Unions has called for building labor rights into the global trading system. This has been endorsed by the preponderance of independent labor federations (Mazur, 2000). Jagdish

Bhagwati (2000) notes, however, that prior to Seattle numerous NGOs from the developing countries issued a statement *against* linkage of labor standards to the WTO. Although unions all over the globe desire the advancement of labor rights, southern workers see possible trade sanctions as threatening their competitive position (Bhagwati, 2000).

GLOBALIZATION AND INTERGOVERNMENTAL ORGANIZATIONS

Today, IGOs bear the brunt of negative publicity concerning the deficiencies of globalization—shortcomings that became abundantly apparent with the reverberating ill effects of the 1997 Asian financial crisis. The big targets are the WTO, the International Monetary Fund (IMF), and the International Bank for Reconstruction and Development (IBRD or World Bank).[5] Violence in Seattle was flashed across television screens throughout the world. Denouncers of the WTO were also very much in evidence at the Geneva Social Summit in June 2000. There was even an effigy of WTO Director General Mike Moore depicting him as a vampire (*Poughkeepsie [NY] Journal*, 2000). Wallach contends that Moore and his staff are "accountable to no one" (see Naim, 2000, 36).

The IMF has been so unpopular in developing countries that it has been the cause of riots. Critics of the IMF often call for its complete overhaul or elimination (Soros, 1998–1999). One of the IMF's alleged sins is said to be the asymmetrical manner in which it treats lenders and borrowers. By imposing conditions on borrowing countries, but not on lending financial institutions, the IMF helps banks recover unsound loans. When Mexico could not pay back the United States in the midst of its 1995 financial crisis, the IMF (and the U.S. Treasury Department) relieved investors of all risk (Soros, 1998–1999, 64).

Billionaire financier George Soros (1998–1999) believes the proper medicine for the world's economic system includes measures (for example, deregulation, privatization, and transparency) to make financial markets more efficient and disciplined. Yet he states that "public-policy measures are needed to stabilize the flows of international finance" (62). He advocates the establishment of an International Credit Insurance Corporation that could eventually become part of the IMF. Yale's Jeffrey Garten, on the other hand, would forget about the IMF and the IBRD. Garten would create a new global central bank, which among other things would provide liquidity to poor countries by the purchase of bonds from national central banks (see Soros, 1998–1999, 63).

Proponents of IGOS are appalled at their precarious positions. IGOs, which are not world governments, frequently have a very difficult time enforcing their decisions and/or collecting assessments from members. The United Nations, the grandfather of all IGOs, is the perfect example. The International Court of Justice, the legal arm of the United Nations, was unable to compel the Ayatollah Khomeini to release American diplomats during the Iran hostage crisis in 1979.

With respect to money, the United Nations manifests a "quantitative/ qualitative problem." Eight wealthy member-countries are responsible for about 75 percent of the UN regular budget. But, members tagged for under 1 percent of the budget control almost 50 percent of the votes in the UN General Assembly. For years the United States has been the largest debtor; in mid-1988, it owed the United Nations over $1.5 billion (Rourke and Boyer, 2000).[6]

Although the United States is almost universally criticized for its failure to pay its dues, there is a more sinister side to the United Nations that many, perhaps, do not appreciate. Individuals on Capitol Hill who attack the United Nations note it has been extraordinarily inefficient and poorly administered. More seriously, they allege that the United Nations has had the audacity to use American dollars for anti-American purposes. Indeed, there is ample empirical evidence that, at times, the United Nations has used a dual standard with respect to human rights—criticizing the U.S. allies of transgressions while simultaneously letting U.S. foes totally off the hook (Donnelly, 2000).

The ILO and the United Nations Educational, Scientific and Cultural Organization have also been accused by the United States of mismanagement and "politicization." This culminated in American withdrawal from these UN specialized agencies respectively in 1977 (under Democratic President Jimmy Carter) and 1984 (under Republican President Ronald Reagan). In the case of the ILO, the U.S. pullout translated into a 25 percent drop in that organization's budget until the superpower returned in 1980 (Riggs and Plano, 1994).

The aforementioned illustrations show inherent weaknesses of some international organizations—defects that, in one form or another, will likely continue into the twenty-first century. There is much less controversy, on the other hand, with other highly successful international organizations such as the Universal Postal Union, the International Civil Aviation Organization, and the World Meteorological Organization (Baehr and Gordenker, 1994).

A CASE STUDY: DEALING WITH CHILD LABOR IN THE AGE OF GLOBALIZATION

A brief examination of the dilemmas associated with contemporary child labor demonstrates the intricate relationships between nation-states, IGOs, and INGOs. According to even extremely conservative estimates, across the globe at least 250 million children work. Yet eradication of child labor is an extremely thorny problem. Preventing youngsters from working may, in some instances, force other family members to go hungry (Bechman, 2000).

For about twenty years, an international movement has been forged to ameliorate the situation. It is made up of different parts with varying perspectives and motivations: ILO, UNICEF, IBRD, governments, trade unions, human rights advocates, journalists, academics, and so forth.

Despite the best of intentions, policies eventually enacted had adverse effects on the children they were designed to assist. Sarah L. Bechman (2000) argues that "although globalization has popularized notions of universal norms, values and solutions, it is misleading and even dangerous to assume that one-size-fits-all policies will solve the problems that lead millions of children into abusive labor" (548).

Bachman stresses a major lack of understanding among the various elements of the Anti-Child Work Movement; namely, child labor is first and foremost a reality of the *informal* domestic economy. However, child labor laws almost always deal with the formal economy. Some solace may be found in ILO and UN treaties that provide international standards outlawing the worst forms of abuse. Nevertheless, there is much more work to be done by, for example, the IMF and even perhaps the WTO, which attempts to avoid the issue altogether (Bechman, 2000).

Experts say there are many reasons for child labor and that a limited number of hours of work may actually be good for children. Not all kinds of child labor perpetuate poverty. Indeed, juveniles themselves of late have been forming working children's movements that defend the benefits of work (Bechman, 2000).

PRIMACY OF POLITICS

By the year 2000, globalization was a reality that was happening one way or another and could not be stopped (Naim, 2000, 12 [Editor's Note]). As Keohane and Nye (2000) suggest, globalization "does not merely affect governance; it is affected by governance" (113). And, it will be accompanied by pervasive uncertainty. Despite its many supporters, globalization, according to UN Secretary-General Kofi Annan, has largely failed its promise to benefit the masses of the world: "some have lost their jobs. Others see their communities disintegrating. Some feel their very identify is at stake. . . . Even in the richest and most democratic countries, people wonder if the leaders they elect have any real control over events" (*Poughkeepsie [NY] Journal*, 2000).

Annan's remarks were made in conjunction with the beginning of the weeklong UN "Social Summit" held in Geneva during the last week of June

2000. The United Nations estimates that since 1995 the number of people living in absolute poverty has actually increased by 200 million to a figure of 1.2 billion. The millions of destitute have an exceedingly hard time just meeting the basic necessities of life. One-third of the Earth's people do not have access to telephones, let alone personal computers (Naidoo, 2000).

In a world characterized by such uneven effects of the positive fruits of globalization, the primacy of politics remains. Power, not economics, is still the key concept explaining international relations. Notwithstanding "global village" rhetoric, the system of sovereign nation-states marked by self-help and frequent threat or use of force will persist for the foreseeable future (Shapiro, 1999; Waltz, 1999). This system is not likely to change drastically because those powers strong enough to implement change do not have the incentive to alter a framework from which they benefit.

However, nation-states and IGOs are free to adapt to changing world circumstances and may make substantial improvements in the human condition. They will take pains to deflect harsh criticisms that have come their way lately; but according to RAND analyst John Arquilla, the nation-state will be in some jeopardy if it does not incorporate NGO viewpoints (see Donnelly, 2000). By circumventing governments, IGOs may actually contribute to NGO prominence.

NGOs, for their part, surely will continue to grow in size and scope. They will attempt to check the power and practice of nation-states. Their delegates will continue to play an active role in fora such as the 1992 Rio Earth Summit and the 1995 Beijing Women's Conference. They will have occasional, sometimes significant, victories. Thus, Jodi Foster won a Nobel Peace Prize for her work in coordinating the International Campaign Against Landmines. College students were influential in forcing Nike to reveal its sweatshops. Threatening demonstrations, the group Global Exchange achieved concessions from Starbucks. The corporation pledged in the future to buy more coffee beans at higher prices in order for Third World farmers to make a better living (Donnelly, 2000).

Many so-called global organizations, however, have very little representation in densely populated China, Russia, Indonesia, and Japan. There are also concerns that some leaders of the global activist movement are too self-righteous to compromise with those with whom they disagree (Naidoo, 2000). Most important, NGOs are not yet authoritative decision makers in international law (Gamble and Ku, 2000).

While some global activists actively try to undermine the nation-state system, others do not. The latter emphasize the positive role the system may play. Kumi Naidoo, secretary general of CIVICUS: World Alliance for Citizen Participation, observes that many activists from the developing world now view the necessity "for effective, accountable and efficient nation-state infrastructures" to check globalization's negative aspects

(Naidoo, 2000, 35). Therefore, whether the influence of NGOs will ever severely challenge the nation-state system—even in an age of globalization—is very much open to question.

NOTES

1. IGOs are a type of international organization in which individual governments become members. The United Nations is the premier example of an IGO.

2. NGOs are private organizations. The UN Charter refers to NGOs, but does not define them. There has been much scholarly debate on a proper definition (see Gamble and Ku, 2000). This chapter will concentrate on international nongovernmental organizations (INGOs), a special category of NGOs. It will reflect contemporary practice by often using the two terms synonymously. INGOs are comprised of private individuals and groups, which act transnationally. A classic case is the Nobel Peace Prize–winning Amnesty International. This human rights INGO, headquartered in London, boasts over one million members and supporters in 140 countries. It has in excess of seventy-five hundred groups in 90 countries. Multinational corporations, also called transnational corporations, are important transnational actors in international relations, as well. Unfortunately, due to spatial limitations, consideration of their special role lies outside the scope of this work.

3. *New York Times* columnist Thomas L. Friedman, author of *The Lexus and the Olive Tree*, emphatically dismisses the notion that globalization is just a passing fad. See Friedman and Ramonet (1999).

4. In 2000, by one count, there were 272 IGOs and nearly 5,000 INGOs (Rourke and Boyer, 2000, 51). By another tabulation, at the same time there were some 26,000 NGOs (Keohane and Nye, 2000, 116).

5. For a taste, read the "Statement from Members of International Civil Society Opposing a Millennium Round or a New Round of Comprehensive Trade Negotiations" and opposition to the proposed Global Free Logging Agreement (*A Seed*, 1999). Some think there is a risk in singling out such organizations. The IBRD has been giving NGOs a bigger say in its funding projects for the developing world. Protests, especially violent ones devoid of well-articulated alternatives, may be seen as the adolescent incantations of rich brats biting the hand that feeds them. On the other side of the coin, "broad, blunt, email-fueled demonstrations are likely to flower" because they are effective in enabling activists to bring light to unpopular policies (Donnelly, 2000).

6. Financially strapped IGOs may be tempted to use NGO intermediation to tap sources of private wealth. A result may be a grossly overrated perception of the abilities of NGOs to conduct wide-ranging activities (Gamble and Ku, 2000).

REFERENCES

A Seed. 1999. Statement from Members of International Civil Society Opposing a Millennium Round or a New Round of Comprehensive Trade Negotiations. wysiwyg://mainframe.86/http://antenna.nl/aseed/trade/index. html.

America. 2000. Editorial, June 3.

Bechman, S. L. 2000. A New Economics of Child Labor: Searching for Answers behind the Headlines. *Journal of International Affairs* 53 (Spring): 545–573.

Baehr, Peter R., and Leon Gordenker. 1994. *The United Nations in the 1990s.* New York: St. Martin's.

Bennett, A. LeRoy. 1988. *International Organizations.* Englewood Cliffs, NJ: Prentice-Hall.

Bhagwati, Jagdish. 2000. Letter to the Editor. *Foreign Affairs* 78 (May/June): 182–183.

Cutter, W. Bowman, Joan Spero, and Laura D'Andrea Tyson. 2000. New World, New Deal: A Democratic Approach to Globalization. *Foreign Affairs* 79 (March/April): 80–98.

Donnelly, John. 2000. New Wave Takes on the World Bank, IMF Citizen Activists Seek to Mobilize More Americans. *Boston Globe*, April 16.

Fishman, Joshua. 1998–1999. The New Linguistic Order. *Foreign Policy* 113 (Winter): 26–40.

Friedman, Thomas, and Ignacio Ramonet. 1999. Dueling Globalizations. *Foreign Policy* 116 (Fall): 110–127.

Fukuyama, Francis. 1999. Economic Globalization and Culture. http://www.ml. com/woml/forum/global.htm.

Gamble, John King, and Charlotte Ku. 2000. International Law—New Actors and New Technologies: Center Stage for NGOs? *Law and Policy in International Business* 31 (Winter): 221–262.

Held, David. 1997. Democracy and Globalization. https:wwwc.cc.columbia.edu/sec/dlc/ciao/wps/hed02/hed02.html.

International Forum on Globalization. 2000. http://www.ifg.org/.

Keohane, Robert O., and Joseph S. Nye Jr. 2000. Globalization: What's New? What's Not? (And So What?). *Foreign Policy 118* (Spring): 104–106.

Kobrin, Stephen J. 1998. The MAI and the Clash of Globalization. *Foreign Policy* 112 (Fall): 97–109.

Libicki, Martin. 1999–2000. Rethinking War: The Mouse's New Roar? *Foreign Policy* 117 (Winter): 30–43.

Magstadt, Thomas M., and Peter M. Schotten. 1999. *Understanding Politics.* New York: St. Martin's/Worth.

Mazur, Jay. 2000. Labor's New Internationalism. *Foreign Affairs* 79 (January/February): 79–93.

Moisy, Claude. 1997. Myths of the Global Information Village. *Foreign Policy* 107 (Summer): 78–87.

Multinational Monitor. 2000. An Interview with Alice Kwan. *Multinational Monitor* 21 (May): 19–28.

Naidoo, Kumi. 2000. The New Civic Globalism. *The Nation* 270 (May): 34–36.

Naim, Moisés . 2000. Lori's War. *Foreign Policy* 118 (Spring): 28–55.

Newhouse, John. 1997. Europe's Rising Regionalism. *Foreign Affairs* 76 (January/February): 67–84.

Newman, David. 2000. Why Disciplines Split on Globalization? *Tikkun* (May/June): 19–21, 57.

Pennell, John. 1997. Re: What is Globalization? http://csf.colorado.edu/mail/ipe/sep97/0039.html.

Poughkeepsie (NY) Journal. 2000. World Poverty Summit Begins Today. June 26.

Public Citizen. 1997. Public Citizen's Global Trade WatchBackgrounder. http://www.ifg.org/backgrounder.html.

Riggs, Robert E., and Jack C. Plano. 1994. *The United Nations: International Organization and World Politics* Belmont, CA: Wadsworth.

Rodgers, Jayne. 1998. NGO Use of Computer-Mediated Communication: Opening New Spaces of Political Representation? https:wwwc.cc.columbia.edu/sec/dlc/ciao/conf/roj02/roj02.html.

Rothschild, Emma. 1999. Globalization and the Return of History. *Foreign Policy* 115 (Summer): 106–116.

Rourke, John T., and Mark A. Boyer. 2000. *World Politics: International Politics on the World Stage, Brief—Sluice Dock.* Guilford, CT: Dushkin/McGraw Hill.

Shapiro, Andrew L. 1999. The Internet. *Foreign Policy* 115 (Summer): 14–15.

Skjelsbaek, Kjell. 1971. The Growth of International Nongovernmental Organization in the Twentieth Century. In *Transnational Relations and World Politics,* ed. Robert O. Keohane and Joseph S. Nye Jr., 70–92. Cambridge, MA: Harvard University Press.

Soros, George. 1998–1999. Capitalism's Last Chance. *Foreign Policy* 113 (Winter): 55–66.

Sutherland, Peter. 1998. Expand the Debate on Globalization. *Time.com* 5 (February 2): 1–3.

Swerdlow, Joel et al. 1999. Global Culture. *National Geographic* 196 (August): 2–33.

Turning Point Project. 1999. Global Monoculture. *New York Times,* November 15.

Waltz, Kenneth N. 1999. Globalization and Governance. *PS: Political Science and Politics* 32 (December): 693–700.

Women's Environment and Development Organization. 1998. Global Survey Finds Progress on Women's Rights and Equality Compromised by Economic Globalization. http://www.wedo.org/monitor/mapping.htm.

9

Globalization, Internationalization, and the Not-for-Profit Sector

Eve Sandberg

To understand the effects of today's globalization processes on nongovernmental organizations (NGOs) in the not-for-profit sector, it is useful first to identify many of the processes attributed to globalization that are distinct from processes that may be considered transnational, international, or interdependent in nature.[1] While a number of authors have written comparatively on these processes, there is little agreement on the terms they employ when discussing these broad analytical categories. Therefore, I will consider some of the globalization processes identified by prominent political scientists and sociologists in the 1990s and how they analytically distinguish these processes from other internationalizing processes.

When I analyze the effects of globalization on nongovernmental organizations operating in the not-for-profit sector, I find that, like the processes of globalization itself, the effects of globalization on nongovernmental organizations are complex and multidirectional. In the not-for-profit world, globalization accelerates the speed by which reactive and proactive programmatic activities must be undertaken because of the reduced costs and accelerated pace of information exchanges as well as because of the influence that one issue arena imposes on another. Globalization increases the cultural complexity of any programmatic initiative. Globalization influences the status of state power and state sovereignty, legitimacy, and capacity with varying possible outcomes for not-for-profits. Often, for example, the withdrawal of state activity or capacity in a given sector offers opportunities for not-for-profits to move into that sector. However, globalization's tendencies toward privatization may favor the private sector over the not-for-profit sector in responding to new demands in areas where the state has withdrawn even though the effects of the responses by the for-profit sector and not-for-profit sector may vary greatly for local citizens. The diminution of the state also affects its ability to contribute to the funding of programs undertaken by nongovernmental organizations. Thus, NGOs are often forced to curtail programmatic initiatives and divert scarce human resources from their major missions (altering the agendas of the not-for-profits) in order to pursue new sources of funding. Globalization highlights the power differentials of actors in various issue and programmatic arenas; and I will discuss how those active in the not-for-profit sector are affected by this spotlighting. Globalization has definitive effects on employment in that it increases unemployment, part-time employment, and disguised employment with consequences for the not-for-profit sector as well as for the individuals and families who suffer from these effects. Finally, globalization offers both new opportunities and obstacles for resource mobilization by representatives of nongovernmental organizations. In the following section, I discuss some usage of general terms for globalization and internationalization. Then, in the section that follows, I identify what appear to be some major differences in the usage of these terms. Finally, I analyze the effects of many of the processes and themes of globalization for nongovernmental organizations in the not-for-profit sector.

CONSIDERING SOME UNDERSTANDINGS OF GLOBALIZATION AND INTERNATIONALISM

Robert Keohane and Joseph Nye Jr., who popularized the phenomena of "interdependence" in the 1970s, have observed that *globalization* was the buzzword of the 1990s and that while it has had many meanings, it implies something quite different from interdependence.[2] Whereas interdependence could increase or decrease, globalization implies that something has been increasing.[3]

Keohane and Nye define *globalism* as "a state of the world involving networks of interdependence at multicontinental distances with linkages occurring through economic and social exchanges." They distinguish this from interdependence, which implies "reciprocal effects among countries or among actors in different countries." Globalism, therefore, is a form of interdependence but it refers to multiple networks although "changes in each area do not necessarily occur simultaneously." Keohane and Nye claim that today's globalism differs from older international or transnational concepts not because it is new, but because its processes are "thicker." They suggest that globalism's thickness can be viewed according to its increased density of networks, its increased institutional velocity of networks, and its increased transnational participation. They note, for example, that greater activity in the trade arena can mobilize environmental activists across borders and thus invigorate a different network. Further, such thick interconnectedness affects uncertainty and the ability of states to govern. Network activities are, however, in turn, affected by states' governance activities. Additionally, borrowing the economists use of the term *network effects*, Keohane and Nye note that chain reactions can occur because the value of something increases when many people use it.

When assessing the effects of globalization they note that real changes have come not in the velocity of informational flows but rather in the reduced costs of communications. Thus, more intensive communicating, rather than extensive communicating, has resulted. Keohane and Nye argue that among the greatest changes has been the expansion of channels of contact among societies as a result of decreasing costs.

In specific references to nongovernmental organizations they note that due to the processes of globalism, the size of a nongovernmental organization hardly matters to its ability to have a hearing. Its voice can be heard through new channels of communication as was never before possible. Thus, nongovernmental organizations can now affect issues that were formerly within the exclusive domain of states, thus advancing the cause of pluralism.[4]

The work on globalization of Barrie Axford supports the concerns of both Anthony Giddens and Roland Robertson and contributes to our understanding of globalization as a phenomenon of multiple processes and systems that must be analyzed for the power differentials inherent in each of its composite systems.[5] Axford's explication of Anthony Giddens's work on globalization as a system reinforces "Gidden's [sic] injunction to see such systems as formed through the intersection of multiple systems with power differentials but where no one level or component is assumed to dominate."[6] Axford also keeps the focus on the systemic features of globalization through his support for Roland Robertson's assertion that "the idea of uniquely global features does not obscure the extent to which all social systems are embedded in or otherwise overlap with other such systems."[7] Thus, Axford argues that it is a mistake to see the global system as one that is imposing its imperatives on various actors within the system. Rather, actors at various levels of the global system act in ways that mediate the impact of global processes that involve money, goods, services, and people, on different parts of the system and the people who reside in different parts of the system. Axford, thus, takes issue with authors such as Paul Kennedy who argue that migration across boundaries is creating a cognitive global order. Rather, Axford notes that where such global consciousness may be attempting to redefine local or national identities, often locals use the perceived external pressures as a way to mobilize against the foreigner or the "other."

Axford offers an interesting discussion of the structure/agent problematic within the processes of globalization. On the one hand, he cautions that structures are not external to individuals but are produced through social practices that both constrain and enable action. He further notes that structures and institutions are not merely an extension of individual's agency or self-identity. However, within a globalizing context, Axford argues that local agents may have limited resources for transforming international structures and certainly lack the face-to-face contact that can sometimes empower effective intervention in institutions and domestic structures.

While Axford is particularly interested in the political dynamics of globalization, many of those who address issues of globalization focus mainly on the economic dimensions of its processes. The South Centre located in Geneva, Switzerland, but serving as a coordinator for Third World states and interests, defines globalization as "the integration of production facilities in different countries under the aegis or ownership of the multinational corporation and . . . the integration of product and financial markets facilitated by liberalization."[8] The processes of globalization are seen as cumulative and uneven, extending over a period of many decades though having accelerated since the 1980s.

According to officials of the South Centre, ably headed by the former president of Tanzania, Julius Nyerere, until his tragic death in 1999, the record of even the advanced industrial countries under liberalization and globalization has been problematic. Instability in terms of output, employment, and interest rates have characterized the performance of the these countries. Unemployment, argue those at the South Centre, is one of globalization's most prominent failings, noting that, historically, unemployment is associated with creating social and political strife in states. Moreover, those at the South Centre worry that the issues given prominence by globalization and liberalization advocates have displaced other issues of development such as resource flows, debt relief, improved access to Northern markets, and special treatment for late industrializing states. Paradoxically, argue those at the South Centre, globalization makes the concept of the South itself more relevant today than ever before and makes the "need for North–South cooperation all the more essential."[9]

Scholars writing within the Marxist tradition also focus on the economic dimensions of the processes of globalization as well as on the class dimensions. Priyatosh Maitra has argued, for instance, that according to Marx, the primary objective of a capitalist state is to suppress the contradictions inherent in capitalism, creating favorable conditions for capitalists' accumulation and maintaining the legitimacy of the system in order to achieve political stability for the wealthy class.[10] From Maitra's perspective, the Keynesian policies of the welfare capitalist state that thrived on domestic consumption and full employment no longer work for capitalist state officials. Costly wage rates even during recessions and the already low cost per unit of output make further gains in accumulation difficult. Thus, while capitalists target market share, especially in the Third World, through policies of globalization promoted by the International Monetary Fund, and through continuing technological changes, the unemployment problems in the advanced industrial countries that accompany globalization deserve attention. Unemployment, part-time employment, and disguised employment (often without medical benefits) are major outcomes of globalization processes. According to Maitra, such outcomes affect the not-for-profit sector, not just the for-profit sector as I will discuss later.

Charles Morrison addresses the issue of the consequences of the dynamics of globalization by noting that "[i]f a central fault line exists in the globalization debate . . . it comes between those who emphasize the macroeconomic benefits of globalization and those who focus on its social adjustment costs."[11] He further notes that it is often the leadership of nongovernmental organizations who draw attention to this dichotomy, as when during the Asian Pacific Economic Cooperation (APEC) meetings, Philippine demonstrators coordinated by several domestic Philippine NGOs demonstrated and made their views known that when APEC leaders adopted globalizing policies of trade and investment liberalization they were not sufficiently attentive to the concerns of the poor.[12] Yet Morrison argues that the very forces of globalization that economically are disadvantaging the poor are also strengthening those who can represent their interests including those organized by and through nongovernmental organizations. According to Morrison, "[G]lobalization has increased pluralization, enhanced international education opportunities, and strengthened awareness of the global issues of importance to civil society, including the environment, social justice, and political representation. The international mass media and telecommunications revolution have encouraged the rise of NGOs and promoted the international transmission of independent perspectives."[13]

Richard Falk has argued that when we speak of globalization, we must acknowledge that two sorts of globalization processes are occurring: globalization from above, and globalization from below.[14] Falk argues that the New World Order of globalization from above is led by political elites within leading states and the main agents of capital formation. Globalization from below is led by a multitude of citizens around the globe (this would include many in the not-for-profit sector) who do not seek a New World Order but rather a "one-world community" in a setting of "democracy without frontiers."[15] Falk notes that Europe, "the birthplace of the modern territorial state" with its ideology of sovereignty and its institutional forms, is "giving rise to a political reality that is intermediate between a territorial state and a globally unified political order."[16] For Falk, globalization from below includes a new concept of citizenship that includes not merely an activism across borders in which alliances are formed but rather a sense of individuals acting across borders, as global citizens, often militantly and out of a sense of necessity.

Margaret Keck and Kathryn Sikkink, too, have focused their work on transnational advocacy networks. However, they do not make a clear distinction between transnational globalizing activity from the top or from the bottom. Rather, they see such networks comprised of multiple agents and these networks can include individuals from civil society allied with those from corporate, professional, academic, or state institutions, depending on the issue area and the communities of knowledge that form network associations. In fact, their point is that there is now a "blurring of boundaries between a state's relations with its own nationals and the recourse both citizens and states have to the international system."[17] For Keck and Sikkink, boundaries have so blurred that they find plenty of evidence of what they call the "boomerang pattern." In this pattern, for example, State A blocks nongovernmental and other organizations within State A, so they, in turn, activate their global network whose members pressure their own states and third party organizations to pressure State A to change its policies vis-à-vis its internal organizations.[18]

Moreover, when comparing activism beyond borders today to earlier forms of internationalism, Keck and Sikkink note that whereas international actions obviously existed in the past, opportunities for network activities have increased in the past two decades. They note that, previously, internationalization was often measured by increased access to foreign travel, increased contact among foreign nationals, and so on. However, they claim that today's new networks are dependent on "a new kind of global public (or civil society), which grew as a cultural legacy of the 1960s."[19] They go on to explain how activism of the 1960s differs from that of today with only labor internationalism surviving the decline of the Left but not really qualifying as a global international network because most labor organizations represent bounded constituencies.[20] According to Keck and Sikkink, the strategic tactics of transnational advocacy networks (which include nongovernmental organizations) in an age when a global public supports them include information politics, symbolic politics, leverage politics, and accountability politics.[21]

CHARACTERIZING THE PROCESSES OF GLOBALIZATION AS DIFFERENTIATED FROM INTERNATIONALIZATION

Keohane and Nye observed that globalization connotes a thicker, denser network system than does internationalization. Some effects of this thicker network are to raise the uncertainty of states because of the spread of network effects (increases in value) and also to increase transnational participation in the international system. Moreover, they noted that in a globalizing world the size of the actor is no longer relevant to its ability to have a hearing. Axford's, Giddens's, and Robertson's work reminds us that globalization is seen as a multiple system phenomenon in which all actors must respond and adjust to the challenges of the processes and initiatives of the various systems utilizing their own abilities, resources, and cultures. Likewise, the pressures of each system are uneven as it encounters various actors in various parts of the globe. They likely would argue that internationalization is but one system in a globalizing world of overlapping systems.

For those particularly interested in the economic aspects of globalization versus internationalization, it is clear that globalization, in particular, is accompanied by problems of unemployment, part-time employment and disguised employment. In contrast with those who attempted to measure internationalization through increased border contacts, globalization connotes much more. Globalization seems to include an outlook of global citizenship on the part of those making cross-border contacts that can be described as embracing democracy beyond territorial boundaries as the scholarship of Falk, Keck, and Sikkink has demonstrated.

Additionally, whereas internationalization has been perceived as contacts among states or among diads of individuals communicating across borders, globalization is seen as having increased contacts among societies. The question I now consider is, What have these and the other aspects of globalization I have discussed meant for nongovernmental organizations in the not-for profit sector?

THE EFFECTS OF GLOBALIZATION ON NONGOVERNMENTAL ORGANIZATIONS IN THE NOT-FOR-PROFIT SECTOR

As I have noted, globalization's effects on nongovernmental organizations are complex and multidirectional. One of the most noticeable patterns of globalization with which NGOs must cope is the accelerated speed necessary for proactive and reactive programming. Due to the reduced costs of communications and due to new technologies, NGOs receive feedback, new information for evaluation, and new information concerning improved strategies and technologies at a much greater pace than was previously the case. Because new information often comes from funding agencies and stakeholders (those whom the NGO serves or those who have some connection to its organizational well-being), NGOs must devote time and human staff hours to quickly access the demands, inputs, and so on of various communicators and then NGO staff members must fashion responses. Not to do so would be to risk funding from funders and to risk the legitimacy and community goodwill from the NGO's stake-holders. However, it is difficult for NGOs to devote the time and human staff hours now being demanded due to the accelerated speed of communications and new technologies. Devoting additional time and human staff hours requires an increase in budget outlays and this request is being made at the same time that NGOs are also being pressured to increase their budgets in order to globalize their governance structures so that they can function effectively and morally in a globalizing world.

Moreover, efforts to address both of these demands are occurring simultaneously with still another effect of globalization on nongovernmental organizations—one that comes from the sea change in the funding of relief and service delivery programs. One of the observations now commonly exchanged among those working in the not-for-profit sector is that while the processes of globalization are creating new wealthy elites (even as it also creates new forms of poverty) in advanced industrial countries, these new elites are not committed to community philanthropy as were many old-money elites. Or to put it as many in the not-for-profit world now ask, who is assuming a sense of stewardship for the new globalization processes? Newly enriched individuals are not financing the not-for-profit sector as might have been hoped for, and simultaneously, globalization carries with it state officials' commitments to cut government budgets, including government programs to help the poorest. Thus, governments, too, are cutting funding for NGO program concerns.

Globalization is pushing governments to withdraw from service delivery in favor of letting the market and multinational corporations make decisions in realms that used to be the responsibility of government. In late industrializing countries, this phenomenon has meant that nongovernmental organizations face additional demands for their programs and services in addition to the increased demands discussed previously (that are derived from globalism's accelerated speed and changes in technology). But they face these demands during a period when there is little financial support available from the private sector or from governments. Their new financial elites have few models of economic philanthropy and most of their populations are stretched economically by structural adjustment programs and so are unable to spare financial assistance to support their local NGOs. Under adjustment programs, governments also are cutting budgets for citizen programs. Thus, just as NGO tasks have expanded, the possibilities for financial support within many Southern countries have eroded.

In Northern countries, this phenomenon is moderated by the fact that as governments withdraw from directly servicing needy populations, they are offering financial assistance in the short run to nongovernmental organizations and to private service providers or to partnerships of both to fill the service gap left by governmental withdrawal. This creates a competition, however, among NGOs servicing similar populations. Such competition can make NGOs unwilling to learn from each other's successes, as they all have to "sell" their own success in the new marketplace in order to garner their share of government funding. Such competition, therefore, may hinder the advance of excellence in community care and services. Additionally, such competition hinders the great need for increased cooperation in areas of coordinating relief work and in undertaking advocacy campaigns.[22]

Additionally, the competition between the for-profit and the not-for-profit sectors carries its own dilemmas. First, as Marc Lindenberg and J. Patrick Dobel have pointed out, many NGOs were organized "in response to what they perceived to be private sector abuses" and have often viewed the private sector as "an enemy of community social well-being and a source of exploitation."[23] Collaborations and partnerships require trust. Yet, such trust will be difficult to achieve between some NGOs and private sector service providers. Moreover, NGO leaders worry that such collaboration will compromise their mission and autonomy as well as compromise their "own legitimacy in the eyes of funders and recipients."[24] Additionally, such competition has brought NGOs under greater public and funder scrutiny adding to the need to spend more staff hours monitoring and assessing activities and filing reports even when funds for these activities are short and staff is limited. The NGOs report, with much frustration, that they would rather be spending their limited resources on community services and program initiatives.[25] Such scrutiny, when it has revealed corruption or adminstrative bungling, as the recent trial of South African antiapartheid activist Allen Boesak has done, also undermines the reputation and integrity of NGOs. Such revelations have the potential to critically affect funding to the sector.

Finally, scrutiny of their activities and competition with the for-profit sector is causing NGO staff to defend themselves from observations of those like Norman Uphoff who has noted that "clients and beneficiaries of NGOs are in a 'take it or leave it' relationship similar to that of customers and employees of private firms."[26] Today, NGOs are at pains to explain how their services differ from the for-profit sector even as they are being urged by government funders to collaborate with the for-profit sector.

However, this observation of the availability of new, short-term government funding for Northern NGOs resulting from multiple globalizing effects must be modified as well. At the end of the 1990s, leaders of major U.S. and European international development and relief work NGOs met in Bellagio, Italy, under the auspices of the Rockefeller Foundation to evaluate the work of their organizations in light of the challenges of globalization. Michael Edwards summarized one of their findings: "[A]lthough aid budgets are declining everywhere (bar a small recent increase in the United

Kingdom), the proportion of foreign aid allocated to NGOs is still rising. Increasingly, however, aid is flowing directly to NGOs in Africa, Asia, and Latin America rather than passing through the traditional northern NGO intermediaries."[27] Thus, another effect of globalization is that Northern NGOs that work in Southern states are increasingly being questioned about what they contribute to the benefits of development programming that cannot be accomplished by going directly to local recipients in Southern countries. Thus, Northern developmental and relief NGOs are themselves questioning their missions and rethinking their programs as a result of the shifting of resources that is occurring by their funding sources when those funding sources are government aid programs or foundations. Foundations, which of course come under the generic umbrella of nongovernmental organizations, are immune from funding issues because they are self-financing (though, they too face other challenges from globalization).

One of the challenges globalization brings to all NGOs is that of professionalization of staffing. This concern springs partly from the increased accountability trends noted earlier and also from those who seek to find employment in the growing not-for-profit sector as private sector employment increasingly shifts to service delivery and to specialized employment under the pressures of globalization. The consequences of shifting from largely voluntary staffing drawn from the community will likely have both benefits and costs. Service delivery may improve with trained staffing, and professional assessment may improve program delivery as well. However, input from those close to the communities that the NGOs serve may decline. This could affect the legitimacy of NGOs in a community, and undermine NGO claims to be close to the grass roots and to be democratically oriented (jeopardizing its identity/morale and funding). Limiting volunteer activism in favor of professional staffing may also permit mistakes in programming that input from community individuals might prevent.

The debates on the cultural effects of globalization also have implications for the not-for-profit sector. For example, while Paul Kennedy may see migrations creating a cognitive global order, Barrie Axford has argued that local leaders are often mobilizing local identities against the "other" or the foreigner. The tension between Northern funders (be they NGO program collaborators or foundations) and Southern NGOs mirrors this problem. Under the auspices of the Institute for Development Research and the International Forum on Capacity Building an interorganizational alliance of Southern and Northern NGOs and multilateral and bilateral donors and foundations, Archana Kalegaonkar, Mark Leach, and L. David Brown conducted a survey on cooperation and capacity building and compiled responses from over nine hundred Southern and Northern NGOs. A major finding of theirs is that "Southern NGOs appear to place a higher degree of emphasis on the context-specific nature of NGOs' capacity building needs," with Asian NGOs especially concerned with "negotiating agreements on goals, values and problem analysis" in advance of any programmatic undertakings to prevent the imposition of inappropriate Northern models.[28] However, Northern NGOs that place value on trying to be culturally sensitive to collaborative NGOs in other countries face additional financial burdens incurred from consultations, communications, and building in new components to programs (that are derived from compromises following consultations). Obviously, such collaboration costs Southern NGOs as well. Another current trend of globalization (noted previously) has had the effect of highlighting power differentials while allowing voice to all parties regardless of size. Critical voices are not the results that NGOs seek. Thus, Northern NGOs or foundations ignore the concerns of Southern NGOs, only at their own peril and under the threat of bad press and low moral among their own staff.

One category of Northern NGO, the church, has been especially affected by the multiple processes of globalization in regard to cultural issues. Karen Jenkins, for example, has written on the bind of religious church-affiliated NGOs and the clergy of Northern churches operating in Southern states. Northern-based churches previously were careful to avoid questioning host governments for a variety of reasons that Jenkins explores. New pressures on churches to speak out on human rights and other issues are placing church leaders on the horns of a dilemma and opening them to charges of cultural imperialism when they act in ways that they believe are in keeping with universal precepts or religious teachings.[29] Thus, one could say that Northern churches operating in Southern states today are caught between two processes of globalization. On the one hand, they have been sensitized to power differentials and they do not wish to be accused of cultural imperialism or to jeopardize their freedom of action within Southern states. On the other hand, globalization's democratizing processes have led local Southern citizens to expect more from Northern church leaders operating within their countries with respect to challenging national governments when those governments act immorally or in ways that harm local communities.

The shifts in state sovereignty identified by globalization scholars have also affected the not-for-profit sector. For example, another finding of the survey research done by Kalegaonkar, Leach, and Brown was the high priority placed by Southern NGOs on capacity building to achieve advocacy skills. This results in part from NGOs, especially Latin American NGOs, being aware that liberalization and globalization have created an expanded space in which they can now operate.[30] Recognition of such "mobilization spaces" tracks well with those writing on globalization who argue that state sovereignty is shifting and the state is now more assessible to its citizens and less able to act autonomously as a result of globalizing processes that affect the capacities and expectations of civil society as well as because of the need for states to act within the boundaries of changing international norms. Moreover, now those international norms are often established with input from advocacy NGOs as well as with input from multilateral organizations. And multilateral organizations are no longer just consulting with states on policy decisions but are, like the World Bank and the United Nations, expanding their formal as well as informal collaboration with NGOs.

This collaboration extends to representatives of NGOs from many parts of the world and reinforces and expands globalization's own tendencies to legitimize and expand democratization and to create, as Falk has argued, a global citizenry. It should be noted, however, that the potential and the present achievements of such collaborations are as yet not as successful as global citizens might hope. Some have reported that efforts by both the World Bank and the United Nations to reach out are important initiatives, but it remains a difficult task to achieve consensus among many participants with varying perspectives.

Other multilateral state organizations are also being approached for collaborative work by NGOs. In April 2000, e-mail listservs that include those active in monitoring International Monetary Fund, World Bank, and World Trade Organization activities noted that the G7 countries summit in Havana, Cuba, called for proposals that paralleled the proposals of many of the demonstrators in Seattle, Washington, at the World Trade Organization conference. A number of NGO activists suggested approaching the G7 countries to coordinate their advocacy work vis-à-vis Northern states while one activist went so far as to circulate a petition asking for general support of the G7 positions to forward to the G7 conveners.[31] While this is a slight modification of Keck and Sikkink's boomerang pattern, it clearly supports their central claim about the increasing power of transnational networks.

The penultimate aspect of globalization that I will take up in this chapter is its consequences for unemployment. Liberalization and globalization are affecting employment in both Northern and Southern states. While industry shifts across borders with important political economy effects, it also produces labor migration as job seekers look for states with greater employment potential. Such migration can create a cross-fertilization of national cultures leading to new global cultural practices. Or such migration can also produce displaced communities, causing governments to turn to NGOs for help in administering, servicing, and governing. Relief work of this nature often requires huge resource expenditures by NGOs but also may serve as a means by which NGOs secure more funding from Northern publics who are willing to help with emergencies or displaced communities. Growing unemployment or underemployment, however, contributes mainly to the burdens of NGOs, as fewer citizens in both the North and the South are able or willing to contribute to the needs of non-family members. This phenomenon is compounded by the final aspect of globalization that I will discuss here, that of the increase in ethnic wars owing to the shifting proximities of ethnic communities and to the decline of the state brought about in large part by globalization (as well as the collapse of the Soviet Union).

Ethnic wars continue to appear as a countervailing force to those who might be hopeful concerning the forces of globalization for creating a global citizenry. NGOs increasingly are presented with the dilemma of providing relief but because of this risk the well-being and very lives of their staff members. Like the other processes of globalization, international migration demonstrates the complexities and multidirectional effects of globalization, the major phenomenon through which we are living.

CONCLUSION

Increases in complexity and the network effects of globalization, the acceleration of communications and outreach, increased recognition of cultural complexity, changes in state sovereignty, the processes of decentralization and privatization, and growing unemployment all derive from the overlapping globalizing systems in which we live today. The consequences of these systems are providing both opportunities and challenges for nongovernmental organizations just as they are for states and market organizations. NGOs will need new resources, new collaborations, new funding bases, and an ever-reactive as well as a proactive organizational culture if they are to compete and thrive. Although much is being written about globalization, much more remains to be done if we are to understand and respond effectively and humanely to this composite of complex processes. No doubt, NGOs will be both learners and teachers with regard to these new phenomena.

NOTES

1. My use of nongovernmental organizations refers to those associations or organizations that are not of the state or market. While this includes an enormous range of organizations from sporting clubs to relief agencies, I believe that it is the most useful definition we have and any subsector research should note the parameters of its inquiry.

2. Robert O. Keohane and Joseph S. Nye Jr., "Globalization: What's New? What's Not? (And So What?)," *Foreign Policy* (Spring 2000): 104–119. All of the

quotes and the discussion in this section on Keohane and Nye's comments on globalism are based on this article.

3. Keohane and Nye have also suggested the use of the term *globalism* as a replacement, which they believe will help recapture the dynamic nature of interdependence for dicussions of globalizing processes.

4. Interestingly, Keohane, who spent much of the 1980s analyzing the power differentials among states through complex interdependence and regime lenses as an antidote to the seemingly benign interdependence lens, focuses more on the channels of communication and voice for nonstate actors than the power differentials to be found in globalization. Keohane's work in the 1980s, which also stressed the role of states around various issue systems as opposed to elevating just one international relational security system, does not devote much effort to these issues involved in systemic analysis when discussing globalization

5. Barrie Axford, *The Global System Economics, Politics, and Culture* (New York: St. Martin's, 1995).

6. Ibid., 25.

7. Ibid., 26.

8. South Centre, *Liberalization and Globalization Drawing Conclusions for Development* (Geneva: South Centre, 1996), 15.

9. Ibid., 85.

10. Priyatosh Maitra, *The Globalization of Capitalism in Third World Countries* (Westport, CT: Praeger, 1996).

11. Charles E. Morrison, "Overview," in *Domestic Adjustments to Globalization*, ed. Charles E. Morrison and Hadi Soesastro (Tokyo: Japan Center for International Exchange, 1998), 14.

12. Ibid., 15.

13. Ibid., 17.

14. Richard Falk, "The Making of Global Citizenship," in *Global Visions Beyond the New World Order*, ed. Jeremy Breecher, John Brown Childs, and Jill Cutler (Boston: South End Press, 1993).

15. Ibid., 40.

16. Ibid., 45.

17. Margaret E. Keck and Kathryn Sikkink, *Activists Beyond Borders* (Ithaca, NY: Cornell University Press, 1998), 1–2.

18. Ibid., 12–13.

19. Ibid., 14.

20. Ibid., 15.

21. Ibid., 16.

22. Janet Salm, "Coping with Globalization?" *Nonprofit and Voluntary Sector Quarterly* 28, no. 4 (1999): S94–S95.

23. Marc Lindenberg and J. Patrick Dobel, "The Challenges of Globalization for Northern International Relief and Development NGOs?" *Nonprofit and Voluntary Sector Quarterly* 28, no. 4 (1999): S11.

24. Ibid., S12.

25. This was a common complaint reported to me during many interviews with NGO leaders in Zambia, Namibia, and South Africa during field trips in 1993, 1995, and 1997.

26. Norman Uphoff, "Why NGOs Are Not a Third Sector: A Sectoral Analysis with Some Thoughts on Accountability, Sustainability, and Evaluation," in *Beyond the Magic Bullet: NGO Performance and Accountability in the Post–Cold War World*, ed. Michael Edwards and David Hulme (West Hartford, CT: Kumarian, 1996), 25.

27. Michael Edwards, "International Development NGOS: Agents of Foreign Aid or Vehicles for International Cooperation?" *Nonprofit and Voluntary Sector Quarterly* 28, no. 4 (1999): S27.

28. Archana Kalegaonkar, Mark Leach, and L. David Brown, "Strengthening Civil Societies: NGO Cooperation across the North–South Divide" (paper presented at the annual meeting of the Association for Research on NonProfit Organizations and Voluntary Action (ARNOVA), Seattle, Washington, November 5–8, 1998, 13.

29. Karen Jenkins, "The Christian Church as an NGO in Africa: Supporting Post–Independence Era State Legitimacy or Promoting Change?" in *The Changing Politics of Non-Governmental Organizations and African States*, ed. Eve Sandberg (Westport, CT: Praeger, 1994), 83–99.

30. Ibid., 11.

31. See peoplespost@post4.tele.dk (downloaded April 27, 2000).

10 Women in a Globalized Economy: Is Globalization Gender Blind?

Janet L. Rovenpor

Protestors smashed windows of coffee shops and department stores. Others chained themselves together to form a human blockade near a downtown convention center. A pair of khaki pants was burned and an American flag at a county jail was taken down momentarily. Police officers used tear gas and rubber pellets to disperse the crowd. This is not a description of the civil rights marches and protests of the 1960s. Nor does it depict the antiwar marches, teach-ins, and demonstrations that were held to protest U.S. military action in the Persian Gulf in 1991. The place is Seattle, Washington, and the time is late November/early December 1999. The target of the protests is the World Trade Organization (WTO), a five-year-old organization responsible for the writing and enforcing of new global trading rules. Seattle, home to such large corporations as Microsoft and Boeing, seemed to be the perfect location for a gathering of 135 WTO delegates to discuss agricultural subsidies, industrial tariffs, and electronic commerce. Nonetheless, demonstrators objected to everything from the secrecy that has surrounded WTO closed-door deliberations to the exploitation of labor in developing countries to the manufacturing of genetically engineered food products.

The rallies in Seattle are significant because they push into the forefront the increasing polarization in the debate regarding the extent to which globalization benefits or harms citizens throughout the world. WTO officials predict that the removing of barriers to trade will increase global output by 3 percent and inject an additional $1.2 trillion into the world economy (Nullis, 1999). An April 1999 nationwide survey conducted by the Pew Research Center, however, reveals that not everyone believes that globalization will benefit them personally. Forty-three percent of respondents thought a global economy would help average Americans while

52 percent said it would harm them (Kohut, 1999). Moreover, a recent United Nations report claims that the move toward a global economy is creating greater inequalities between the haves and the have-nots. By the late 1990s, for example, 20 percent of the world's population living in the highest-income countries had 86 percent of world gross domestic product while the bottom 20 percent had just 1 percent. Organization for Economic Cooperation and Development (OECD) countries with 19 percent of the global population had 71 percent of global trade in goods and services, 58 percent of foreign direct investment, and 91 percent of all Internet users. The assets of the top three billionaires were more than the combined gross national product of all least developed countries and their 600 million people (United Nations Development Programme, 1999b). The report concludes: "The collapse of space, time and borders may be creating a global village, but not everyone can be a citizen. The global, professional elite now faces lower barriers, but billions of others find barriers as high as ever" (United Nations Development Programme, 1999a, 31).

The purpose of this chapter is threefold. It will (1) provide some overall statistics on the global employment status and well-being of women, (2) review the literature on the types and levels of participation of women in the labor force in a select number of countries, and (3) examine the impact of globalization (and the economic changes it brings) on women's work. Will women be able to participate fully in the new global village? Are women considered equal citizens with the same rights and responsibilities as men in today's global economy? To what extent does job discrimination and stereotypical attitudes toward women around the world prevent them from obtaining meaningful employment? The answers to these questions are complex. As will be discovered, the ability of women to succeed in today's global economy depends on such factors as who the woman is, to which socioeconomic group she belongs, in which region of the world she resides, what her educational opportunities have been, and whether local economic conditions are favorable or unfavorable.

WOMEN IN THE GLOBAL ECONOMY: A SNAPSHOT VIEW

Key population statistics available from multiple sources provide insights into the general well-being and employment status of women worldwide (Hall and Laird, 1995; Bhatti, 1998; Feldmann et al., 1998; Hilary, 1999):

- Life expectancy has risen from forty-nine to sixty-eight years since the 1950s.
- Of the world's nearly one billion illiterate adults, two-thirds are women.
- Of the world's 1.3 billion poor people, nearly 70% are women.

- Worldwide labor force participation increased from 33% of women in the 1960s to 54% in the 1990s.
- Of the twenty-seven million people working in 850 export-processing zones worldwide, 90% are women.
- Women earn on average about three-fourths the pay of men for the same work.
- The average minutes of work per day in developing countries is 514—544 for women and 483 for men; in industrial countries it is 419—430 for women and 408 for men.

Thus, while women are living longer and entering into the workforce in greater numbers, they also work longer hours for less pay than their male counterparts. Others are still indigent and bereft of educational opportunities.

In some countries, employment practices remain particularly harsh. In Brazil, for example, companies are unwilling to hire women who are pregnant or who might become pregnant during the course of their employment. On occasion, a woman is asked to present a certification of tubal ligation as a prerequisite to employment or to sign a prepared letter of resignation that could be used later in case she becomes pregnant (Hinchberger, 1991). When the Islamic Taliban regime first rose to power in Afghanistan, women were not allowed to work and girls were not allowed to attend school. Females were not allowed to leave their homes, even to seek medical care or receive humanitarian aid, without a male relative. A few mullahs have been able to use their mosques as classrooms (although instruction is mostly religious). Other schools for girls have opened up in secrecy (Bearak, 2000).

Interestingly, even in countries like Sweden, which provide women with generous benefits for child care, the system may ultimately fail women. After the birth of an infant, working mothers are permitted to work on a part-time basis—at lower pay—for up to twelve years. Women also receive lengthy vacations, free day care and job protection. These policies, however, encourage women to drop out of the workforce and assume traditional roles. Less generous maternity leaves provided by such countries as the United States may be more detrimental to the family unit but they keep working mothers on a forward-moving career track (Milbank, 1995).

GLOBALIZATION'S IMPACT ON WOMEN:
A LITERATURE REVIEW

The literature examining globalization's impact on women from the period 1994 to 2000 can be broken down into three categories: (1) books and articles that offer an in-depth portrayal of women from a particular socioeconomic group working within a single country (Crompton, 1997; Cravey, 1998; Mills, 1999; Renshaw, 1999; Freeman, 2000); (2) books and articles that provide a comprehensive analysis of women's status in society and career opportunities across several countries (Adler and Izraeli, 1994; Afshar and Barrientos, 1999; Rubery, Smith, and Fagan, 1999); and (3) official reports, briefs, and conference working papers on women's employment made public by various nongovernmental organizations (for example, the International Confederation of Free Trade Unions, the International Labor Organization, the Panos Institute, the Third World Network, the United Nations).

In the "single-country" category, two books are worthy of mention. Jean Renshaw's *Kimono in the Boardroom: The Invisible Evolution of Japanese Women Managers* (1999) describes the discrimination that exists against women in the traditional Japanese management system. Help wanted advertisements specify sex and age requirements and set limits on the percentage of women college graduates who can be hired. Other practices restrict women to staff positions, exclude them from informal meetings, and prevent them from participating in off-site training sessions. Nonetheless, some Japanese women have become successful managers in business, government, and education.

Based on interviews with over 160 Japanese women managers, Renshaw finds that women were more likely to discard typical gender roles and become successful managers when the economy was expanding, when their companies had an open organizational culture, when they were the youngest child in the family or grew up without older male siblings, when good work habits were formed early in life, and when they possessed skills of observation and speaking out. Living in a foreign country, learning a second language, and obtaining parental support were also helpful. Renshaw is convinced that in an increasingly competitive business world, future organizations in Japan will need to capture the "best" and the "brightest" whether male or female.

Mary Beth Mills's *Thai Women in the Global Labor Force: Consuming Desires, Contested Selves* (1999), a case study on Thailand, provides an example of how today's global economy relies on rural migrants, especially women, as a source of inexpensive, compliant labor. When the Thai government made urban-based export manufacturing and international tourism the cornerstones of its economic expansion plans in the 1980s, women began their migration from the impoverished countryside to urban areas. Migration surveys for 1987 and 1989 found that women made up 62 percent of total migrants to Bangkok and over 50 percent of migrants to other major urban areas. Mills finds that women had a complex set of motives for seeking employment in urban centers. Unmarried women wanted to help their families in the country meet their household obligations. They also desired to experience "modernity." Being able to work and live in Bangkok provided them with cash, with opportunities to participate in new forms of entertainment, and with the means to acquire pop culture items (for example, blue jeans). Never before had rural women experienced such levels of independence and self-sufficiency. Tensions were raised, at home, however, when parents began to fear that their daughters would sexually degrade themselves.

Mills explains how the rural ties women maintained to agricultural communities affected their lives, families, and the companies they worked for. Part of a woman's wages was sent home to family members on the farm. In return, the worker often received supplements of rice and other foods. Children were sent to live with grandparents or hired help in the country. Rural households also provided shelter to urban women when they became ill or unemployed. Thus, inadvertently, these patterns of support provided a subsidy to industrial enterprises. Village homes supplied important benefits to women workers, which in turn made it easier for employers to keep wages low.

One of the prime examples of a book using a "multiple-country" perspective on women's work in a global economy is *Competitive Frontiers: Women Managers in a Global Economy* (1994), edited by Nancy Adler and Dafna Izraeli. Articles, written by different authors, appear on women managers in twenty-one countries spanning four continents (including China, Indonesia, Japan, Malaysia, Canada, the United States, Finland, Singapore, Taiwan, Thailand, Israel, and South Africa). Adler and Izraeli find that in each country, the move toward a global economy and the rise of multinational companies has brought more and more women into the workforce. Nonetheless, although women represent over 50 percent of the world population, in no country do they represent one-half or even close to one-half of the corporate managers. Many barriers—sexual harassment, traditional attitudes toward women's family roles, and limited access to social networks—prevent women from further upward job mobility. Adler and Izraeli, however, remain optimistic. They believe that if corporations want to be successful global competitors, they must take advantage of the skills and creative abilities of women. According to the editors, gender diversity fosters innovation in organizations.

In *Women, Globalization, and Fragmentation in the Developing World* (1999), Haleh Afshar and Stephanie Barrientos explore the effects of globalization on the lives of women at the grassroots level in such countries as India, Iran, Egypt, Indonesia, Chile, and Thailand. In some of these countries, the integration of women into the workforce through the process of globalization has led to new forms of participation and empowerment. In other countries, it has had a detrimental effect on marriage, motherhood, and family life. Egypt is an example of the latter. Noha El-Mikawy describes Egypt's efforts in implementing International Monetary Fund and World Bank recommendations for structural adjustment and in shifting its focus to an economy based on export-oriented production. Less investment in the public sector and slow growth in the private sector, however, led to high rates of unemployment. As a result, a majority of women could find employment only in the informal sectors of agriculture and services—where work is characterized by long hours, low pay, and no benefits. Professional women who were able to obtain managerial positions in the formal sector came from the middle and the upper classes, and enjoyed family connections and educational privileges. Globalization produced a conservative and populist reaction in Egypt, stemming from fear of the market and distrust of the free movement of capital and ideas. The view that women should remain in their private roles as mothers became predominant. The public roles of women as civic participants and decision makers were undermined. Globalization led to political isolation and disempowerment.

Representative of the third category of literature are reports, briefs, and conference working papers on women's issues posted on the Internet by nongovernmental organizations (NGOs). The Third World Network, an independent nonprofit group, has a section devoted to "Women, Globalization and Economic Crisis" and "Women's Rights and Gender Equity." In one reading, globalization is found to have a negative impact on women as consumers and producers. Transnational corporations are blamed for promoting unsafe products and novel food items that lack nutritional value to women in Third World countries. These countries have become the dumping grounds for dangerous contraceptives (for example, Depo Provera, the Dalkon Shield, and Norplant). Infant formula, cigarettes, junk food, and soft drinks are being advertised and sold to poor women who cannot afford them and who do not benefit from a nutritional perspective. Transnational corporations that have located their manufacturing operations in Third World countries have positioned themselves to take advantage of cheap, hardworking, and docile labor. Thus, as producers, women toil for low wages. They suffer from stress and are exposed to radioactive materials, pesticides, and bacteria that threaten their health and the health of their unborn children (Hong, 1995).

The Web site maintained by the International Labor Organization (ILO) includes proceedings notes, magazine articles, working papers, and press releases on women employment throughout the world. One reads, for example, that women make up 60 percent of the population in Papua New Guinea. They produce and process 80 percent of the country's food, without much technical assistance. Nonetheless, the quality of life for women remains poor. The country has one of the highest infant and maternal mortality rates in the world. The life expectancy of women is forty-seven years; most women die of preventable diseases. There are very few women managers. Most young women do not receive adequate training to participate in the formal labor sector or to function productively in their own village (International Labor Organization, 1998a).

The news is not all negative for women in developing countries. NGOs sometimes can play a significant role in raising the standard of living for women. The Self-Employed Women's Association, a registered trade union in India, for example, helped poor, self-employed women in the *chikan* industry (devoted to a type of embroidery) organize and renegotiate terms with middlemen who were exploiting them. The union provided the women with skills training, management, accounting, and market development assistance for their products (Mehra and Gammage, 1997). In Africa, women followed a custom of putting their money in a tontine or common pool. The women drew straws, with the winner taking all. In 1993, the National Council of Negro Women set up a matching savings and credit plan around a women's tontine in a Senegal village. The annual income of the village doubled and the women were able to open a general store and build the first health clinic (Feldmann et al., 1998).

The literature reviewed above indicates that globalization is a contributing force to both the advances and the reversals suffered by women in recent years. There appears to be two faces of globalization: an ugly one and a benevolent one. This is the topic of discussion in the next two sections of this chapter.

THE UGLY FACE OF GLOBALIZATION: SLAVERY, PROSTITUTION, AND SWEATSHOPS

Globalization has been blamed for many ills in society such as the use of slave labor, the increase in prostitution, and the exploitation of workers in sweatshops. Kevin Bales (1999) believes that there are twenty-seven million slaves in the world today. Most of the stories Bales recounts are about female slaves. Girls as young as ten are sometimes sold by their destitute parents to work in domestic services or brothels. Others are captured and forced to work on government construction projects. For example, the Yadana natural gas pipeline is being constructed in Myanmar (formerly Burma) by its military regime in partnership with the U.S. oil company Unocal, the French oil company Total, and the Thai company PTT Exploration and Production. In the early years of its construction, old men, pregnant women, and children were forced at gunpoint by soldiers guarding the pipeline to clear land and build a railway adjacent to the pipeline. Local villagers were even placed at the heads of military columns to detonate mines and booby traps, and spring ambushes (Iritani, 1998). Bales estimates that the total yearly profit generated by slaves around the world is roughly $13 billion. As he cautions, "Slaves in Pakistan may have made the shoes you are wearing and the carpet you stand on. Slaves in the Caribbean may have put sugar in your kitchen and toys in the hands of your children. In India they may have sewn the shirt on your back and polished the ring on your finger. They are paid nothing" (3–4).

According to a *New York Times* article, "Selling naïve and desperate young women into sexual bondage has become one of the fastest growing criminal enterprises in the robust global economy" (Specter, 1998). Worldwide, it has been estimated that each year, two million women are sent into lives of sexual bondage, usually as prostitutes. To get an idea of the magnitude of the problem, Laura Lederer of Harvard University's School of Government notes that the number of women that have been trafficked in the past ten years is similar to estimates of the number of Africans who were enslaved in the sixteenth and seventeenth centuries (Bennett and Colson, 2000). The women often come from rural areas and city slums. They seek a better life and are attracted to job opportunities in foreign countries that promise work as dancers, models, waitresses, or secretaries. While en route to their new jobs, their "employers" (sometimes gang members) seize their passports and force them to work in brothels serving fifteen to twenty clients a day. If they refuse, they are beaten or raped. Other women have chosen this line of work, albeit with a heavy heart, for economic reasons. As a recent ILO report found, "Sex work is usually better paid than most of the options available to young, often uneducated women, in spite of the stigma and danger attached to the work . . . [it] is often the only viable alternative for women in countries coping with poverty, unemployment, failed marriages and family obligations, in the near absence of social welfare programs. For single mothers with children, it is often a more flexible and less time-consuming option than factory or service work" (International Labor Organization, 1998b, 4).

Conditions for women working in sweatshops found around the world are deplorable. Following are a few poignant descriptions of how women are treated in such places of work. Sri Lanka's garment industry employs 350,000 people, almost all of them women. The factories located in free trade zones are heavily guarded and unions are not allowed. Women work fourteen hours a day, seven days a week. Conversation between workers is discouraged. Injuries occur because of fatigue and women do not receive compensation while they take time off to recuperate. One worker described a supervisory practice in which unattainable output quotas are purposely set. When the quotas are not met, women are shouted at and beaten. After work, six to ten women share a single room, sleep on mats on concrete floors, and haul water from a well for bathing and cooking (Goldenberg, 1997).

In an El Salvador factory that manufactures clothes for the sportswear company Adidas, women as young as fourteen worked for seventy hours and more a week. They were allowed to visit the rest room only two times a day, with one day's wages deducted if they stayed more than three minutes (Echikson, 1999). In New Delhi, India, women work from dawn to midnight for $42 a month and live in overcrowded slums that lack sanitation, clean water, and access to government schools and health services. Pregnant women are denied work and employees who get pregnant resort to unsafe abortions to keep their jobs. Meanwhile, the value of exports generated by the zone rose from $16.8 million in the period 1990–1991 to $141 million in the period 1997–1998 (Rajalakshmi, 1999).

The question that must be asked is whether globalization is to blame for slavery, prostitution, and poor working conditions of women around the world. At best, there seems to be an indirect link. Globalization has resulted in freer movement across national boundaries and in greater foreign investment in developing countries. It has encouraged the transition from an agrarian economy to an industrialized economy in previously underdeveloped countries. These economic forces have led to migration and lifestyle changes. Peasants and farmers are migrating in increasing numbers to urban areas in search of employment. Young women become easy prey for various forms of exploitation. One must be careful, however, not to blame globalization for everything that is wrong in society today. As UN Deputy Secretary-General Louise Frechette said, "Some people are tempted to view globalization as the root case of crisis and insecurity, or even as the embodiment of economic and social evil. The reality is more complex. Globalization has brought about as many benefits as it has engendered new risks" (see Hilary, 1999, 3). I shall discuss some of these benefits for women in the next section.

THE BENEVOLENT FACE OF GLOBALIZATION: OPPORTUNITIES IN SMALL BUSINESSES, MULTINATIONAL CORPORATIONS, AND HIGH-TECHNOLOGY FIRMS

The forces of globalization seem to be helping some women, especially those with special skills and high levels of education, to open small businesses, accept overseas assignments in multinational corporations, and choose careers in high-technology companies. "Entrepreneurship among women is a vibrant and growing trend internationally. Women business owners are making significant contributions to economic health and competitiveness in countries around the world," states Julie Weeks, director of research at the National Foundation for Women Business Owners (NFWBO; 1997). NFWBO surveys conducted during the 1990s found that women-owned firms typically comprise between one-fourth and one-third of all businesses worldwide. The fast-growing sectors in the United States and Canada for women are in construction, wholesale trade, transportation, and agribusiness. In Australia, small businesses are concentrated in finance, property, and business services; recreation and personal services; wholesale and retail; and community services. Most women-owned firms in developing countries are in service and retail trade (Weeks, 1997).

The literature suggests that women-owned businesses are quite successful. A 1996 report by the International Labor Organization claims that women-owned businesses are as financially sound and creditworthy as the average U.S. firm. Companies owned by women remain viable for longer periods of time, are more likely to offer flex-time and tuition reimbursement to employees, and encourage employees to volunteer for social causes. Similar findings were found for women-owned businesses in Australia (Clayton, 1998).

Women entrepreneurs around the world possess similar characteristics—they are likely to be married, have children, be between thirty-five and fifty-four years old, and be more highly educated than the typical woman in the community. All women expressed a concern about maintaining profitability and managing cash flow. Women in developing countries had additional concerns. In Africa, 77 percent of women surveyed at a conference stated that they feared problems with infrastructure (roads, bridges, and utilities) while 60 percent were worried about political instability. In Russia, more than one-half of the women surveyed felt that tax policies, business laws, banking system instability, and government corruption were serious issues (Weeks, 1997). Women are also interested in overseas expansion. A survey of women business owners in sixteen countries found that between 22 percent and 40 percent of women-owned firms engage in some form of international trade (Rosenthal, 1999).

Why are women opening businesses at such a rapid rate? A survey of 763 women in the United States conducted by Working Solo Incorporated found that 30 percent said they started their own businesses for greater freedom while 13 percent said that prospects of more money motivated them. Among the reasons given for choosing to work in small businesses in Australia were the desire to work independently, job satisfaction, flexibility of lifestyle, financial security, and the personal challenge of operating one's own business (Kravetz, 1999).

There has been a slight increase in the number of women working for companies with international operations that are being sent overseas. The Global Relocation Trends 1999 Survey Report by Windham International, the National Foreign Trade Council, and the Institute for International Human Resources indicates that 13 percent of the expatriate population were women in 1998 compared to 10 percent in 1993. While hard data are not available, it seems that the countries with the most liberal attitudes toward women are Sweden and Norway. The German, French, Spanish, Russian, Latin American, Middle Eastern, and African business environments are not as favorable to women. Italy, on the other hand, has an increasing number of highly respected women-led family businesses; China apparently accepts women in business at all levels while Japan is receptive to foreign women (Kemper, 1998).

American women working overseas may be more successful than their male counterparts. According to Cornelius Grove and Associates (an international staffing consultancy), traits generally associated with women—consensus building, relationship-orientation, and greater sensitivity to nonverbal cues—give them an advantage over men in expatriate assignments. As one women said, "I feel more respected as a manager in China than I do in the U.S. The Chinese value two qualities in their leaders: competence and ren: warm-heartedness, benevolence, and readiness to care for others. If a leader is ren, he or she will receive subordinates' loyalty in turn. Adopting ren behavior is more common by American female assignees than by American males." When a competent female professional starts her overseas assignment, local colleagues do not necessarily place her in the same category as local female coworkers. Either the men are unsure how to classify her (because she is outside their range of experience) or they view her as a high-status professional deserving respect. The woman expatriate must be able to prove herself and create a new positive classification (Grove and Hallowell, 1997).

Unfortunately, the finding that women may be more effective than men in overseas assignments runs contrary to the current thinking of male managers. Men assume that women are less mobile because of family ties, they may not be able to cope with gender discrimination abroad, and they are likely to face sexual harassment. In a study of 323 managers in Germany, Mexico, and the United States, researchers at Loyola Marymount found that U.S. male managers were significantly more doubtful about the effectiveness of American women working overseas than their U.S. female counterparts or German and Mexican managers of either gender. Similarly, in a study of 261 women working abroad and 78 of their mostly male supervisors in multinational corporations, researchers at Loyola University of Chicago found that women saw their ability to adapt to foreign cultures and the attitudes of foreigners toward female expatriates more favorably than their bosses did. Despite these stereotypical attitudes, the researchers believe that women possess important traits—knowing when to be passive, being a team player, knowing when to solicit a variety of perspectives—that help them achieve high levels of success in international assignments (Koretz, 1999; Lancaster, 1999).

The Bureau of Labor Statistics estimates that the computer industry will need more than 1.3 million information technology workers by 2006 (Edwards, 2000). In the Silicon Valley alone, there are reportedly 160,000 unfilled information technology (IT) positions, which cost companies $3–4 billion in lost production each year (Gaudin, 1999). IT careers are attractive to women because of the flexibility they provide. Women in IT firms can take advantage of flexible hours, telecommuting, a condensed workweek, and on-site day care facilities. Statistics show an increasing number of women in Internet companies. According to VentureOne, a San Francisco research firm, 6 percent of the chief executives of venture capital–financed Internet companies were women in 1999, compared to 4 percent in 1998. In 1999, 45 percent of senior-level positions in venture capital–financed Internet companies were held by women, compared to 21 percent in 1998. Women are getting more and more involved in managing Internet firms while their ability to attain high-level positions in Fortune 500 corporations remains minimal. According to a 1998 Catalyst study, only 1 percent of chief executive officers of Fortune 500 companies were women while only 3.8 percent of top management positions were held by women (Kaufman, 2000).

Women seem to feel that new Internet startups have a different culture, one that is devoid of stereotypical views of women, compared to the culture of traditional, old-economy corporations. One reason, according to experts, is that men in high-tech firms have matured in a work environment that fosters greater gender equality compared to previous generations of male executives. There has not been enough time for the old-boys network to develop. E-commerce also requires a new set of rules. Internet companies are realizing that the nontechnical skills of women are needed. Online businesses can only succeed if they build good Web sites, establish strong consumer loyalty, and communicate effectively with customers. Women seem to have a natural talent for developing lasting and mutually beneficial relationships with customers. Women also make 80 percent of a family's buying decisions and are now a majority of Internet users (Hoffman, 2000). Women know how to market to women.

It is even helping the impoverished women of the world. In Lethem, Guyana, for example, a group of three hundred indigenous women from two local tribes revived the ancient art of hand-weaving large, brown-and-white hammocks made from village-grown cotton. The first hammock the women sold was to the British Museum of London. Their business received unexpected support when the chief executive officer of Guyana Telephone and Telegraph gave the weavers two telephone lines, free Internet access, and $12,000 worth of equipment. The company even sent one of the young women to a Web site development course. Through the Internet, the women sold seventeen hammocks at $1,000 a piece. Unfortunately, regional male leaders felt threatened by the weaver's success and took control of the organization (Romero, 2000).

CONCLUDING REMARKS

This chapter has examined how well women have fared in the global economy. It concludes that globalization is *not* gender blind. However, women have not reached equality with men in the workforce. We find a global economy in which women receive less pay for the same work. We find a global economy in which teenage girls drop out of school to work for a few dollars a day to pick coffee, assemble shoes in a sneaker factory, or sew labels on jeans (Ramdas, 1998). We find a global economy in which garment factories manufacturing clothing in Saipan, for such companies as Tommy Hilfiger and Jones New York, are able to label their merchandise "Made in the USA" and pay their Chinese women workers $3.05 an hour, evading the U.S. minimum wage of $5.15 an hour (Lin, 1998).

Even in the areas in which women have made the most progress, significant obstacles remain. It was noted that women have created opportunities for themselves as owners of small businesses, as expatriates working overseas, and as information technology professionals in Internet companies. Nevertheless, it is harder for female entrepreneurs to obtain bank financing for their small businesses than for male entrepreneurs (Dickerson, 1998). Female managers are infrequently offered international career opportunities even though they are just as willing as men to accept overseas assignments, even though male spouses of female managers are just as willing to relocate as female spouses of male managers (Brett and Stroh, 1999). On the average, female IT staff members earn $6,000 less than male IT staff members while female IT managers earn $5,000 less than male IT managers (McGee, 2000). Moreover, women hold only 10 percent of chief investment officer positions in the United States, the United Kingdom, and France (Schneider, 1999).

Gail Collins, a *New York Times* columnist, writes that "at the present rate, it will be 2270 before women are as likely as men to become top managers in corporations and 2500 before there is gender parity in Congress. So far, no culture has constructed a truly level playing field for sharing family responsibilities and job opportunity" (1999, 78). Even so, Helen Fisher (1999), a Rutgers University anthropologist, is optimistic. She believes that the skills and talents of women are crucial for success in today's complex and fast-paced global marketplace. Companies will need women who can perform multiple tasks at once, consider a broad range of consequences, build consensus, prepare fallback options, devise long-term plans, and remain mentally flexible. Fisher predicts that in some economic sectors, women will predominate, becoming the "first sex." It is hoped that her view will prevail and that the new millennium will bring positive change to the women of the world.

REFERENCES

Adler, Nancy, and Dafna Izraeli. 1994. *Competitive Frontiers: Women Managers in a Global Economy*. Cambridge, MA: Basil Blackwell.

Afshar, Haleh, and Stephanie Barrientos. 1999. *Women, Globalization, and Fragmentation in the Developing World*. New York: St. Martin's.

Bales, Kevin. 1999. *Disposable People: New Slavery in the Global Economy*. Berkeley and Los Angeles: University of California Press.

Bearak, Barry. 2000. Afghanistan's Girls Fight to Read and Write. *New York Times*, March 9.

Bennett, William J., and Charles W. Colson. 2000. The Clintons Shrug at Sex Trafficking. *Wall Street Journal*, January 10.

Bhatti, Robina. 1998. The World Economy, Development, and Women. *Peace Review* (March): 21–26.

Brett, Jeanne M., and Linda K. Stroh. 1999. Women in Management: How Far Have We Come and What Needs to Be Done as We Approach 2000? *Journal of Management Inquiry* 8 (December): 392–398.

Clayton, Kerrie. 1998. Women's Work: Success in Small Businesses. *Australian CPA* 68 (November): 36–39.

Collins, Gail. 1999. A Social Glacier Roars. *New York Times Magazine*, May 16, 77–80.

Cravey, Altha J. 1998. *Women and Work in Mexico's Maquiladoras*. Lanham, MD: Rowman and Littlefield.

Crompton, Rosemary. 1997. *Women and Work in Modern Britain*. New York: Oxford University Press.

Dickerson, Marla. 1998. Small Business: Women Finding More Financing, Still Lag Men. *Los Angeles Times*, November 1.

Echikson, William. 1999. It's Europe's Turn to Sweat about Sweatshops. *Business Week*, July 19, 96.

Edwards, Cliff. 2000. Women Out to Break Silicon Ceiling? Anita Borg Recruits Females, Minorities for Male-Dominated High-Tech Industry. *Houston Chronicle*, March 9.

Feldmann, Linda, Howard LaFranchi, Sarah Gauch, Nicole Gaouette, Kevin Platt, and David Hecht. 1998. Around the World, Women Find Very Different Roads to Wider Rights. *Christian Science Monitor*, July 22.

Fisher, Helen. 1999. *The First Sex: The Natural Talents of Women and How They Are Changing the World*. New York: Ballantine Books.

Freeman, Carla. 2000. *High Tech and High Heels in the Global Economy*. Durham, NC: Duke University Press.

Gaudin, Sharon. 1999, November 22. The Critical Shortage of Women in IT. *Network World*. www.nwfusion.com/news/1999/1122women.html.

Goldenberg, Suzanne. 1997. Stitched Up in Sri Lankan Sweatshops. *The Guardian*, November 7.

Grove, Cornelius, and Willa Hallowell. 1997, November. Guidelines for Women Expatriates: Benefits and Compensation Solutions. http://www.grovewell.com/pub-expat-women.html.

Hall, Cindy, and Bob Laird. 1995. USA Snapshots: World's Women Work Longer. *USA Today*, August 18.

Hilary, John. 1999, May. Globalisation and Employment: New Opportunities and Threats. *Panos Briefing No. 33*. http://www.oneworld.org/panos/briefing/brief33.htm#SECTION1.

Hinchberger, Bell. 1991. Fighting for Women's Lives: Corporate Sterilization. *Multinational Monitor* (November): 13–15.

Hoffman, Lisa. 2000, April. Women Move to the Top of dot.coms, but Salaries Lag. Nando Media. http://www.techserver.com/noframes/story/0,2294,500187392-500250939-501259264.

Hong, Evelyne. 1995, September/October. Women as Consumers and Producers in the World Market. *Third World Resurgence*, no. 61/62. http://www.twnside.org.sg/title/consu-cn.htm.

International Labor Organization. 1996. Enterprise and Jobs: Job Generation by Micro, Small, and Medium Sized Enterprises. ILO Enterprise Forum 96, Bureau for Workers' Activities. http://www.itcilo.it/english/actrav/telearn/global/iol/seura/mikro.htm.

———. 1998a. Papua New Guinea, South-East Asia, and the Pacific Multidisciplinary Advisory Team, On-Line Gender Learning and Information Module. http://www.iol.org/public/english/region/asro/mdtmanila/training/unit2/pngplat.htm.

———. 1998b. Sex Industry Assuming Massive Proportions in Southeast Asia. Press Release, August 19. http://www.ilo.org/public/english/bureau/inf/pr/1998/31.htm>

Iritani, Evelyn. 1998. U.S. Bolsters Labor Charge against Unocal; Asia: Labor Department Lends Credence to Claims of Worker Abuse on Myanmar Pipeline. Oil Firm Alleges Report Is Biased. *Los Angeles Times*, October 23.

Kaufman, Leslie. 2000. The dot.com World Opens New Opportunities for Women to Lead. *New York Times*, March 9.

Kemper, Cynthia. 1998. Attitudes Abroad Vary for Women. *Denver Post*, January 11.

Kohut, Andrew. 1999. Globalization and the Wage Gap. *New York Times*, December 3.

Koretz, Gene. 1999. A Woman's Place Is . . . *Business Week*, September 13.

Kravetz, Stacy. 1999. A Special News Report about Life on the Job—and Trends Taking Shape There. *Wall Street Journal*, June 8.

Lancaster, Hall. 1999. To Get Shipped Abroad, Women Must Overcome Prejudice at Home. *Wall Street Journal*, June 29.

Lin, Jennifer. 1998. Clothes Makers Flock to Saipan, "Made in U.S.A." Masks Low Pay. *Times-Picayune (LA)*, February 22.

McGee, Marianne Kolbasuk. 2000. Women at Work. *Informationweek*, February 28, 63–69.

Mehra, Rekha, and Sarah, Gammage. 1997, March. Employment and Poor Women: A Policy Brief on Trends and Strategies (available from the International

Center for Research on Women, 1717 Massachusetts Avenue, NW, Suite 302, Washington, DC 20036).

Milbank, Dana. 1995. Sweden: Laws Help Mom, but They Hurt Her Career. A Special Report: Women in Business: A Global Report Card—Around the World, Women Have Achieved Different Things, Fought Different Battles—and Made Different Sacrifices. *Wall Street Journal*, July 26.

Mills, May Beth. 1999. *Thai Women in the Global Labor Force: Consuming Desires, Contested Selves*. New Brunswick, NJ: Rutgers University Press.

Nullis, Clare. 1999. Globalization Juggernaut: WTO Talks May Have Collapsed, but Its Work Continues. The Associated Press. ABC News Internet Ventures. http://more.abcnews.go.com/sections/business/dailynews/wtotalks 991206.html.

Rajalakshmi, T. K. 1999, May 1. Sita and Her Daughters: Women Workers at an Indian Export-Processing Zone. *PANOS Features*. http://www.twnside. org.sg/title/sita-cn.htm.

Ramas, Kavita. 1998. Women and the New Global Economy. *San Francisco Chronicle*, August 20.

Renshaw, Jean R. 1999. *Kimono in the Boardroom: The Invisible Evolution of Japanese Women Managers*. New York: Oxford University Press.

Romero, Simon. 2000. Weavers Go dot-com, and Elders Move In. *New York Times*, March 28.

Rosenthal, Bruce. 1999, March 5. Characteristics of Women Entrepreneurs Worldwide Are Revealed. National Foundation for Women Business Owners 1-301-495-4975. http://www.womenconnect.com/LinkTo/mar0599_rptBIZ. htm.

Rubery, Jill, Mark Smith, and Colette Fagan. 1999. *Women's Employment in Europe: Trends and Prospects*. London: Routledge.

Schneider, Polly. 1999, July 1. Women IT Leaders: Sense and Sensibility. *CIO Magazine*. www.cio.com/archive/070199_women.html.

Specter, Michael. 1998. Trafficker's New Cargo: Naïve Slavic Women. *New York Times*, January 11.

United Nations Development Programme. 1999a. Chapter 1: Human Development in This Age of Globalization. *Human Development Report 1999*. New York: Oxford University Press. http://www.undp.org/hdro/report.html.

———. 1999b. Overview: Globalization with a Human Face. *Human Development Report 1999*. New York: Oxford University Press. http://www.undp.org/ hdro/report.html.

Weeks, Julie. 1997. Women Entrepreneurs as a Growing International Trend. Center for Women's Business Research. http://www.nfwbo.org/Research/ 2-28-1997/2-28-1997.htm.

Windham International, the National Foreign Trade Council, and the Institute for International Human Resources. 1999. Survey Highlights. *Global Relocation Trends 1999 Survey Report*. http://www.windhamint.com/html/ purposemethodology.html.

11

Toward Universalism?: Human Rights and Cultural Relativism in the Globalization Process

Shawn Shieh

We live in an age of unparalleled optimism about human rights. As early as the first half of the twentieth century, human rights rarely entered international discourse. The Covenant of the League of Nations, to take one prominent example, did not even mention human rights. All that changed dramatically after the war. The discovery of the concentration camps, and the establishment of the Nuremberg War Crimes Trials to prosecute Nazi war criminals on the charge of crimes against humanity, were landmark events that focused the world's attention on the importance of human rights. The United Nations, established in 1945, made human rights a prominent principle in its charter and moved to elaborate international human rights standards. Since then, we have seen the proliferation of human rights conventions and institutions at the national, regional, and global levels that form what international relations theorists call a "regime." In addition, hundreds of nongovernmental organizations associated with human rights causes have emerged around the world to monitor and publicize human rights abuses and to campaign for specific human rights causes. More recently, the international community has taken stronger actions to try to enforce human rights violations initiated by states against their citizens, most prominently in the cases of ethnic cleansing and genocide.

Yet in spite of, or perhaps even because of, this progress, the human rights crusade still elicits skepticism and even opposition from various circles. One of the most contentious human rights debates in recent years has revolved around two very different perspectives: universalism and cultural relativism. The universalist position claims that human rights, such as those enumerated in the Universal Declaration of Human Rights, applies to all peoples across cultures. This claim is often justified using theological or natural law principles (Brown, 1999, 106–110). The former argue that human rights are given to us by God, while the latter holds that humans, by nature, are born with certain rights.[1] The cultural relativist, on the other hand, rejects any universal foundation for human rights and argues that because values are culturally specific there can be no values or laws regarding human rights that can have universal applicability. Cultural relativism is often associated with the positive law school that argues that rights do not stem from God or some higher source, but rather are a formalization of a society's values and customs.

This chapter examines how the process of globalization is shaping this debate. Is globalization, as some claim, creating a homogeneous global culture that can serve as a foundation for a universal moral code? Or is globalization aggravating long-standing divisions between cultures, or even creating new ones, thereby weakening the universalist position? Has globalization changed the terms of the debate, or has it perhaps made the debate altogether obsolete? On the surface, it would appear that globalization would lend more weight to the universalist view. Globalization, after all, has exposed more people than ever before to transnational flows of goods, services, money, information, and ideas, thereby breaking up the insularity and provincialism of national and subnational cultures. This chapter argues, with some reservations, that globalization is indeed tipping the balance toward the universalist position. But one should be cautioned that the very nature and significance of globalization and human rights is missed if the struggle for human rights is only seen from these two perspectives. A fuller understanding of globalization's impact on human rights can only be reached if one looks at the many ways in which so-called universal human rights are negotiated by different cultures.

DEFINING GLOBALIZATION, HUMAN RIGHTS, AND UNIVERSALISM

Before examining the impact of globalization on the debate between universalism and cultural relativism, it is necessary to clarify what is meant by *globalization* and *universalism*. Robert Keohane and Joseph Nye (2000) define globalization as the process of increasing globalism. *Globalism*, in turn, they define as a network of relationships with a multicontinental, not just regional, reach. "Globalization refers to the shrinkage of distance on a large scale. It can be contrasted with localization, nationalization or regionalization" (105). Globalization is also multidimensional in that it refers to a number of different types of networks. Much of the writing on globalization has explicitly or implicitly been about economic globalization, which refers to the growth of transnational flows of goods, services, capital, and information. But globalization also has a social and cultural dimension that pertains to the movement of ideas, images, and people, and an environmental dimension that refers to the flow of chemical and biological substances and species that affect the world's ecology (Keohane and Nye, 2000). Globalization is also said to be an evolving process that started centuries ago. The concern here, however, is with the most recent period of globalization, when one could argue that something qualitatively different is happening. Globalization is now, more than ever, about the proliferation of networks between nonstate actors, whether they be international organizations, international nongovernmental organizations, transnational social movements, or multinational corporations (Held et al., 1999; Keohane and Nye, 2000).

In examining how globalization processes affect human rights, it is useful to distinguish between human rights in two senses of the word: as a set of moral values and as a set of legal obligations. The two are interrelated of course. Laws can be an important source of social norms and values. On the other hand, as positivists remind us, a society's values are an important consideration in the making of laws. How closely the two are related depends on the kind of society one is talking about. In domestic societies where laws have a legitimate basis, there is said to be a close relationship between morality and law. In other words, people in those societies are more likely to find law acceptable because the laws, and the procedures followed in making them, conform to their value system. At the level of international society, which is characterized by the absence of a central lawmaking body, there remains a large gap between moral values and legal obligations, particularly in the area of human rights. Here I am interested in how the globalization process affects human rights at both of these levels, but realize that globalization may have different consequences depending on whether one is talking about the possibility of universalizing human rights at the level of legal norms or at the level of moral values. For example, the fact that substantial progress has been made in the area of international human rights law does not necessarily mean that one is witnessing greater convergence among cultures over human rights values. If such a convergence were taking place, then this would lend greater weight to the universalists. But if not, then the emergence of an international human rights regime may just be a smoke screen for fundamental disagreements between cultures over human rights. Or worse, it may further conflict between cultures over human rights if the legal infrastructure is viewed by many nations as imperialistic and thus illegitimate.

There is also the thorny question of what it means to say that human rights are becoming (or not becoming) universal values. How one defines universalism is crucial to how one answers the question I started out with, which is whether globalization strengthens the conditions for a moral consensus on human rights. One standard of universalism put forth by natural rights thinkers is that all humans have rights by virtue of their humanity (Donnelly, 1999). This standard, however, is not helpful because it assumes that universal human rights are a given, rather than a historical work-in-progress. A more useful standard comes from the positive law assumption that rights cannot be abstracted from their political and legal context. In this view, universal human rights would require a universal political and legal infrastructure needed to define, monitor, and enforce those rights. Chris Brown (1999) raises the bar even further in arguing that human rights requires the existence of an ethical community that has less to do with the liberal view of rights, and more to do with the communitarian model that emphasizes a strong family structure and active civil society and culture as a necessary foundation for the realization of human rights. Universal human rights would, in this view, require not only a universal political and legal infrastructure to protect one's rights, but also a universal ethical community to ensure that a proper balance was maintained between individual rights and community interests. Amartya Sen (1999) seems to set a lower standard when he argues that values such as democracy are universal not because it is but because "people anywhere might have reason to see it as valuable" (12). In this view, human rights become universals when they are seen worldwide as a desirable goal. I do not use any one standard in this chapter, but I feel it is important to keep in mind that there are multiple standards, some having a stronger requirement for universalism than others.

GLOBALIZATION AND UNIVERSALISM

No one at this point would deny that the world is still a diverse place and that there are few values, if any, that enjoy a universal consensus. Yet a number of arguments have been put forth supporting the claim that globalization as defined above has, in many respects, strengthened the conditions for arriving at such a consensus.

One such argument is that the processes of globalization are creating fundamental worldwide changes in cultural values that strengthen the prospects for universal human rights.[2] Globalization accomplishes this by narrowing the range of desirable values or expanding the range of values and norms shared by all cultures. E. J. Hobsbawm's work (1975) on the spread of global capitalism and Immanuel Wallerstein's world systems theory (1974) drew my attention early on to the centuries-old evolution of a world capitalist system, and the growing networks of transportation and communication it fostered, as a powerful source propelling the global diffusion or imposition of values. While they did not speak about human rights, they do point to a growing international standardization not just of economics and technology, but also of culture as a result of the evolution of a world system. Hobsbawm, for instance, speaks of a bourgeois culture disseminated across the world by popular movies, music styles, television programs, and lifestyles. It is worth quoting him on the parallels between 1970 and 1870: "There is no doubt that the bourgeois prophets of the mid-nineteenth century looked forward to a single, more or less standardized, world where all governments would acknowledge the truths of political economy and liberalism carried throughout the globe by impersonal missionaries more powerful than those Christianity or Islam ever had; a world reshaped in the image of the bourgeoisie, perhaps even one from which, eventually, national differences would disappear" (55).

More recent commentators have extended this observation to argue that this growing standardization of culture is no longer a goal to be attained but a reality or near-reality. Francis Fukuyama's much-cited essay "The End of History" (1989) is a pronouncement in this vein. He argued that with the collapse of communism and fascism, liberalism in both its economic and political forms no longer had any major ideological challengers. While religious and nationalist conflicts would continue, the post–Cold War world would see the spread and universalization of liberalism as the only desirable global ideology. Fukuyama does not elaborate on what globalization processes might sustain the spread of liberalism, but he does point to the inroads that Western consumer culture has made into other parts of the world, thereby foreshadowing later writings about the diffusion of values propelled by the globalization of markets. Benjamin Barber's essay "McWorld and Jihad" (1992) is more explicit about the processes behind the worldwide diffusion of a consumer culture built on McDonald's and Levi's. In that essay, Barber identifies economic interdependence, information technology, and an ecological worldview as powerful forces contributing to a global culture, although, as will be seen in the next section, he is more skeptical than Fukuyama about whether this global consumer-based culture can so easily translate into political values respectful of democracy and human rights. Still others have pointed to the globalization of communications as a powerful force for informing people around the world about human rights abuses, and disseminating human rights norms (McCorquodale and Fairbrother, 1999, 760–761). Now, more than any time in our history, governments are less able to hide human rights violations from public scrutiny, and more people know more about human rights abuses and are more informed about human rights.

Ronald Inglehart's well-known thesis on the rise of postmodern values (2000) presents a somewhat different, yet potentially more powerful, set of arguments and evidence about the global diffusion of a core set of values. Based on his extensive, long-term analysis of the World Values Survey database, Inglehart finds persuasive evidence of a fundamental intergenerational shift to what he calls "postmodern values" in countries moving to higher levels of development and experiencing prolonged periods of prosperity.[3] In response to this new economic and cultural environment, later generations gradually adopt a new set of "postmodern" value priorities. Unlike the previous generations that put a great deal of value on economic security, Inglehart finds that this postmodern generation tends to value quality of life concerns such as environmental protection and lifestyle issues, and values conducive to liberal democracy such as freedom of speech and political participation. In this regard, Inglehart's findings posit a strong correlation between economic development and value changes that are conducive to human rights. While his thesis recognizes ongoing value differences between developed and developing countries, the implication of his message is clear: if globalization proceeds at the current rate, and has the effect of raising the overall level of development around the world, then one should see greater convergence among countries toward "postmodern values" that emphasize the protection of human rights. This message has interesting implications for the debate over civil and political rights versus economic and social rights because it suggests that this is not so much a debate over fundamental values but over the issue of whether different values should be emphasized at different stages of development. Inglehart's thesis implies that, in the end, these disagreements will subside once developing societies pass a certain threshold.

For others, globalization is not an exogenous process, like global capitalism or global communication networks, that transmits or imposes political values around the world; rather, globalization is the very process by which political culture becomes globalized. While this process by no means implies that cultural diversity is disappearing, some would argue that it is resulting in a growing standardization of core political norms and values worldwide. A number of scholars, for instance, have pointed out that the governance models different societies use to organize themselves are more similar than thought. They point, in particular, to the modern nation-state as a cultural model that has become the preferred norm around the world. John Meyer and his colleagues (1997) argue that the modern state has been transmitted not only through economic and military processes of globalization, but also through social processes like isomorphism, the borrowing of practices and institutions from other society's and from an overarching world culture. Furthermore, the state as culture contains within it a complex of features that many would list as necessary for the realization of human rights: "constitutional forms emphasizing both state power and individual rights, mass schooling systems organized around a fairly standard curriculum, rationalized economic and demographic record keeping and data systems, antinatalist population control policies intended to enhance national development, formally equalized female status and rights, expanded human rights in general, expansive environmental policies, development-oriented economic policy, universalistic welfare systems, standard definitions of disease and health care" (Meyer et al., 1997, 87). In this view, the universalization of human rights has been made a possibility, though not yet a reality, through the universalization of the modern state.

A related argument is that globalization in its various manifestations is creating the institutional–legal conditions for universalizing human rights. This is similar to the previous argument, which identifies the globalization of the modern state as providing an important set of institutional conditions. The arguments and evidence we have in mind here, though, are those that point to what some would call "political globalization," or the spread of international institutions—international governmental organizations, international law, and nongovernmental organizations—as powerful universalizing forces. In the area of human rights, a host of international institutions has emerged since the end of World War II to disseminate, define, monitor, and seek to enforce human rights standards worldwide (Donnelly, 1998, ch. 1). These political institutions have come about as a response to economic, military, and environmental globalization to manage the problems associated with the increasingly complex interactions between states and nonstate actors that can no longer be adequately regulated by states themselves.

The United Nations has been the most important of these institutions. Under its auspices, a number of international human rights conventions were adopted that have become the basis for international human rights law. The precursor to these conventions is the Universal Declaration of Human Rights, which was adopted as a resolution by the UN General Assembly in 1948. This resolution was followed by a series of human rights covenants that were signed and ratified by member-states and thus were legally binding (see the Appendix at the end of this chapter). The most important of these has been the International Covenant on Civil and Political Rights and the International Covenant on Economic, Social and Cultural Rights. Together with the declaration, these covenants form what is know as the International Bill of Human Rights. Each of these conventions have now been ratified by over 140 of the 190 member-states of the UN and more are expected to ratify them (Held et al., 1999, 67). One of the latecomers has been the United States, which finally ratified the International Covenant on Civil and Political Rights in 1992, but not the Covenant on Economic, Social and Cultural Rights (Donnelly, 1998, 15). The United Nations also houses the Commission on Human Rights, which is the organization responsible for monitoring abuses to these conventions and bringing them to the attention of the Security Council and the International Labor Organization, which is charged with monitoring workers' rights.

There is a similar institutional and legal human rights infrastructure at the regional level in many areas of the world, and a burgeoning human rights nongovernmental organization (NGO) movement. According to one source, there are over two hundred NGOs associated with human rights issues in the United States, a similar number in Europe, and a growing number in the developing world (Held et al., 1999, 67). One census of human rights NGOs lists over two hundred worldwide (Smith and Pagnucco, 1998, 382).

As many have noted, these international institutions have significant limitations. While international laws are legally binding, international organizations have no coercive authority to enforce those laws. At best, they can set and promote standards, monitor abuses, and press for corrective action. But they are constrained by the sovereign power of states. As one study notes, "[I]nternational human rights law, despite its concern with the protection of the rights of humans, remains largely contained within a state-based framework where the responsibility for violations of human rights is by states alone and the sovereign power of states is affirmed" (McCorquodale and Fairbrother, 1999, 741)

These limitations and problems notwithstanding, the evolution of these international organizations over the years is the story of the gradual institutionalization of international human rights norms worldwide (Donnelly, 1998, ch. 1). As Jack Donnelly (1998) and others have shown, the institutionalization of human rights norms has been particularly striking during the post–Cold War period. There has been a distinct move away from placing state sovereignty above human rights in all cases. More recent human rights conventions contain provisions that democracy is the form of government most associated with state legitimacy (Held et al., 1997, 69). The most dramatic evidence has come in international humanitarian responses to genocide and politicide. In these cases, human rights concerns are seen to outweigh state sovereignty. It is an important statement that certain areas of domestic conduct now fall under the scrutiny of international law (Held et al., 1997, 700). In recent years, steps have been taken to create an enforcement mechanism by establishing international criminal tribunals, specifically in Rwanda and the former Yugoslavia, and the 1995 decision to create an International Criminal Court (Donnelly, 1998, 16). Furthermore, unlike the Cold War period, human rights goals have become incorporated into multilateral peacekeeping missions. As Donnelly (1998) notes, "UN peacekeeping operations in Namibia, El Salvador, Cambodia, Somalia, Northern Iraq, Mozambique, Bosnia, Croatia and Guatemala have had explicit human rights responsibilities, and the operations in Haiti and Rwanda had primarily human rights mandates" (16).

Another argument favorable to the universalist position is that globalization, primarily the economic form, strengthens political institutions favorable to human rights, such as liberal democracy, civil society, and the rule of law, by promoting growth based on neoliberal principles of the free market. Liberal democracy here refers to a political system that has free and fair elections, a multiparty system, and the protection of individual liberties. There are two parts to this argument. One is that globalization, on the whole, promotes neoliberal principles such as free markets, private property, and constitutional government. The second is that economic liberalism, in turn, fosters the conditions conducive to liberal democracy, civil society, and the rule of law. The evidence for the first claim comes not only from the nature of globalization but also from the nature of institutions that support it. The present era of globalization is based on neoliberal ideas of free markets and trade. These ideas are reflected in the long-term decline in tariffs, the demise of socialism as an effective alternative to capitalism with the collapse of communism, and the emergence of neoliberal institutions such as the World Trade Organization (WTO) and the International Monetary Fund (IMF), which serve as the core of the Bretton Woods system (Held et al., 1997, ch. 3). Some would argue that these institutions, as well as multinational corporations, tend to strengthen human rights guarantees by demanding that a country meet certain "democratic governance" conditions before investing in them. These conditions, which include "the acceptance of the rule of law, clear and transparent practices by government and local institutions, and international dispute resolution" help ensure judicial guarantees of human rights in those countries (McCorquodale and Fairbrother, 1999, 751–752). The second claim, that economic development based on free market principles creates the conditions for democracy, is controversial. But there is evidence showing that development along these lines enlarges the private sector and promotes the formation of an economically powerful middle class, a stable legal environment, and greater integration into the international community. While these trends do not by themselves result in democratic change, they do contribute to social and international pressures for democratic change and create the conditions needed for the consolidation of democracy.[4]

GLOBALIZATION AND CULTURAL RELATIVISM

As the title of this book suggests, globalization is not necessarily a panacea that fosters greater cooperation and agreement among cultures and nations. Globalization, as many have noted, has a darker side that provokes global conflict and disagreement over values and thereby provides ammunition for supporters of the cultural relativist view. One prominent view is that the processe of globalization reinforces cultural differences and inequalities around the world because it is associated with liberal, capitalist values that are peculiarly Western. This is the argument that usually emanates from the developing world. It does not contest the worldwide spread of values, so much as the legitimacy of the values being spread. Two distinct criticisms of these values can be found in this camp. One is that these values are illegitimate because they were imposed on the rest of the developing world through formal colonial rule, and continue to be perpetuated through the West's military and economic dominance and its control of international organizations such as the UN Security Council, the IMF, and the WTO. In other words, these values have become global values because they are values of the powerful. To these critics, the human rights crusade is neoimperialism masquerading as universalism (Muzaffar, 1999). The other and more fundamental critique is that these values do not always mesh, and sometimes undermine, non-Western values. To proponents of this view, the globalization of human rights norms represents the West's imposition of liberal values on much of the non-Western developing world. They point out that human rights norms derive from the historical, political, and cultural legacy of the West and thus reflect a particular bias that undermines their universality. This bias favors individualism, and political and civil rights, and downplays communal values rooted in economic, social, and cultural rights that are seen as just as important, if not more, in many non-Western cultures (Aziz, 1999; Muzaffar, 1999).[5]

Economic globalization has fueled this critique of universalism as particularism because it is seen as part of the same liberal project, driven by free trade and free market ideologies, supported by Western political and military power, and serving the interests of the West. While global capitalism is credited with promoting unprecedented levels of prosperity worldwide, it is also blamed for creating a familiar set of social problems that disproportionately affect the poor in the developing world: inequalities of wealth, unemployment, exploitation of labor, and environmental pollution (McCorquodale and Fairbrother, 1999). The Asian financial crisis that started in Thailand in 1997, and spread to Malaysia, Indonesia, and South Korea, made many people painfully aware of the speed by which global capitalism can devastate national economies. While early analyses of the crisis pointed to close ties between governments and business in those countries as a major cause of the crisis, many now recognize that a more important factor was the ability of investors, bond traders, and multinational banks to move massive sums of money across borders with astonishing ease and speed (Friedman, 1999, ch. 6; Beeson, 2000, 357–358). In other words, the culprit was economic globalization or, more specifically, the integration of Asian economies into the global financial marketplace. The immediate social consequences of the crisis were rising inflation, unemployment, and inequalities of wealth. In Indonesia alone, the number of people below the poverty line was expected to quadruple from 22 million in 1997 to 88 million in 1998, almost one-half of Indonesia's 202 million people (Emerson, 1998). As real incomes declined through unemployment and inflation of more than 70 percent, the Central Bureau of Statistics projected that almost one-half of Indonesia's 202 million people would fall below the poverty line by the end of 1997, compared with less than one-fifth in 1996. The International Labor Organization estimated that 5.4 million Indonesian workers would lose their jobs in 1998 as a result of the downturn, and that two-thirds of the population would subsist on less than 50 cents (U.S.) a day by the following year (Liebhold, 1998).

At a general level, economic globalization is associated with growing inequality between the industrialized and developing nations. In 1990, per capita gross domestic product in the North was $18,750 more than per capita gross domestic product in the South. By 1998, that gap had grown to $24,260 (Rourke and Boyer, 2000, 309). While inequality may not fit into the usual category of human rights abuses, it can be seen as a deprivation of one's economic and social rights guaranteed under various international human rights covenants. Moreover, the social problems generated by global capitalism can only undermine the legitimacy of liberalism in the eyes of the developing world. Events such as the Asian financial crisis, and its precursors, such as the peso devaluation in Mexico, have prompted calls for global governance mechanisms for managing large-scale flows of capital, goods, and services in ways that protect the welfare of the more needy (Annan, 1999).

Multinational corporations have taken much of the blame for the social costs of global capitalism as their power and influence grows, particularly in the developing world. Currently, fifty-one of the largest economies in the world are multinational corporations, while the other forty-nine are states. As Amnesty International (1998) puts it, "Mitsubishi is bigger than Indonesia . . . General Motors is bigger than Denmark, Toyota is bigger than Norway, Philip Morris is larger than New Zealand" (187). Increasingly, multinational corporations are associated with human rights abuses ranging from child labor to complicity with repressive governments for silencing human rights activists. Shell Oil, to cite just one prominent example, was accused of playing a role in the execution of Nigerian human rights activist Ken Saro-wiwa in 1995 when it asked the military government to put a stop to protests that Saro-wiwa was organizing against Shell in the Ogoni region of the country (Lewis, 1996).

These cases reinforce a belief that was common during the Cold War era, which is that Western nations only promote human rights when it serves their own national interests (Mahbubani, 1998, 57–80; Donnelly, 1998, ch. 1). They also drive home the tenuous link between economic and political liberalization, a point made by Benjamin Barber (1992) who argues that economic interdependence and the rise of a global consumer culture do not, by themselves, foster ideas and institutions needed to promote human rights and democracy: "The primary political values required by the global market are order and tranquillity, and freedom—as in the phrases 'free trade,' 'free press,' and 'free love.' Human rights are needed to a degree, but not citizenship or participation—and no more social justice and equality than are necessary to promote efficient economic production and consumption" (62).

The association of Western hegemony with other globalization processes has tainted the effort to universalize human rights and revived calls to protect local values and norms. Cultural globalization, driven by global capitalism and the communications industry, is provoking demands around the world for cultural preservation and autonomy in the face of an increasingly homogenized global culture that looks to many like an imitation of American popular culture. Barber (1992) has coined this trend "Jihad" and counterpoised it to the other dominant cultural trend taking place in the post–Cold War world, which he terms "McWorld." As examples of Jihad, he refers to the ethnic conflict in the former Yugoslavia and Soviet Union, the resurgence of Hindu nationalism in India in the early 1990s, Palestinian nationalism, and of course the September 11, 2001, attacks in the United States. One might add to this list fundamentalist religious movements— that the Asian values debate fueled—by Asian leaders such as Singapore's Lee Kwan Yew and Malaysia's Muhammad Mathathir who have argued for a distinctive Asian approach to human rights and democracy. These are frequently characterized as movements reacting against a global consumer capitalism, backed by Western political and military muscle, that is seen as imperialistic, individualistic, and inegalitarian, while also seeking meaning and identity in local traditions and values. Their participants are likely to be critical of the effort by the international community to set forth universal standards, and thus proponents of cultural relativism.

Western hegemony is also associated with the political globalization process that has given rise to global bureaucracies that have been criticized for being undemocratic, coming under the control of the industrialized countries, and making decisions that undermine national legislation and are insensitive to the needs of local cultures. These kinds of criticism usually come from the developing countries that complain about the liberal bias of international organizations such as the IMF and the World Bank. Critics of these organizations point out that the structural adjustment programs they impose on developing countries are based on neoliberal economic policies that require cuts in government spending on social programs and the privatization of government industries and services.

These cuts end up denying many people rights to jobs, education, and development opportunities (McCorquodale and Fairbrother, 1999; Amnesty International, 2000). But even in the West, there is a growing sense among many that globalization is giving rise to governance institutions that are inherently authoritarian, unresponsive to popular interests and national norms, and bad for human rights.[6] One only has to look at the protests in the last two years in Seattle, Washington; Washington, DC; and Prague, Czechoslovakia, against the WTO and the IMF, and the concerns raised by those protesters about international bureaucrats making policies that undercut national and international labor rights laws, and environmental legislation. While not directly opposing a universalist view of human rights, these protests sound a note of skepticism concerning efforts to impose universal standards and tend to support a positivist view of rights that derive from government legislation.

CONCLUSION: TOWARD UNIVERSALISM?

Not surprisingly, the examination in this chapter of some of the arguments and evidence linking globalization to the debate between universalism and cultural relativism shows support for both sides of the debate. I would argue, however, that a closer look at the arguments and evidence suggests greater support for universalism than skeptics might lead one to believe. By universal, I do not mean that human rights are now accepted by everyone but, to use Sen's formulation (1999), that they have become accepted by almost everyone as a viable and desirable goal. As a result of globalization, certain conditions have been put in place that make human rights a universal possibility: a political condition in that all states have accepted the idea of human rights in some form; and a legal–institutional condition in the various human rights conventions and transnational organizations that have emerged in the last half of the twentieth century. In creating the political and legal infrastructure needed to define, monitor, and enforce human rights, these trends also bring us closer to the standard of universality erected by the positive law school. In the realm of culture, morality, and philosophy, and in terms of creating what Brown (1999) calls an "ethical community," universalism is still a long ways off, although optimists such as Charles Taylor (1999) and Louis Henkin (1989) have argued that there may be certain core universal values accepted by all cultures (that is, right to life and freedom from torture, slavery, and arbitrary detention), and Ronald Inglehart's work (2000) suggests that the conditions for a postmodern value consensus are present. Clearly, then, a standardization of human rights norms is occuring slowly through the universalization of the modern state, and the growth of global institutions.

Moreover, many of the arguments on the side of cultural relativism do not seem to find fault with human rights norms or values, as much as they do with the global political and economic power structures in which these norms are embedded. In other words, if people from different nationalities and cultures came together as equals, they might find substantial agreement on human rights norms.[7] As recent scholarship has pointed out, local efforts to redefine human rights norms in terms acceptable to those cultures may be a way to relegitimate human rights norms, especially in developing non-Western countries.[8] Local social movements in these countries often seek to negotiate their own understanding of human rights in relation to the "universal" norms contained in international agreements. These movements indicate that human rights norms are gaining a foothold in cultures that relativists argue have a very different conception of human rights than the Western, liberal notion.

Where globalization may present problems for the universalist position is in the broadening of human rights norms to embrace rights that are not always compatible and may even contradict one another. Over the past few decades, the notion of a human right has been expanded to include political and civil rights, as well as economic, social, and cultural rights, including the right to an adequate standard of living, to education, to be free from hunger, and the right of self-determination for all peoples.[9] An example of how these rights might conflict can be found in governments that justify silencing dissidents on the grounds that certain kinds of dissent may endanger national security or disrupt economic growth, and thus deprive the majority of basic economic rights. Another example might be international covenants protecting local cultures whose customs deny women the same rights as men. If all these rights are regarded as universal, there certainly is no universal consensus about whether these rights are equally valid or whether there should be a hierarchy of rights with some taking priority over others. The Asian values debate, as some have pointed out, is not so much about embracing or rejecting human rights as currently defined in international agreements, but about whether certain rights should take precedence over others (see Kausikan, 1997).

Finally, it may be that globalization is accelerating changes that will change the terms of the debate between universalism and cultural relativism, and perhaps even make the debate obsolete altogether. In the end analysis, universalism and cultural relativism are not very useful frameworks for understanding the dynamic and fluid ways in which globalization shapes the struggle over human rights. Universalism and cultural relativism tend to reify cultures and gloss over the tremendous cultural changes and interactions that are going on as a result of globalization. There is a tendency in this debate to contrast broad categories such as West versus the non-West, North versus South, or Western versus Asian values.

Such categories ignore the diversity of cultures in Asia, as well as the contentious debates over liberalism heard in the West. More important, the broad categories used in this debate divert our attention from efforts made by local social movements and human rights activists in many parts of the world to interpret human rights norms in light of their own cultural practices and values.[10] These local movements are part of what Richard Falk (1993) calls "globalization from below," a set of processes that are not adequately captured by universalism and cultural relativism because they often involve cross-cultural attempts to mediate between the universal and the particular. In contrast to "globalization from above," which involves international institutions, multinational corporations, and states imposing values and institutions in a top-down process that many have criticized as homogenizing and imperialistic, "globalization from below" is a grassroots, pluralistic process that may lend greater legitimacy to human rights norms (Aziz, 1999). Ironically, as some scholars have pointed out, while this process may have originated from a universalistic impulse to see all peoples as human, the end result may well be the construction of multiple, competing universalisms (Monshipouri and Englehart, 2000).

APPENDIX: IMPORTANT INTERNATIONAL AND REGIONAL HUMAN RIGHTS DOCUMENTS AND TREATIES

- Universal Declaration of Human Rights (December 10, 1948)
- Convention on the Prevention and Punishment of the Crime of Genocide (January 12, 1951)
- European Convention for the Protection of Human Rights and Fundamental Freedoms and Its Nine Protocols (September 3, 1953)
- Convention Relating to Status of Refugees (April 22, 1954)
- International Convention on the Elimination of All Forms of Racial Discrimination (January 4, 1969)
- International Covenant on Economic, Social and Cultural Rights (January 3, 1976)
- International Covenant on Civil and Political Rights (March 23, 1976)
- American Convention on Human Rights (July 18, 1978)
- Convention on the Elimination of All Forms of Discrimination Against Women (September 3, 1981)
- The African Charter on Human and Peoples' Rights (October 21, 1986)
- Convention Against Torture and Other Cruel, Inhuman or Degrading Treatment or Punishment (June 26, 1987)
- European Convention for the Prevention of Torture and Inhuman or Degrading Treatment (February 1, 1989)

- The Cairo Declaration on Human Rights in Islam (signed on August 5, 1990)
- The Convention on the Rights of the Child (September 2, 1990)

Source: Center for the Study of Human Rights (1994).

NOTES

1. For a defense of universal human rights using the latter approach, see Donnelly (1999).
2. On the need for a global ethic, and what it might look like, see Kung (1998).
3. A more thorough presentation and analysis of this data can be found in Inglehart (1997).
4. For the classic statement of this argument, see Lipset (1959). Also, see Rueschemeyer, Stephens, and Stephens (1992).
5. Similar criticisms were voiced in the Asian values debate during the 1990s. See Mahbubani (1998).
6. See Stiglitz's criticisms of the IMF (2000).
7. This point was reinforced by a discussion with Siamack Shojai about the Iranian Revolution of 1979. While I had used the revolution as an instance of an Islamic reaction against global consumer capitalism and in defense of Islamic values, Professor Shojai pointed out that important segments of Iranian society saw the revolution's goals as consistent with democratic, and even capitalist, values.
8. See Bell (1996) and An-Na'im (1991).
9. See the three documents referred to collectively as the International Bill of Human Rights: the Universal Declaration of Human Rights; the International Covenant on Civil and Political Rights; and the International Covenant on Economic, Social and Cultural Rights.
10. There is a burgeoning literature on these grassroots movements. For representative works, see An-Na'im (1991) and Monshipouri (1998) and the essays by Abdullah Ahmed An-Na'im, Norani Othman, and Suwanna Satha-Anand in Bauer and Bell (1999).

REFERENCES

Amnesty International. 2000. AI on Human Rights and Labour Rights. In *The Globalization Reader*, ed. Frank J. Lechner and John Boli, 187–190. Oxford: Blackwell.

An-Na'im, Abdullah Ahmed, ed. 1991. *Human Rights in Cross-Cultural Perspectives: A Quest for Consensus.* Philadelphia: University of Pennsylvania Press.

Annan, Kofi. 1999. Business and the U.N.: A Global Compact of Shared Values and Principles (speech presented to the World Economic Forum in Davos, Switzerland, January 31).

Aziz, Nikhil. 1999. The Human Rights Debate in an Era of Globalization: Hegemony of Discourse. In *Debating Human Rights*, ed. Peter Van Ness, 32–55. London: Routledge.

Barber, Benjamin. 1992. Jihad vs. McWorld. *Atlantic Monthly* (March): 53–65.

Bauer, Joanne R., and Daniel Bell, eds. 1999. *The East Asian Challenge for Human Rights.* Cambridge: Cambridge University Press.

Beeson, Mark. 2000. The Political Economy of East Asia in a Time of Crisis. In *Political Economy and the Changing Global Order*, ed. Richard Stubbs and Geoffrey R. D. Underhill, 352–361. Toronto: Oxford University Press Canada.

Bell, Daniel A. 1996. The East Asian Challenge to Human Rights: Reflections on an East–West Dialogue. *Human Rights Quarterly* 18 (3):641–667.

Brown, Chris. 1999. Universal Human Rights: A Critique. In *Human Rights in Global Politics*, ed. Tim Dunne, Nicholas J. Wheeler, and Timothy Dunne, 103–127. New York: Cambridge University Press.

Center for the Study of Human Rights. 1994. *Twenty-Five Human Rights Documents.* New York: Columbia University.

Donnelly, Jack. 1998. *International Human Rights.* 2nd ed. Boulder, CO: Westview.

———. 1999. Human Rights and Asian Values: A Defense of "Western Universalism." In *The East Asian Challenge for Human Rights*, ed. Joanne R. Bauer and Daniel Bell, 60–87. Cambridge: Cambridge University Press.

Emerson, Tony. 1998. Just How Bad Can It Get? *Newsweek*, August 24.

Falk, Richard. 1993. The Making of Global Citizenship. In *Global Visions: Beyond the New World Order*, ed. Jeremy Brecher, John Brown Childs, and Jill Cutler, 39–50. Boston: South End Press.

Friedman, Thomas L. 1999. *The Lexus and The Olive Tree: Understanding Globalization.* New York: Farrar, Straus, Giroux.

Fukuyama, Francis. 1989. The End of History. *National Interest* (Summer): 3–18

Held, David et. al. 1999. *Global Transformations: Politics, Economics, and Culture.* Stanford, CA: Stanford University Press.

Henkin, Louis. 1989. The Universality of the Concept of Human Rights. *Annals of the American Academy of Political and Social Science* 506:10–16.

Hobsbawm, E. J. 1975. The World Unified. In *The Age of Capital 1848–1875.* London: Weidenfeld and Nicolson. Excerpted in Frank J. Lechner and John Boli, eds., *The Globalization Reader*, 52–56. Oxford: Blackwell.

Inglehart, Ronald. 1997. *Modernization and Postmodernization: Cultural, Economic, and Political Change in 43 Societies.* Princeton, NJ: Princeton University Press.

———. 2000. Globalization and Postmodern Values. *Washington Quarterly* 23 (1):215–228.

Kausikan, Bilahari. 1997. Governance That Works. *Journal of Democracy* 8 (2):24–34.

Keohane, Robert O., and Joseph S. Nye Jr. 2000. Globalization: What's New? What's Not? (And So What?). *Foreign Policy* (Spring): 104–119.

Kung, Hans. 1998. *A Global Ethic for Global Politics and Economics.* Oxford: Oxford University Press.

Lewis, Paul. 1996. Nigeria's Deadly Oil War: Shell Defends Its Record. *New York Times*, February 13.

Liebhold, David. 1998. 15,000 Workers Losing Jobs Everyday. *Asia Today* (October).

Lipset, Seymour M. 1959. Some Social Requisites of Democracy: Economic Development and Political Legitimacy. *American Political Science Review*, 53 (1):69–105.

Mahbubani, Kishore. 1998. *Can Asians Think?* Singapore: Times Books International.

McCorquodale, Robert, and Richard Fairbrother. 1999. Globalization and Human Rights. *Human Rights Quarterly* 21 (3):735–766.

Meyer, John W. et. al. 1997. World Society and the Nation-State. *American Journal of Sociology* 103 (1):144.

Monshipouri, Mahmood. 1998. *Islamism, Secularism, and Human Rights in the Middle East*. Boulder, CO: Lynne Rienner.

Monshipouri, Mahmood, and Neil Englehart. 2000. Constructing Universalisms: Human Rights in an Age of Globalization. Unpublished manuscript.

Muzaffar, Chandra. 1999. From Human Rights to Human Dignity. In *Debating Human Rights*, ed. Peter Van Ness, 25–31. London: Routledge.

Rourke, John T., and Mark A. Boyer. 2000. *World Politics: International Politics on the World Stage, Brief*. 3rd ed. New York: Dushkin/McGraw-Hill.

Rueschemeyer, D., E. H. Stephens, and J. D. Stephens. 1992. *Capitalist Development and Democracy*. Chicago: University of Chicago Press.

Sen, Amartya. 1999. Democracy as a Universal Value. *Journal of Democracy* 10 (3):3–17.

Smith, Jackie, and Ron Pagnucco, with George A. Lopez. 1998. Globalizing Human Rights: The Work of Transnational Human Rights NGOs in the 1990s. *Human Rights Quarterly* 20 (2):379–412.

Stiglitz, Joseph. 2000. The Insider. *New Republic* (April 17/24): 56–60.

Taylor, Charles. 1999. Conditions of an Unforced Consensus on Human Rights. In *The East Asian Challenge for Human Rights*, ed. Joanne R. Bauer and Daniel Bell, 124–144. Cambridge: Cambridge University Press.

Wallerstein, Immanuel. 1974. The Rise and Future Demise of the World Capitalist System: Concepts for Comparative Analysis. *Comparative Studies in Society and History* 16: 387–415. Excerpted in Frank J. Lechner and John Boli, eds., *The Globalization Reader*, 57–63. Oxford: Blackwell, 2000.

12 Globalization: The Impact on the Global Environment

Hank Hilton

The "Battle in Seattle" placed the debate in bold headlines. Protestors at the World Trade Organization's Seattle Summit contended that globalization imposes onerous burdens, including severe environmental burdens, on countless people. The charges, of course, drew sharp rebuttals from the World Trade Organization and its supporters. Although the conflict failed to generate new insights about the link between globalization and the environment, it did highlight the complexity of that connection and the intense feelings surrounding it. The battle also reminded people that evaluations of globalization should consider its environmental impact.

This chapter explores three aspects of the globalization/environment connection. The first section considers foreign direct investment's influence on pollution. It analyzes that link in terms of the Pollution Haven Hypothesis. The second section considers trade's impact on pollution, both its technology effect and its income effect. The third section examines the manner in which electronic commerce alters pollution. In focusing on these links, this chapter is not suggesting that globalization consists only of foreign direct investment (FDI), trade, and e-business. It simply treats these as aspects of globalization with highly publicized links to pollution. Similarly, in focusing on pollution, the analysis is not dismissing key environmental issues such as resource depletion or species extinction. The chapter concludes that FDI and trade have mixed influences on pollution while e-commerce tends to reduce it. It seems that Seattle's generalizations call for a careful review.

FOREIGN DIRECT INVESTMENT AND POLLUTION

This issue often dominates the "globalization/environment" debates, especially as nations ratify trade pacts such as the North American Free Trade Agreement (NAFTA), the General Agreement on Tariffs and Trade (GATT), and U.S. trade treaties with China. Some contend that globalization, by encouraging FDI, increases global pollution; others dismiss that view. Participants frequently frame the debate in terms of the Pollution Haven Hypothesis. The paradigm's basic claims enjoy broad acceptance. Efforts to substantiate those claims, however, encounter serious challenges.

The Pollution Haven Hypothesis: The Basic Claims

A few intuitively appealing claims can summarize the Pollution Haven Hypothesis. First, many factors, including the globalization wave, encourage firms, especially multinational manufacturers, to produce in one nation and export to others. Second, environmental regulations and pollution-control costs influence firms' location decisions. All other things being equal, firms would prefer to operate in a nation with lower pollution-control costs. Third, low-income countries (LICs) have lower environmental standards and lower pollution-control costs. Therefore, fourth, globalization encourages firms to locate their dirty operations in LICs with low pollution-control costs (the pollution havens). Fifth, globalization consequently leads to a rise in pollution intensity (the amount of pollution generated per unit of output) as firms move from regulated to unregulated locations and, sixth, to increases in polluting activity as lower production costs stimulate price reductions, growth in demand, and more output by the polluters.

The Pollution Haven Hypothesis enjoys widespread acceptance. Most people who endorse it want to control the pattern it describes. In a letter to the *New York Times*, Walter Cronkite (1980) urged the government to restrict trade with nations that had slack environmental regulations. In 1991, Senator David L. Boren (D-OK) unsuccessfully sponsored legislation designed to do just that: The International Pollution Deterrence Act of 1991 (U.S. Congress, Senate, 102nd Cong., 1st sess., S.984). As hearings on the bill opened, Senator Max Baucus (D-MT) (1993) warned that other nations' "inadequate environmental protection creates a competitive advantage vis-a-vis [*sic*] nations that protect the environment" and that the United States needed to "level the playing field." However, others who accept the hypothesis seek simply to go with its flow. U.S. Treasury Secretary Lawrence Summers, while still chief economist at the World Bank, speculated, "[S]houldn't the World Bank be encouraging more migration of dirty industries to LDCs?" (*The Economist*, 1992, 7). Beneath these various statements and policy proposals, one finds implicit but widespread endorsement of the Pollution Haven Hypothesis. Notwithstanding its intuitive appeal, however, the hypothesis merits careful consideration.

The Pollution Haven Hypothesis: Problems with the Basic Claims

Each claim that underlies the hypothesis requires some qualification. For example, the first claim that globalization encourages multinational manufacturers to produce in one nation and export to others faces a mild but noteworthy challenge. Charles Pearson (1987) and Peter Thompson and Laura Strohm (1996) underscore the importance of domestic firms. If export markets grow, there seems little reason, a priori, to presume that domestic firms will not be the first to seize those export opportunities. A large role for domestic firms could limit both FDI and the relevance of the Pollution Haven Hypothesis.

The second claim—that environmental regulations, and their resulting pollution-control costs, influence firms' location decisions—rests, in part, on the valid claim that environmental regulations and pollution-control costs are rising steeply and, because of this surge, are becoming more of a consideration for corporate strategists. A report by the U.S. Environmental Protection Agency (1990, 2) shows that annualized pollution-control costs, measured in real 1986 dollars, rose from $26 billion in 1972 to $100 billion in 1990. The report predicted that the costs would reach $160 billion in 2000. As a portion of gross national product (GNP), these expenses amount, respectively, to 0.9 percent, 2.14 percent, and 2.83 percent of GNP.

Despite this surge, however, pollution-control costs remain a very small portion of total production costs. Ingo Walter (1973) estimates that pollution-control costs amount to 1.75 percent of the value of U.S. exports and 1.52 percent of the value of import substitutes. Although Walter's estimates must be considered with caution, the costs are certainly higher in 2000 than they were in 1970, and his estimates face all the data difficulties described below, they suggest that pollution-control costs are generally a very small piece of overall cost considerations. It seems implausible to suggest that lower pollution-control costs could provide large incentives to relocate manufacturing facilities. Other factors and costs surely provide much stronger incentives. Moreover, it is probably not always the case that, all other things being equal, firms would prefer to operate in the nation with lower pollution-control costs. Eric Neumayer (2000) raises the issue of disincentives for environmentally based capital migration. He observes that firms might well forego lower environmental costs since migration to pollution havens could increase exposure to liability, endanger corporate reputations, and alienate "green" consumers.

The third assertion—that LICs have lower environmental standards and lower pollution-control costs—remains unsubstantiated. Starting in the 1970s, many organizations, including the United Nations Conference on Trade and Development (1972, 1976), the United Nations Conference on Environment and Development (UNCED; 1992), a collection of nongovernmental organizations (for example, Natural Resources Defence Council, 1994), and many academic researchers (for example, Walter and Ugelow, 1979), have attempted to assemble systematic descriptions of nations' environmental legislation. Although the efforts generated a great deal of very valuable data, none has provided a basis for systematic comparison of these regulations. Moreover, to the extent that they have provided useful data, they provide many exceptions to the assumption that low GNP implies low environmental regulations and low pollution-control costs. The reports, especially UNCED's (1992), clearly indicate that many LICs have established impressive regulations and enforcement mechanisms. As described in the next section, I found in a 1999 study that many LICs were among the first to get rid of leaded gasoline. Claims that all LICs have less stringent environmental regulations should be accepted with great caution.

Caution should also be used when considering the claim that LICs have lower pollution-control costs. To "prove" these claims, researchers would first have to quantify international differences in pollution-control costs. In the best of all worlds, they would assemble site-specific cost data for many plants, in many industries, in many nations, over many years. They could then compare pollution costs and identify pollution havens (that is, nations with relatively low pollution-control costs). Unfortunately, however, no one has yet produced such a data set. In a 2000 study, I, and my colleague Arik Levinson, describe the difficulty of that important task. We indicate that pollution-control costs can be far more difficult to identify than one might presume. Newer equipment, for example, tends to be more environmentally friendly and is already equipped with pollution-reducing features. Determining what portion of total capital cost is accounted for by those features can be a most challenging effort. On the other hand, older equipment tends to be less environmentally friendly and requires more pollution-control expenses. In many places however, older equipment enjoys "grandfather" exemptions. This too complicates the effort to isolate pollution-control costs. We also indicate that efforts to collect the data face serious hurdles. The presumed suppliers of such data are frequently unable or unwilling to do so. Past efforts to collect relatively simple information on environmental regulations (described previously) encountered serious delays. Many of the respondents in the selected nations either could not or would not answer the questions in a timely fashion. Efforts to collect relatively complex data on pollution-control costs will certainly encounter even more serious obstacles. In theory, of course, the required data could materialize, but it will require an exceptionally well-organized, well-funded effort. Meanwhile, some have developed impressive proxies for measuring pollution-control costs. Others use anecdotal data. In either case, without the needed data, claims about international differences in environmental legislation and pollution-control costs should be treated as highly qualified.

A substantial body of empirical research also challenges the fourth assertion—that firms will locate their dirty operations in low-income nations with low pollution-control costs (the pollution havens). Jeffrey Leonard, focusing on U.S. firms and their responses to tighter environmental regulation, finds little evidence that pollution-control costs have actually caused polluting activities to relocate. He instead argues that "there are only a relatively small number of American industries whose international location patterns have been significantly affected by environmental regulations in the United States" (1988, 111). He further observes that enhanced environmental legislation has prompted many U.S. firms to pursue "technological innovation, change in production processes, more efficient process controls, and other adaptations" that "have proved more economical and less drastic than flight abroad" (113). Patrick Low and Andrew Yeats (1992) also question the notion that differences in pollution-control costs prompt polluters to relocate. They observe that dirty industries account for a growing share in the total exports of some developing countries and that this development "has occurred against the backdrop of a reduction in the share of dirty industry exports of industrial countries" (102). They do not hold, however, that differences in pollution-control costs explain the relocation of dirty industry. The authors cite many possible explanations, including the commonly held belief that, in the early stages of development, LICs "naturally" move from reliance on agriculture to reliance on industry. Thus, one could view this growth in dirty industry as a predictable development, not as a response to pollution-control costs. Industrial relocation due to pollution-control costs has probably been limited.

Substantial research results also challenge the fifth claim—that globalization increases pollution intensity (the amount of pollution generated per unit of output) as it prompts firms to move from regulated to unregulated locations. This claim suggests that firms would find it profitable to "unbundle" their technologies. That is, they could increase profits by using one production process in a regulated setting and another production process, presumably a dirtier low-cost process, in a pollution haven. Intuition and evidence argue against this assumption. Nancy Birdsall and David Wheeler, examining the environment/investment relationship in

Latin America, argue that unbundling makes little economic sense because "multinational corporations may face high costs in implementing different business practices (different pollution standards) in different settings" (1993, 140). In this regard they concur with the Neumayer's (2000) claim that unbundling creates more costs than it eliminates.

The sixth claim—that globalization will, on balance, increase polluting activity as lower production costs stimulate price reductions, growth in demand, and more output—also faces serious questions. Much of the analyses described previously concur that pollution-control costs constitute a small share of overall production costs. Hence, reductions in these costs are unlikely to spur the price cuts that could stimulate demand for the pollution-generating output. Moreover, without knowledge of the prevailing market structures and demand elasticities, one cannot draw any conclusions about the extent to which those cost savings will be passed along to the consumer. Thus, there seems little reason to presume that FDI increases, on a global scale, either polluting activity or pollution intensity.

Taken together, many factors argue against broad-based acceptance of the Pollution Haven Hypothesis. It does not seem to be the case that globalization's encouragement of FDI necessarily harms the environment. In fact, there are ample reasons to believe that, in some circumstances, FDI helps reduce pollution. Neither does it seem to be the case, however, that the Pollution Haven Hypothesis completely lacks anecdotal support. Eban Goodstein (1995) describes the migration of certain furniture manufacturers (from Los Angeles to Mexico) as, in part, an example of the Pollution Haven Hypothesis. Thus, while one can find individual examples to illustrate the Pollution Haven Hypothesis, it seems imprudent to draw broad generalizations that globalization, by encouraging FDI, increases pollution on a global scale.

TRADE AND POLLUTION

The international exchange of goods and technologies can constrain pollution in important ways. Conventional wisdom identifies an income effect and a technology effect as two of the most important. Both of these effects tend primarily, but not exclusively, to cut pollution.

The Income Effect

The "income effect" describes a two-step process by which trade reduces pollution: first, trade increases income; and second, income growth encourages improvements in environmental quality, including reductions in pollution. The notion that trade increases income finds support in centuries of theoretical and empirical work. Adam Smith (1776) made the point persuasively in *The Wealth of Nations*. Sebastian Edwards (1993) finds empirical support for "the policy view that more open and outward oriented economies have outperformed countries with restrictive trade regimes" (1360). David Dollar's research (1992) also upholds that position. Using distortions in real exchange rates to measure openness in 117 developing economies, Dollar finds that between 1976 and 1985, real per capita income in the most open economies grew at an annual average rate of 2.9 percent. In the least open economies, it decreased by 1.3 percent. Ross Levine and David Renelt (1992) identify many other works that link openness with growth. Rudiger Dornbusch (1992) and Jay R. Mandle (2000) also argue persuasively that openness and trade stimulate income growth.

The view that income growth discourages pollution also enjoys widespread support. The GATT (1992) contends that trade is "a source of increased wealth . . . [that, in turn] enhances societies' ability to protect and upgrade the environment" (19). The World Bank (1992) maintains that "demand for a better environment rises as per capita income grows" (39) because "higher income frees people from worries about their daily survival and enables them to devote resources to environmental quality" (10). Marian Radetzki (1992) holds a similar view, claiming that income growth (a) lets people meet survival needs and (b) allows them to "abstain from consumption known to harm the environment, spend [more] on repairing the environment, and adopt preventive measures" (132). A sizable body of theoretical and empirical literature supports these claims about the inverse relation between income and pollution. Still, however, they should be accepted with a number of caveats.

First, income growth can encourage environmental improvement, but it does not guarantee it; income growth is not a "sufficient condition" for pollution reduction. Nemat Shafik and Sushenjit Bandyopadhyay (1992) claim that "it is possible to 'grow out' of some environmental problems but there is nothing automatic about doing so" (1). Hilton and Levinson (1998) find that "[s]ome government action such as taxes or bans on leaded gasoline appears to be behind much of the decline in automotive lead pollution. This undermines the claim that income growth is itself a panacea for environmental problems" (140). Pollution reduction does not result automatically from rising per capita GDP.

Second, many factors other than income growth can help the environment; income growth is not a "necessary condition" for pollution reduction. In the efforts to remove lead from gasoline, in my 1999 study I found that a number of low-income nations moved in the vanguard of the worldwide phase-out. Many poor nations got rid of lead before many of their industrialized counterparts. Factors such as human rights, grassroots movements, and idiosyncratic factors have, in some instances, influenced lead phase-out far more than has income growth. Alan Durning (1990) asserts that "[i]f we want to help citizens of the Third World save their environment, our top priority should be to help them protect their human rights. They, in there hundreds of thousands of local organizations, will take care of themselves" (18). Improvements in education systems have also been known to encourage environmental quality. Anne Forrest (1995) maintains that "it may not be development itself, but factors that occur along with development that produce the turning point" toward pollution reduction (11). Similarly, the World Bank (1992) describes many improvements other than income growth that can prompt pollution reduction. Clearly, environmental improvements can unfold before incomes rise.

Third, in considering the income/pollution relationship, it is important to recognize that the relationship changes as income changes. As explained in the Environmental Kuznets Curve (EKC) literature, environmental damage tends to increase in the early stages of income growth, reach a peak, and then decline as income increases further. Gene Grossman and Alan Krueger (1991) use an EKC-approach in exploring the ways in which income growth, associated with NAFTA, might influence Mexico's air quality. They conclude that ambient concentrations of many pollutants rise as the country approaches an income level of $5,000, reach an inflection point, and decline thereafter. Thomas Selden and Daqing Song (1994), studying four pollutants in thirty countries between 1973 and 1984, find inflection points of $5,963 for carbon monoxide, $8,709 for sulfur dioxide, $10,289 for suspended particulate matter, and $11,217 for nitrogen oxide. Similarly, Hilton and Levinson (1998), studying gasoline-based lead pollution in fifty nations over twenty years, find that the pollution increases with income growth, reaches a peak, and then declines. They determine, however, that estimates of the inflection point vary from $4,000 to $11,000, depending on the functional form of the analysis. Altogether, the EKC literature makes a persuasive argument that income growth has an inconsistent effect on pollution levels. In the early phases of income growth, it tends to increase certain pollutions. Starting from higher levels, income growth tends to reduce them.

The evidence thus suggests that trade probably does stimulate income growth. However, it is not possible to generalize about income's subsequent effect on pollution. The idea that income growth encourages environmental quality is both intuitively appealing and empirically justified—in certain circumstances. However, income growth is neither a necessary nor a sufficient condition for pollution reduction. The effect of income growth on pollution also changes across the income spectrum.

The Technology Effect

Trade can also reduce pollution by contributing to a technological exchange that fosters environmental improvement. Insofar as (a) trade promotes the exchange of the latest goods and technologies and (b) those latest goods and technologies are environmentally friendly, then (c) trade will tend to reduce pollution. Again, an extensive literature supports and reiterates the optimistic view that trade ultimately encourages reductions in pollution.

GATT holds that "trade promotes a diffusion of technology" and that this diffusion promotes environmental quality (1992, 19). The Organization for Economic Cooperation and Development (OECD; 1994) points to similar links between trade, technological change, and the environment, saying that "trade facilitates the international diffusion of environmentally beneficial products and services" (7). Grossman and Krueger (1991) find that trade liberalization encourages firms to trade technologies across international borders and that the traded technologies are "typically cleaner than older technologies due to . . . the urgency of (global) environmental concerns" (4). Birdsall and Wheeler (1993) theorize that "openness and resulting competitive pressure will increase investment in the latest technology, all other factors remaining the same . . . to the extent that new and efficient technology embodies cleaner processes, this will reduce emissions" (140).

Useful evidence, however, challenges the prevailing paradigm. Trade seems not always to promote the exchange of the latest goods and technologies. Santiago, Chile, presents an interesting example of "dirty" trade. Nathaniel Nash (1992) explains that "during the Pinochet years, the (city's) bus system was totally deregulated and the government permitted the import of thousands of used vehicles." These old, imported buses became a significant portion of the city's fleet of 11,000 diesel buses. The bus fleet, in turn, has become a primary source of Santiago's intolerable air pollution. Kenny Bruno (1991), citing similar anecdotal evidence, claims that free trade increases the flow of harmful technologies and products, including leaded gasoline.

Trade can also introduce technologies, which, although modern, are not necessarily good for the local environment. Missionaries in the South Pacific report that trade expansion has encouraged the use of disposable diapers in many small, island states. As the atolls and reefs have little space for garbage dumps, the diapers have been deposited primarily in the sea. Certain wind and tide situations then return most of the used diapers back to the beaches (O'Connor and O'Connor, 2000). Similarly, trade has encouraged many Asian cities to replace bicycles with motorized vehicles as a primary mode of transportation. This trade-based growth in dirty buses, diapers, and fossil-fueled vehicles exemplifies what the OECD (1994) describes as "the negative product effects" of trade (12).

Like the income effect, the (positive) technology effect describes a trend that should not be overgeneralized. The international exchange of goods and technologies frequently, but not always, promotes the diffusion of the latest and the cleanest technologies. Moreover, because of the inconsistent results produced by both the income effect and the technology effect, trade's overall influence on pollution resembles FDI's and is mixed.

ELECTRONIC COMMERCE AND POLLUTION

Electronic commerce (e-commerce) adds great force to the globalization wave. It enables firms of every proportion to globalize as long as they have an Internet connection. Because of e-commerce, large corporations no longer have a monopoly on "multinational" status. Electronic commerce also constitutes a rapidly growing force. Virtually nonexistent in the early 1990s, e-commerce transactions expanded to $150 billion in 1998 and could easily reach $3 trillion by 2003. Though business-to-business exchanges now account for three-quarters of all electronic commerce, all sectors including business-to-consumer and consumer-to-consumer are likely to undergo impressive growth (*The Economist*, 2000, 26).

Electronic commerce, like every aspect of globalization, influences pollution. Unlike the established environmental consequences of FDI and trade, however, the emerging environmental implications of e-commerce have undergone relatively little analysis. Discussions thus far have focused on the ways in which e-commerce can reduce energy use and its associated pollutions. The Earth Day 2000 issue of *Time*, for example, explained "Why Mother Nature Should Love Cyberspace." It presented reductions in paper use and energy consumption as the two most important environmental benefits of e-commerce with a clear suggestion that the energy gains were most important. *Time*'s focus typifies the prevailing view. In keeping with this focus, and with standard practice in energy analysis, the following considers how electronic commerce could help limit energy use in the industrial sector, the transportation sector, and the residential/commercial sector (which includes agriculture).

Even before the advent of the Internet, growth in the world's energy demand had started to slow. Between 1970 and 1975, the world's primary energy consumption rose by 16 percent. Between 1980 and 1985 it grew by only 7 percent, and in the five-year period from 1990 to 1995 total energy consumption increased by only 5 percent (Cambridge Energy Research Associates, 1996, 18). This period of decelerating energy demand coincides with a slight reduction in dependence on fossil fuels. Although they continue to satisfy the majority of fuel needs, fossil fuels have become a marginally less important part of the global energy market. In 1971, they satisfied 97 percent of global energy requirements; in 1995, they accounted for 91 percent. The OECD (1997, xxiii) explains that most of this reduction in the world's fossil fuel dependence comes from the growth of nuclear power in OECD nations. Despite their relative decrease, combustion of fossil fuels remains a primary cause of many pollutions, including carbon dioxide (CO_2) pollution, and climate change. CO_2 remains "the single most important anthropogenic greenhouse gas," and "fossil fuel production and use represent about three-quarters of man-made CO_2 emissions" (OECD 1997, xi). To the extent that e-commerce reduces the growth in energy use, it can reduce the growth in CO_2 pollution and other fuel-related pollution.

Electronic commerce could impose a particularly strong constraint on industrial fuel use. Viewed from a number of perspectives, that sector's demand growth has already weakened. Worldwide, industry's use of energy grew from 1,925 million tons oil equivalent (MTOE) in 1980 to 2,145 MTOE in 1997 (OECD, 1999). However, during the same period, total global energy use rose from 4,827 MTOE to 6,660 MTOE. Thus, industry's share of total global energy use declined from 40 percent to 32 percent. Industrial energy use in the OECD has taken an even more noticeable downturn, actually falling from 1,071 MTOE in 1980 to 1,065 MTOE in 1997. This decline reduced industry's share of OECD energy use, from 36 percent to 30 percent. Thus, e-commerce is starting to constrain industrial energy demand at a time when demand has already started to weaken.

Testifying before a subcommittee of the U.S. Congress, Joseph Romm, executive director of the Center for Energy and Climate Solutions and author of *Cool Companies* (1999), pointed out three primary ways in which e-commerce could restrict the growth in industrial energy demand. First, Romm observes that the growth in e-commerce and its associated industries (for example, Internet companies, computer manufacturers, information technology firms) requires relatively little energy (U.S. Congress, House, 2000). Unlike periods when the expansion of heavy, energy-intensive industries generated a large share of economic development, growth in these industries suggests significant increases in industrial output with only meager increases in industrial energy demand. Second, e-commerce will enable existing industries to improve efficiency and reduce energy use. Romm asserts that "as traditional manufacturing and commercial companies put their supply chain on the Internet" they will be better able to "reduce inventories, overproduction, unnecessary capital purchases," and other actions that waste energy. Hence, they could achieve "greater output with less energy." Finally, in terms of industry's energy use, Romm expects that e-commerce will continue to facilitate "energy outsourcing"— the arrangements by which energy service companies agree to manage the energy needs of large firms, especially manufacturers (U.S. Congress, House 2000, 2). Taken together, these e-commerce influences could substantially limit industry's demand for energy.

Electronic commerce could also limit the demand for transportation fuels. Worldwide demand for transportation fuel increased by over 500 MTOE between 1980 and 1997, from 1,145 MTOE to 1,653 MTOE. Most of that growth (338 MTOE) came from OECD nations. These developments increased the transport sector's share of energy demand from 24 percent to 25 percent for the world in general but from 27 percent to 33 percent for the OECD. Thus, unlike industry's energy demand, the transportation sector's demand is positioned to expand.

Romm's congressional testimony indicates two basic ways in which electronic commerce could constrain the growing demand for transportation fuels. First, electronic business promises to reduce the number of trips between home and office. He testifies that "as e-commerce itself grows . . . more jobs will involve spending a considerable amount of time on the Internet," and these jobs "can be done as easily from home as from traditional workplaces" (U.S. Congress, House, 2000, 3). To the extent that it limits commuting, electronic commerce can slow the rise in consumption of transportation fuels. Electronic commerce could also reduce the amount of fuel used to travel from homes to stores. As Chris Taylor (2000) notes, online purchases require a fraction of the fuel that goes into purchases made in traditional retail locations. Most importantly, it takes far less energy to deliver a book to a home than it does to deliver a shopper to the bookstore. Romm cautions that these fuel savings will materialize only if the packages are delivered by the Post Office, or other firms already visiting most neighborhoods. Heavy reliance on special delivery mechanisms could significantly reduce the projected efficiency gains in this area. As Romm claims, "The great unknown question at this point is whether or not a significant fraction of Americans will change their driving habits over the next few years once it is possible to make a critical mass of cyber-trips on the Internet" (U.S. Congress, House 2000, 3).

Finally, electronic commerce might also limit the growth in the residential/commercial sector's demand for energy. Recent strength in this sector contrasts sharply with the other two sectors. Of the 1,833 MTOE growth in total world energy demand—from 4,827 MTOE in 1980 to 6,660 MTOE in 1997—over one-half (1,073 MTOE) came from the residential/commercial sector. Moreover, of that 1,073 MTOE increase in residential/commercial energy demand, the vast majority (893 MTOE) originated outside of the OECD.

Electronic commerce could well constrain this sector's energy needs, albeit in different ways in different subsectors. The OECD itself estimates that electronic commerce could substantially reduce the world's need for

retail space and, by doing so, could reduce the sector's energy requirements by $5 billion per year (Wyckoff and Colecchia, 1999). Romm (1999)
identifies two ways in which the shift from retail to warehouse will reduce
the sector's overall energy requirements. First, warehouses contain far
more products per square foot than do retail spaces. Second, warehouses
require far less energy per square foot than do retail spaces. Less space
using less energy per unit of space could translate into noticeable energy
savings. Taylor (2000) reports that "[o]nline retailers that employ nothing
but warehouses have about eight times the number of sales per square
foot of space used" (82). Less need for office space (produced by the increase in cybercommutes) will further limit this section's demand for energy. The dynamics described previously have already started to unfold.
They suggest that electronic commerce will continue to limit energy use in
the industrial, transportation, and residential/commercial sectors. To the
extent that it does, e-commerce will also help to reduce CO_2 concentrations, climate change, and other forms of pollution associated with fossil
fuel combustion. Notwithstanding the encouraging reports, various factors currently limit the degree to which electronic commerce can curtail
the growth in energy use. First, the surge in e-commerce is still primarily
a U.S. phenomenon. *The Economist* (2000) reports that "[s]omething like
three-quarters of all e-commerce currently takes place in the United
States" and that "the country also accounts for 90 percent of commercial
websites" (49). E-commerce is quickly becoming a global reality, one that
will reinforce the globalization wave even more in the future. For the near
term, however, both e-commerce and its influence on energy will be concentrated in the United States. Second, the interaction between electronic
commerce and energy use seems particularly far off for the many nations
where energy growth is likely to accelerate quickly and most profoundly.
It remains difficult to predict how long it will take for e-commerce to influence energy demand in China, India, and many other countries where
energy demand is poised for impressive growth. Third, "cleaner" energy
is expected to account for a growing share of the world's overall energy
mix (OECD, 1997). To the extent that energy markets move away from fossil fuels, owing to influences such as the Kyoto Protocol, electronic commerce will have a smaller influence on environmental quality. Finally,
even in the places where e-commerce does influence energy demand, it
will have a mixed influence. For example, as discussed previously, e-commerce encourages reductions in commuting and thereby reduces the need
for transportation fuels. These fuel gains must, however, be weighed
against the extra fuel required to light and heat homes and to power home
computers during the day. Similarly, growth in online shopping will require more fuel for delivery purposes. On balance, it seems that e-commerce will limit the growth in energy demand, but the influence, at least

when viewed from a global perspective, could remain moderate for quite some time.

CONCLUSION

The Battle in Seattle prompted many of its participants to speak in sweeping terms about the connection between the globalization wave and the environment. News coverage of the incident provides an extensive collection of such statements. The generalizations are not limited to that setting. As described in this chapter, they have emerged at the World Bank, the U.S. Senate, and throughout the popular press. For many, the topic remains a neuralgic one that quickly raises larger issues and carefully selected data.

This chapter has argued that broad statements about the globalization/environment link will probably be misleading. The three aspects of globalization considered here have very different influences on pollution levels. Both foreign direct investment and trade exert mixed influences on pollution, albeit for different reasons. Electronic commerce promises to limit the growth in fossil fuel use and the pollution it produces, though those influences will unfold gradually.

Analyses of globalization need not be constrained to issues of FDI, trade, and electronic commerce. Similarly, considerations of the environment need not be constrained to pollution. Subsequent studies of the globalization/environment connection might consider issues such as air traffic's influence on sensitive habitats or the ways in which different nations' legal systems resolve deforestation. Such reviews might provide conclusions that sharply oppose those presented here. Based on this review, however, it seems appropriate to conclude that globalization is neither the sinister opponent nor the shining champion of environmental quality. For the foreseeable future, globalization is best considered a mixed blessing.

REFERENCES

Baucus, M. 1993. *Hearing before the Subcommittee on International Trade of the Committee on Finance.* United States Senate, 102 Congress, First Session on S.984, October 25, 1991. Washington, DC: U.S. Government Printing Office.

Birdsall, N., and D. Wheeler. 1993. Trade Policy and Industrial Pollution in Latin America: Where Are the Pollution Havens? *Journal of Environment and Development* 2 (1):137–149.

Bruno, K. 1991. Poison Petrol: Leaded Gas Exports to the Third World. *Multinational Monitor* 12:24–27.

Cambridge Energy Research Associates. 1996. *World Oil Trends—1996.* Cambridge, MA: Cambridge Energy Research Associates.

Cronkite, W. 1980. To Save Our Industry and Environment. *New York Times*, October 14.

Dollar, D. 1992. Outward-Oriented Developing Economies Really Do Grow More Rapidly: Evidence from 95 LDCs, 1976–1985. *Economic Development and Cultural Change* 40:203–233.

Dornbusch, R. 1992. The Case for Trade Liberalization in Developing Countries. *Journal of Economic Perspectives* 6 (1):69–85.

Durning, A. 1990. Environmentalism South. *Amicus Journal* 12 (3):12–18.

Edwards, S. 1993. Openness, Trade Liberalization, and Growth in Developing Countries. *Journal of Economic Literature* 31:358–393.

The Economist. 1992. The Freedom to Be Dirtier Than the Rest: Why Differing Environmental Priorities Cause Problems for Trade. May 30.

———. 2000. Shopping around the Web. February 26.

Forrest, A. 1995. *Turning Points: The Development-Environment Relationship.* Research Brief No. 5 (July). Washington, DC: Environmental Law Institute.

General Agreement on Tariffs and Trade. 1992. *International Trade 90–91.* Vol. 1. Geneva: General Agreement on Tariffs and Trade.

Goodstein, E. S. 1995. Economics and the Environment. Englewood Cliffs, NJ: Prentice-Hall.

Grossman, G., and A. Krueger. 1991. *Environmental Impacts of a North American Free Trade Agreement.* Discussion Papers in Economics No. 158. Princeton, NJ: Princeton University/Woodrow Wilson School.

Hilton, F. G. H. 1999. Income, Liberties, Idiosyncracies, and the Decline of Leaded Gasoline, 1972 to 1992. *Journal of Environment and Development* 8 (1):49–69.

Hilton, F. G. H., and A. Levinson. 1998. Factoring the Environmental Kuznets Curve: Evidence from Automotive Lead Emissions. *Journal of Environmental Economics and Management* 35:126–141

———. 2000. Measuring Environmental Compliance Costs and Economic Consequences: A Perspective from the United States. In *Quantifying the Trade Effects of Standards and Regulatory Barriers: Is it Possible?* (Proceedings of the Symposium in Washington, DC, April 27, 2000, by the Development Research Group, World Bank). Washington, DC: World Bank.

Leonard, H. J. 1988. *Pollution and the Struggle for World Product: Multinational Corporations, Environment and International Comparative Advantage.* New York: Cambridge University Press.

Levine, R., and D. Renelt. 1992. A Sensitivity Analysis of Cross-Country Growth Regressions. *American Economic Review* 82:952–963.

Low, P., and A. Yeats. 1992. Do "Dirty" Industries Migrate? In *International Trade and the Environment.* World Bank Discussion Papers No. 159, 89–103. Washington, DC: World Bank.

Mandle, J. 2000. Trading Up: Why Globalization Aids the Poor. *Commonwealth,* June 2.

Nash, N. 1992. Santiago Journal: Scrubbing the Skies over Chile. *New York Times,* July 6.

Natural Resources Defence Council. 1994. *Four in '94: Focus on Two Years after Rio.* Washington, DC: Natural Resources Defence Council.

Neumayer, E. 2000. Trade and the Environment: A Critical Assessment and Some Suggestions for Reconciliation. *Journal of Environment and Development* 9 (2):138–159.

O'Connor, G., and J. O'Connor. 2000. Interviews by authors. Washington, DC, May.

Organization for Economic Cooperation and Development. 1994. *The Environmental Effects of Trade.* Paris: Organization for Economic Cooperation and Development.

———. 1997. *CO_2 Emissions from Fuel Combustion: A New Basis for Comparing Emissions of a Major Greenhouse Gas—1972–1995.* Paris: International Energy Agency, Organization for Economic Cooperation and Development.

———. 1999. OECD Environmental Data: Compendium 1999. Paris: Organization for Economic Cooperation and Development.

Pearson, C., ed. 1987. *Multinational Corporations, Environment, and the Third World.* Durham, NC: Duke University Press.

Radetzki, M. 1992. Economic Growth and the Environment. In *International Trade and the Environment.* World Bank Discussion Papers No. 159, 121–133. Washington, DC: World Bank.

Romm, J. 1999. *Cool Companies.* Washington, DC: Island Press.

Selden, T., and D. Song. 1994. Environmental Quality and Development: Is There a Kuznets Curve for Air Pollution Emissions? *Journal of Environmental Economics and Management* 27:147–162.

Shafik, N., and S. Bandyopadhyay. 1992. *Economic Growth and Environmental Quality: Time Series and Cross-Country Evidence.* Policy Research Working Paper No. WPS 904. Washington, DC: World Bank.

Smith, A. 1776. *An Inquiry into the Nature and Causes of the Wealth of Nations.* London: Strahan and Caldell.

Taylor, C. 2000. Why Mother Nature Should Love Cyberspace. *Time,* Special Edition, Earth Day 2000.

Thompson, P., and L. Strohm. 1996. Trade and Environmental Quality: A Review of the Evidence. *Journal of Environment and Development* 5 (4):363–388.

United Nations Conference on Environment and Development. 1992. *Nations of the Earth Report.* Geneva: United Nations Conference on Environment and Development.

United Nations Conference on Trade and Development. 1972. *Impact of Environmental Policies on Trade and Development in Particular of the Developing Countries.* Geneva: United Nations Conference on Trade and Development.

———. 1976. *Implications of Environmental Policies for the Trade Prospects of Developing Countries: Analysis Based on UNCTAD Questionnaire.* Geneva: United Nations Conference on Trade and Development (mimeograph).

U.S. Congress, House. 2000. Hearings on the Energy Implications of a Digital Economy. Committee on Government Reform, Subcommittee on National Economic Growth, Natural Resources and Regulatory Affairs. February 2.

U.S. Environmental Protection Agency. 1990. *Environmental Investments: The Costs of a Clean Environment* (EPA-230-12-90-084) Washington, DC: U.S. Environmental Protection Agency.

Walter, I. 1973. The Pollution Content of American Trade. *Western Economic Journal* 11:61–70.

Walter, I., and J. Ugelow. 1979. Environmental Policies in Developing Countries. *Ambio* 8:102–109.

World Bank. 1992. *World Development Report, 1992: Development and the Environment*. New York: Oxford University Press.

Wyckoff, A., and A. Colecchia. 1999. *The Economic and Social Impact of Electronic Commerce*. Paris: Organization for Economic Cooperation and Development.

13 Business Education in a Globalized Economy: The Next Millennium

Peter Lorenzi

What are the prospects for business education in a global economy? University-based business schools have been a primary institution for management education for the past fifty years. The study of business at the university level has become both a driver and a reflection of the changes in the theory, practice, and culture of business. University-based business education is a peculiarly American phenomenon, not widely adopted by the rest of the world until recently, and many American theories and practices reflect the unique social and economic culture of the United States, making the transfer of this knowledge technology to other countries and cultures problematic.

The purpose of this chapter is to study the growth and development of university-based business education and its relationship to global economic growth, with special attention to the past twenty-five years and the next twenty-five years. The analysis examines the changing role of university-based business education, the privatization of higher education around the world, and the expansion of corporate universities and for-profit business education firms.

Global business education has been characterized by the development of the MBA degree as a valued, global credential. The MBA has become a global brand directly associated with graduate business study at a university. Marketing, global economic growth, product maturation and segmentation of the educational market, and media scrutiny further refined the MBA brand to become identified with specific schools. In essence, schools have attempted to identify their MBA for a specific niche in the global educational market. The current stage of brand development is characterized by the continued growth, studied segmentation and raucous fragmentation of the market. And now, beyond degree or school brand identity, individual disciplines and specializations, for example, e-commerce, are newly branded. And with near-universal reach made possible by the Internet, low-marginal cost distribution of educational services to the business community has allowed new, nontraditional educational purveyors to enter the market. These new competitors rely on rapid and low-cost distribution, marketing, and global markets to compete with premium brand, traditional faculty and business schools to expand and serve the global market for business education. In this chapter, while recognizing that Canada, Mexico, and South America are important parts of America, "American" will refer to schools and firms based in the United States. "Foreign students" will refer to students earning a degree from a school in a country other than the country where the student grew up and completed the vast majority of their previous education.

INTRODUCTION

The global business of business education is large and growing. With historic roots in the American educational system, universities around the world have adopted or initiated various forms of university-based business studies programs, with the greatest growth of these new programs occurring in the last fifty years of the twentieth century. The 1990s may have been the period of the most accelerated growth, as countries and universities fought to compete in the global knowledge economy, an economy more rooted than ever in university-based business programs.

The primary focus of this chapter will be university-based business schools and educational programs. They constitute the current nexus for research-based knowledge of business practices as well as the critical network for the development of current and future business leadership. Business schools have not always assumed this role; in fact, they are relatively recent developments as an institutional response to the need for management development. Historically, military academies took on these institutional responsibilities, and much of the language and culture of military education still inhabit (and perhaps inhibit) the research archives and jargon of business schools. For example, the field of business policy has direct ties to military strategy.

Much business education occurred by trial and error and outside any institutional structure. For most of their existence, universities provided more intellectual and less practical studies, and certainly not business studies. And the future of business schools is no less problematic to predict or understand. The surges and streams of the information age, knowledge economy, and global markets are major forces working to reduce the institutional role of formal, university-based business education. At the heart of change is the movement to asynchronous, unmediated learning, where students are no longer constrained by time, place, or teacher in mastering their subjects. Yet the role of major brand providers of business education will likely become more important, with information technology allowing students to become more dispersed and providers more concentrated.

Business schools are both the drivers of economic success and the recipients of scorn from a variety of sectors. Scorn or skepticism comes from traditional university academics who think business faculty are not academic enough. The popular and business media, which often show little understanding of education or business, deride business schools for not being what the media elite suppose them to be. Corporate executives criticize business schools for not producing well-rounded graduates, at the same moment they vigorously compete to employ students from the very programs they criticize

A review must begin with an understanding of global economic growth, power, and competitiveness. The globalization of business schools is as much a managerial issue as an academic one, as well as an economic and political concern. Foremost, the current, modern business school is primarily an American contrivance, so let us begin there, with a review of the historic, economic, political, and managerial issues that developed and continue to drive business schools.

America has attained economic growth, power, and competitiveness because of the nation's ability to adapt, to embrace free trade and technology, to develop and maintain productive workers, and to accept the destruction of jobs as part of the process required for the creation of new jobs. Americans operating as customers, consumers, and, in an impersonal sense, a market intuitively understand the role of markets. This understanding is not deep or philosophical. Rather, it is practical, daily, and nearly invisible to people living and working in an economy approaching $10 trillion.

America is not alone in having experienced the recent and ongoing global transformation from an industrial- and a services-driven society to one where information has become the key service. Service remains critical, only now technology, specifically information technology, has replaced much of the human labor of the service economy. Each reader can edit a customized Web newspaper; a search engine rather than a librarian can facilitate a research project. The telephone and telecommunications are being supplanted by the Internet, e-mail, and electronic commerce, as critical networks.

In America, the number of software firms doubled between 1990 and 1998, from 22,000 to more than 45,000. Fax machines, cellular phones, satellite and cable television, Web sites, modems, personal computers, digital assistants, and pagers are just some of the technology that has replaced the dominant information device in use by students, teachers, and businesspeople only thirty years ago: the slide rule. Companies such as Amazon, Microsoft, Wal-Mart, General Motors, IBM, Intel, Dell, Yahoo, and American Airlines have used information technology to sell products, to run their business, and to grow markets. American business schools both lead and reflect this change, recognizing the power of self-employed individuals and small- and medium-sized firms operating in a global, information-rich, knowledge-powered economy, where English and Internet technology are the languages of commerce and customers. Universities are the new factories of the knowledge industry, producing data, information, and knowledge, as well as competitive, informed citizens, all critical currencies in today's global marketplace. Business schools develop the market knowledge and knowledge managers for competing in the twenty-first century, not for reflecting on the twentieth century.

While market and global growth and change have been spectacular for the past ten years, change has not been even, consistent, or especially predictable. And criticisms of American-based models of business education have also mounted, with claims that American business programs produce students who are culturally insensitive and ignorant, short-term in their orientation, unethical and willing to cut corners, and greedy. Some observers predicted the demise of American economic supremacy and based some of those predictions on criticisms of American business education.

Short-term economic realities have intervened. The widely predicted Asian twenty-first century has experienced startup problems. A currency collapse centered in Thailand in 1998 soon spread throughout the region, stalling growth across Asia. Japan's economy contracted. China's boom slowed to a near halt. Indonesia, Thailand, Korea, India, and other Asian tigers saw their teeth grow dull and their appetites exceeding their ability to feed themselves, with real estate devaluation; political instability; generational divides; religious, cultural, and language conflicts; economic sluggishness; and collapsed confidence. Asian thrift, work values, religious tolerance, high levels of savings, and government efforts to preselect and cultivate key industries appear to be much less powerful than once envisioned.

Ironically, repeated predictions of American economic and educational decline have been incorrect. In the 1950s, some economists predicted economic dominance for India by the end of the twentieth century. In the 1960s, the American CIA estimated that Russia would be triple the economic size of the American economy by the end of the century. In 2002, Russian gross domestic product (GDP) per capita is about $1,700, one-twentieth the size of the U.S. GDP per capita. In the 1970s, the blossoming of the European Economic Community prompted predictions of the triumph of an integrated western European economy by the turn of the century. Japanese market successes in the 1980s produced assertions about the inevitability of the century of the rising sun. And the 1990s provided speculation as to Chinese dominance of the world economy. Even America has experienced economic growth problems since 1998, but much of this is a modest correction to almost twenty years of consistent growth. Recent predictions of the profound decline of American economic leadership have proven false. We should apply similar skepticism to predictions of the demise of business schools.

American business schools, like the American economy, have proven adept at adapting to changes in markets, technology, and practices. Like giant corporations, large business schools have built their brands, adopted new technologies, leveraged their comparative advantages, and increased their margins. Business knowledge has become a primary asset for economic growth and the numerous, highly competitive, and diverse (predominantly) American business schools have proven to be quite agile in competing in this market.

WHY BUSINESS SCHOOLS SUCCEED

Business schools succeed because they produce globally competitive products: global business knowledge and knowledge workers. Knowledge workers speak the language and know the basic culture of business and business school graduates provide both the leaders and the front-line troops for the global economy. Business students at all levels—undergraduate, graduate, and executive—learn the culture and language of the new world economy. Despite their higher-paid faculty, business schools are the cash cows for universities, costing little in terms of specialized infrastructure, libraries or facilities, and garnering hundreds of millions in donations. Business faculty straddle the academic and the practical, earning criticism from academic colleagues for being too practical (and too well paid) and from the business community for being to academic.

And, like some corporations, some successful business schools have become large and complacent. An absence of innovation and leadership among the "top" schools is a phenomenon in all industries: leading organizations become rich and self-satisfied and the real change bubbles up from those struggling, niche-building programs competing for the new customers' dollar. And much of the work of business schools is basic, not cutting edge. A well-trained manager may not have the IQ or analytical skills of a rocket scientist, but if there are design flaws in the manager's education, Challenger-like disasters are in the making. Business education is too big and too important to be left to elite, expensive schools. And we should all be grateful that it is not. University-based business education is a competitive, global industry, both helped and hindered by market and nonmarket forces.

American economic historian David Landes (1998) finds cultural values underlying economic success, recognizing diversity as a resource rather than as a goal, and a common value system as a critical ingredient to national, sustainable economic competitiveness in a global market. Landes discovered a historic pattern of cultural characteristics of an "ideal growth and development" economic strategy. Successful global economies knew how to operate, manage, and build the instruments of production. They knew how to create, adapt, and master new techniques on the technological frontier; they have been able to impart this knowledge to the young, by education or apprenticeship. They adopted a national strategy for growth and were able to choose people for jobs by competence and merit. They evaluated workers on the basis of their performance; afforded opportunities for individual or collective enterprise; encouraged initiative, competition, and emulation; and allowed people the opportunity to employ and enjoy the fruits of their labor and enterprise through the ownership of private property and profits.

Landes's "culture" well describes the basic paradigm of any competitive business school. Diversity of inputs, including people, meld to form a culture of common values. It is the pursuit of these values that makes economies successful. It is the development and transmission of these values that make business schools successful.

Landes's work underscores a general thesis: business has led this radical change in global markets with the recognition that the customer is king—in Dutch, *de klant is koning*; in Czech, *nas zakaznik, nas pan* (our customer is our master). This recognition has produced the realization that companies, including business schools, need to adopt new methods that both respond to and anticipate customer wants and needs, in existing, emerging, and untapped markets. Business schools, especially the model based on American business schools, provide the information technology leadership and managers necessary for a new global economy.

A PARADIGM FOR BUSINESS EDUCATION

University-based business education is epitomized and often caricatured by the MBA. Most of the attention goes to full-time, internationally visible programs while the majority of the degrees are granted to students who study on a part-time basis, maintain their current employer during their studies, and forego long-distance moves to enroll. The MBA degree has undergone rapid and profound transformation (by the standard of glacial academic change), from its original intent, to its evolved role, and then to its current popular, if cynical, information age image. Originally, the MBA provided business skills preparation to technically proficient graduates of programs in the sciences, engineering, and other technical fields, preparing high-potential managers for corporate senior management in industrial America, converting technical expertise into management skills. As programs grew, the "modern" version emerged: students seeking more independent employment, entrepreneurial success, and a higher, faster return on their educational investment sought preparation for consulting, financial, and broader global responsibilities, hoping to operate as consultants, investment bankers, or self-employed deal makers. The information age has created an MBA program culture where students aspire to millionaire status by age thirty with dot.com, high-tech startups. The *Wall Street Journal* (Digits, 1999; see also Hill, 2000) noted that Pennsylvania's Wharton School lost 25 members of its class of 765 students in their Class of 2000 to business: "the majority jumped ship to work at dot-coms." By 2002, a large number of students who graduated from prominent MBA programs had returned to school from failed dot.coms. And the other graduates often returned to their previous employer, grateful to have work in the "old" economy.

There is a broader pattern of change at levels below and outside that of the elite, well-publicized business schools. Universities worldwide are under tremendous pressure to earn funding from new sources, to modernize programs and facilities, to provide accessibility to entitled groups, and to be accountable to diverse stakeholders. Philip G. Altbach and Todd M. Davis (1990) claim that although the "basic institutional model and structure of studies are similar worldwide," higher education is "moving from elite to mass to universal access." Demand for access conflicts with funding controversies, with an increased emphasis on individual student "users" paying a higher portion of the cost of what has become perceived to be an individual benefit. Student loans, privatization, and enrollments have all increased, with less funding on facilities and basic research. Education and work form continuous cycles over a person's life, with technology impacting pedagogy and global mobility affecting enrollments, especially from countries like India and China to the developed world, with "stay rates" in excess of 75 percent for graduate students.

Graduate education has been one of the areas of greatest expansion worldwide, with the privatization of higher education a worldwide phenomenon of considerable importance, especially in Latin America and Asia, and also central and eastern Europe. Tenure has come under repeated threats, with more part-time and virtual faculty. Gender, ethnicity, and social class discrimination remain serious issues. Accountability is a contemporary yet misunderstood and distrusted concept in higher education. Demands to measure academic productivity and demands made of professional academic administration have been persistent. Global expansion brought differentiation and new kinds of institutions.

Various roots or sources of managerial or business education can be traced, depending on the precision of the definition of university-based business education. Hundreds of years ago, the Chinese created systems of higher learning to prepare political bureaucrats, at a time when politics meant more than economics in the creation and management of markets. The British system of universities for the elite, combined with assimilation and training through a vast network of trading companies, provided a system for screening and selecting talent for managing a global empire, before any university understood and taught the concept of free markets. Prussian military training and the global system of management development used by the Catholic Church offer alternative, close approximations of systematic development of organizational leaders. Harvard University's MBA program is often cited as the first true, university-based and endorsed system of academic attention to senior management development.

Rapid expansion of the Harvard success can be modeled to increase enrollment, capitalize on profitability of business schools, and develop financial ties to even more successful alumni for subsequent development work (for example, gifts, expansion of the post-MBA or non-MBA executive education track). Phil Ruthven (1999) notes that in Australia, the knowledge industry's share of GDP will have tripled in one hundred years and that education "will have risen from about 1.9 percent of GDP to 4.2 percent" (116). In Japan, disillusionment with some of the cultural elements of American MBA education, along with a falling Japanese economy, led to a decline in Japanese students studying abroad. Instead, foreign schools are opening MBA programs in Japan, and Japanese universities have led a recent upsurge in domestic MBA programs.

From these efforts, we can identify a global business education paradigm, a system of preparation for managing and leading in a global information economy. Michael R. Czinkota and Ilkka A. Ronkainen's (1998) Delphi study of a global set of experts drawn from the policy, business, and academic communities identified geographic areas of key business growth, major sector transformations, shifts in the trade framework and its institution, and strategies for corporate adjustment. Executives ranked globalization high on their strategic agenda, while universities have adjusted their business curricula and research to address global business issues. They concluded that international business causes many changes, but is also the subject of major transformations. The authors offer insights into the thinking among the business, policy, and academic communities with regard to the future of international business and trade in the major market areas of the world: the Americas, Asia-Pacific and Europe.

University-based business education consists of formal coursework, integration of previous and ongoing work experience, and a blend of concepts and skills, art, and science. The domain includes attention to global business, free markets, and the role of customers, based on recognition of the shift from the industrial to information economy and the development of an appreciation of global cultures and differences.

A global business education is similar to studying the language and culture of a country prior to living in that country, only business is the language and the culture. Despite what some critics imagine business education to be, there are certain things that a good business education is not. A global business education is not vocational, nor is it short term in focus. Formal classroom education is not a substitute for actual experience. By the 1980s, large numbers of foreign students increased their share in the North American MBA student market; this resulted in a shift to limit the number of elite Asian students at elite North American schools. Beginning in Europe, alternative models at established universities expanded. American schools moved to offer programs directly in former communist regions and the customer-rich, university-poor Asian market through programs offered overseas, recruitment of large numbers of Asians, and creative programs combining technology, residencies, travel, and executive pedagogies.

GLOBAL PRIVATIZATION OF EDUCATION

There has been strong demand for global business education from many firms, countries, and students. There are high margins in business university-based education, with the recognition that the information economy further leverages the value of highly skilled managers rather than simply low-cost labor; and the inability and unwillingness of governments to pay for the increasing number of university students. Ruthven (1999) characterizes education as being faced with three problems: custodial care (managing young students), tutoring (learning to learn), and information. Other sectors of the knowledge industry need only be concerned with one of these issues and, in the case of most consulting firms, two of these issues (tutoring and information). He notes that the "real cost of full-time university education has barely changed in four decades . . . at a time when the costs are being transferred from the state to the student" (117).

CASE STUDY: LATIN AMERICA

The development of business schools in Latin America (Lorenzi, 1999) is an example of the global exportation of American business school culture, with its features and its flaws. Mexico is a case in point. In the summer of 1999, students from Mexico's largest university—the Autonomous National University of Mexico (UNAM)—draped banners over freeway bridges and demanded to be allowed back to school, protesting a strike by other students concerned by a proposed tuition hike. Classes were disrupted when student protesters shut down the campus. The strike began when authorities announced plans to increase fees to $63 a semester from a small, longtime fee of less than $.02. The rector submitted his resignation. Striking students kept the campus closed during most of two semesters. Even when UNAM capitulated to student demands, making the new tuition entirely voluntary, the strikers refused to leave the campus. Radical students called for a return to the "automatic pass," which guarantees admission to the university. They also demanded that UNAM allow students an unlimited amount of time to graduate from the university.

UNAM is perhaps representative of the problems in Latin America's university education, including business schools. Traditional business programs in state-sponsored universities have become marginalized. The Latin American tradition had been to prepare students for careers in accounting or economics. A broader business education is a more recent phenomenon. For example, the University of the Republic in Uruguay, which fifty years ago was producing internationally recognized programs in jurisprudence and medicine, offered its first marketing course in 1984.

The modernization of academic programs in business have been driven by private universities, similar to the process that took place in France with the Institute Superieur de Commerce model. And now China is moving in this direction. Chinese enrollments in higher education increased from one million to six million in the past twenty years, less than 10 percent of the university-age cohort, while the international average is closer to 13 percent, and 30 percent in industrialized countries. The new Latin American approach had been to emulate the best business programs of American universities. Since the early 1980s and as a result of success stories such as the University of Chile, there has been a rush of Latin schools seeking exchange agreements with American schools. But accurate program information, measures of quality, and benchmarking standards are slow to develop. In many Latin American countries (there are exceptions), academics are basically of two types: distinguished practitioners who do it because they like the profession and appreciate the prestige, or individuals who have a variety of part-time jobs to make ends meet. Relations with American schools are viewed as a one-way street. There are showcases of excellence. INCAE's programs in Costa Rica have a first-rate faculty. The University of Chile hires their best graduates first as teaching assistants and then sends them to America for doctorates.

Public universities in Latin America tend to be either centers of middle-class privilege or of overpopulated poverty. Public spending on higher education in Latin America is 1 percent or 2 percent of GDP. The Organization for Economic Cooperation and Development (see www1.oecd.org/e1s/education/ei/eag/wei.htm) average university participation rate of the college-aged population is about 23 percent; for Brazil and Mexico, about 5 percent; and Argentina about 22 percent. The main response has been to encourage the entry of new, private universities. Public school support has been cut dramatically, requiring high-interest student loans. Private schools spend little on research and selectively skim the cream of top students. Employers prefer graduates from private universities, and thus, graduates of public universities may not find an appropriate job.

CORPORATE AND FOR-PROFIT EDUCATION

To encourage alternatives to public funding for education and to adopt a more free market approach to education, governments have reduced restrictions, regulations, and entry barriers for for-profit firms seeking to capitalize on the high demand for management development (or continuing education).

These new competitors employ the best of traditional university practices. More important, they leapfrog with information technology breakthroughs; avoid highly paid, full-time, and tenured faculty; and satisfy seemingly insatiable demand for management education. Their success is further fueled by corporate frustration with traditional academic progress (that is, slow-to-change accreditation barriers) and processes (that is, arcane admissions, academic selectivity). Corporations exchange their traditional regard for traditional universities for a willingness to pay directly for this management education for their employees (that is, the direct subcontractor model), and seemingly insatiable corporate appetite for management talent. In brief, not everyone wants, needs, can afford, or deserves a Harvard MBA, but many firms need more MBAs, and even more firms want and need more managers with skills produced by a global business education.

In a global, consumer-driven economy, the branding of educational providers will become more important than it was in earlier years and in less competitive conditions. In late 1999, the University of Cambridge and the Massachusetts Institute of Technology announced a $135 million partnership for global education (Tugend, 1999). The goal was to improve British productivity and competitiveness, stimulate research spin-off firm creation, bring MIT executive education courses to Britain, and develop common courses in science, engineering, business, and management. Todd Woody (1999) claims, "Hundreds of millions of dollars will be spent in the next few years on a gamble that middle managers in

Singapore or Heidelberg are as hungry for U.S. education as they are for *Baywatch*" (2). In a $740 billion education industry, branding has earned a place just as it has in traditional durable and consumer goods industries. And education is both a consumer and a durable good. According to former Harvard business dean Kim Clark, "Education used to be done in the early stages of someone's life and maybe once or twice after that. We are moving to an era where organizations are much more fluid, the pace of change is much faster and much more international. There's much more need for just-in-time, just-right education. The Internet is becoming central to education because it allows you to meet these kinds of needs" (cited in Woody, 1999).

The practical paradigm or the stereotypic business school model for success has also changed, as countless levels of management have been supplanted by flat organizations, self-employment, and the dot.com boom of Internet entrepreneurship. Corporate universities, frustrated with colleges' tenured faculties and aging curricula, have taken training and development market share from universities, providing in-house, focused, streamlined training and education not possible to coax from traditional universities. The strategic issue will be whether universities can reassert their traditional comparative advantages. If firms' frustrations grow, they may do for themselves what they once subcontracted. As knowledge management increases in importance and specialization, subcontracting of this task may become inefficient, expensive, or untenable.

BUSINESS OF BUSINESS EDUCATION

What explains the success of the American economy and of university-based business schools in a country of 250 million people, with a GDP of $9.5 trillion? Much of the answer can be found in American history and culture. Private property and free markets have been the cornerstones of economic growth and success. The ability to own and to trade creates economic value. The American culture of individual freedom and choice provides a diverse set of interests in incentives, providing an engine for economic growth. Two hundred years of general if imperfect political and social stability of the country has helped. Despite a civil war and ongoing racial tension, the ability to change governments and to maintain general tranquillity are important to economic growth. Excellent physical and information infrastructure spurs growth. Highways, railroads, commercial aviation, overnight express mail, and electronic networks facilitate commerce, as does a basic and sound uniform commercial code for offering and exchanging credit and goods. Rapid technological diffusion stems from the integration of all four of the previous points, and further accelerates economic growth.

One hundred years ago, agricultural employment dominated the American economy. The industrial manufacturing economy that emerged in the nineteenth century then surpassed farming as the basic mode of life and employment. By the end of World War II, the devastation of major industry in all other countries other than the United States allowed for a moment of absolute dominance of the global industrial economy, just as the importance of the service economy came to the forefront. And the past twenty years has demonstrated the importance of and transition to the information or knowledge economy. The business of America is business. A business school not only teaches business, it is itself a business. A business school has customers, competitors, revenues, employees, and goals. A business school is like an airline. Each group of students studying in one course are passengers on a plane; the professor is the pilot. The school must ensure that the pilot is well trained and that the course and destination for the plane are carefully considered. The plane must be modern and well equipped, with sufficient students on the plane to pay the costs and earn a contribution for overhead and other endeavors. The intellectual journey must be profitable in terms of learning and in terms of the ledger.

To board this plane, students pay a price, and not just in dollars. These customers cannot simply purchase a course credit or a degree. The full price includes an academic admissions standard, showing that the student has the intellectual preparation to partake in the journey. The student will likely have to submit a test score or a curriculum vitae to earn a seat on the plane. Also, the student will be expected to work on the plane, not just sit idly as the pilot flies the plane. Without working hard, the student might fall off or be thrown off the airplane.

Where is this plane going? The faculty determine a complete and meaningful itinerary. That is, there are many segments to the complete journey. This is not a single, nonstop flight but rather an integrated connection of smaller journeys that lead to the ultimate destination. The student will have to change planes and each time show he or she is prepared to continue on the journey. Interest in flying and a large bank account are not enough. Most important, the dean and the faculty must ensure that the journey prepares the student for the rest of his or her life.

EDUCATION IN THE INFORMATION AGE

So what is the future of business education in the information age? Will dot.com madness prevail again in the future? Will the Internet segment the market beyond recognition and destroy the culture of the traditional university? Jiri Zlatuska (2000) writes that "the pattern of changes to the educational activities as well as the structure and shape of the educational institutions can be traced to the underlying fabric of the new time." He notes five elements of these changes:

- *Customization of educational programs.* Specialized, segmented curricula are replacing mass-produced, low differentiation programs.
- *Disintermediation.* Computers have allowed the process of "shipping" knowledge from teacher to student to be removed. Universities can better stick to core competencies and contract with multiple faculty accordingly via dynamic, ad hoc networks and systems for delivering education. This furthers customization interests by making education less time- or place-specific.
- *Convergence.* There is a global convergence of economies, language, culture, and disciplines built around common interests and regular communication.
- *Virtualization.* The three preceding elements—customization, disintermediation, and convergence—allow the creation of large, virtual, university-like systems that will somewhat mimic yet also compete with traditional bricks-and-mortar institutions.
- *Globalization.* The four preceding elements reduce the barrier of geography and distance. The age of information coincides with the era of globalization. (3–5)

TRENDS IN UNIVERSITY-BASED BUSINESS EDUCATION

What are the trends in university-based business education? Business education has never been fully dominated by universities and the university's share of the market for current business knowledge and skills is likely to continue to decline. But the overall growth of the market will continue to make universities the prominent, branded, visible, and the most open purveyors of business education. The following predictions are more speculative than empirical:

- Business schools are profitable. Expect the continuing profitability of business schools—be they traditional, university-based, or private, for-profit corporations—in American and around the globe.
- Despite more opportunities outside the United States, expect an increasing demand for American business schools from foreign markets and students. The American economy and the long-standing success of American business schools in accelerating students into that market will make American programs attractive.
- Expect innovative producers to enter the marketplace, including proprietary schools and Internet-based universities.
- Expect an increasing market demand around the world for global business skills.

The developing globalized system is not invulnerable. The recent crisis in the Asian tiger economies demonstrates some of the vulnerability of this emerging globalized system. There is a chance of a collapse of the system (contagion effect) with global repercussions reflecting the current level of integration. It is more likely that the system will be changed by many small actions and challenges, based on local acts of resistance that affirm the principles of equity, democracy, social justice, and public education.

REFERENCES

Altbach, Philip G., and Todd M. Davis. 1999. Global Challenge and National Response: Notes for an International Dialogue on Higher Education. http://www.bc.edu/bc_org/AVp/soe/cihe/newsletter/News14/text1.html.

Czinkota, Michael R., and Ilkka A. Ronkainen. 1997. International Business and Trade in the Next Decade: Report from a Delphi Study. *Journal of International Business Studies* 28 (4):827–844.

Digits. 1999. *Wall Street Journal*, November 18.

Hill, Miriam. 2000. Wharton's in a Whirl as MBAs Target dot-com Riches. *Philadelphia Inquirer*, March 6.

Landes, David S. 1998. *The Wealth and Poverty of Nations*. New York: Norton.

Lorenzi, Peter. *Issues in Higher Education in Latin America: Business Schools*. http://www.evergreen.loyola.edu/~plorenzi/Research/latin.htm.

Ruthven, Phil. 1999. Knowledge Is the "Soft" Solution. *BRW* (November 26): 116–122.

Tugend, Alina. 1999. U. of Cambridge and MIT Will Collaborate on Technology Institute. *Chronicle of Higher Education*. www.hku.hk/CAUT/Projects/Weekly_Update%5Bitt4_3%50/J19991112.htm.

Woody, Todd. 1999. Ivy Online. *Industry Standard*, October 22.

Zlatuska, Jiri. 2000. *Education as an Information Age Business*. http://www.cvut.cz/Ascii/cc/icsc/NII/papers/Zlatuska.html.

Index